THE ROYAL FAMILY IN GLOUCESTERSHIRE

the photographs of Michael Charity

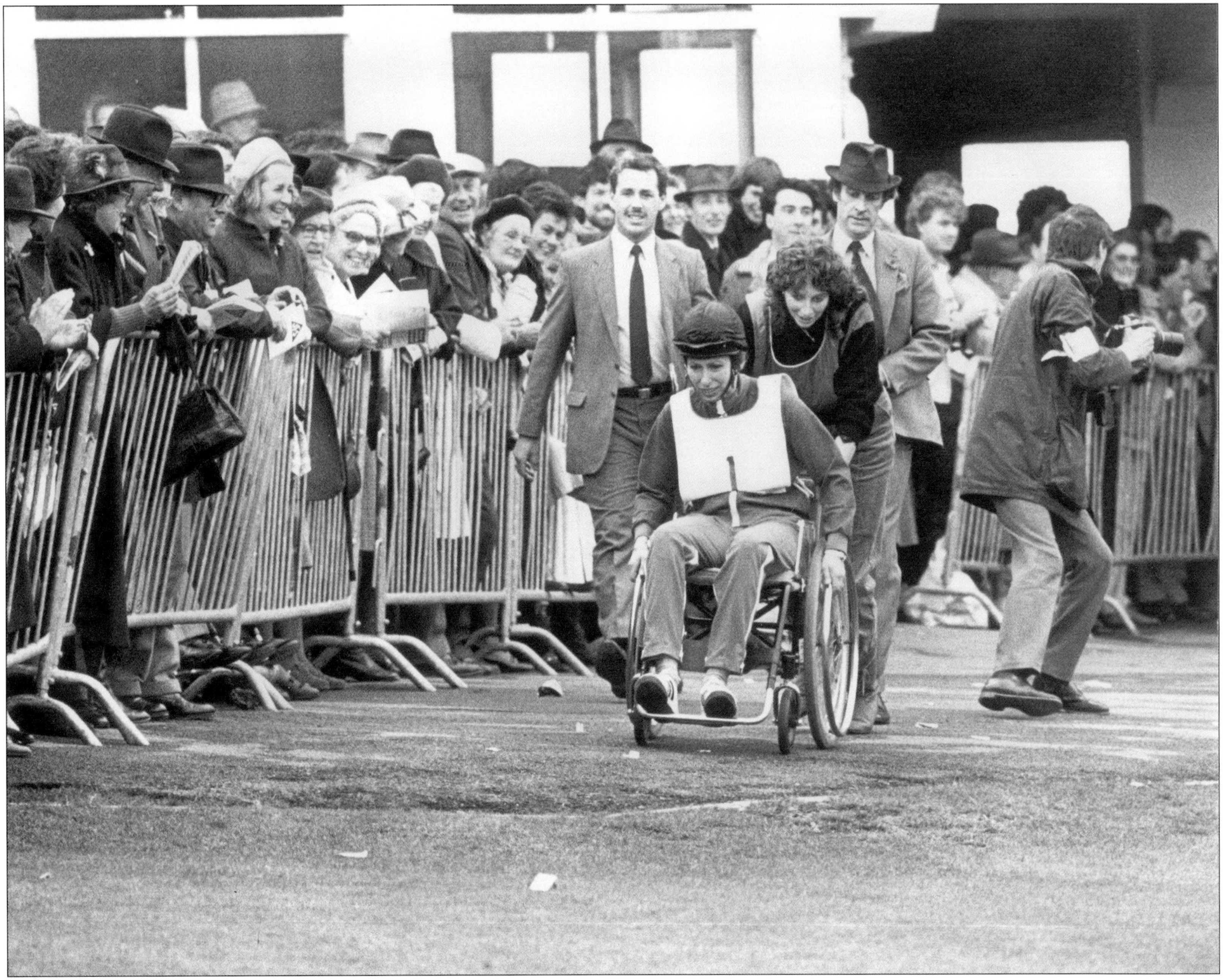

They're off!
In 1984 the princess was at Prestbury Park taking part, with other equestrian personalities, in wheelchair races to raise money for the Injured Jockeys Fund. The light-hearted event delighted the crowd of onlookers and raised a significant amount for the cause.

THE ROYAL FAMILY IN GLOUCESTERSHIRE

the photographs of Michael Charity

TEMPUS

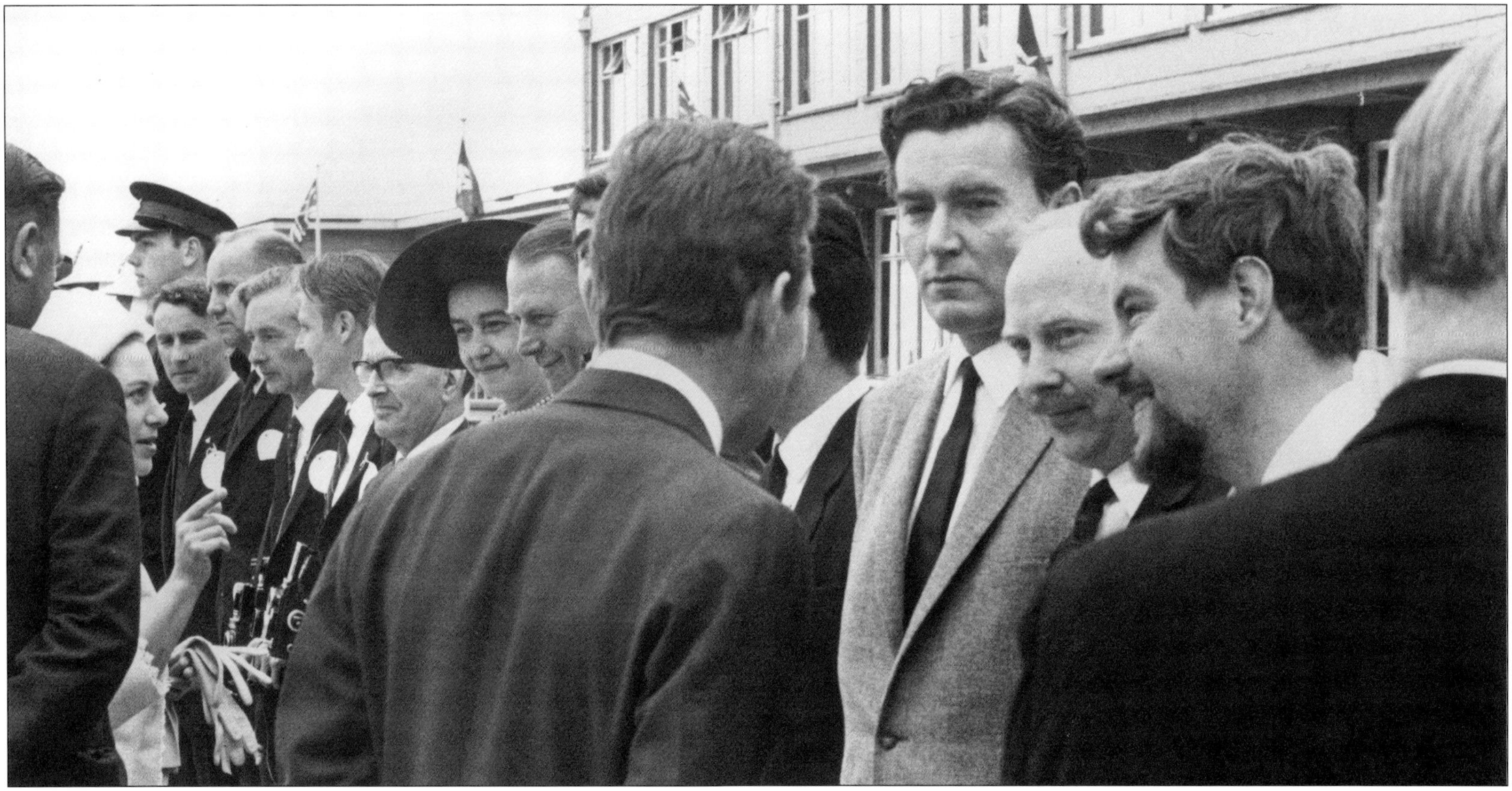

Michael Charity (right, with beard) and newspaper colleagues being presented to Lord Snowdon and Princess Margaret after covering a royal tour of the Isle of Man in 1968.

First published 2003

Tempus Publishing Limited
The Mill, Brimscombe Port,
Stroud, Gloucestershire, GL5 2QG

British Library Cataloguing in Publication Data.
A catalogue record for this book is available from the British Library.

ISBN 0 7524 2871 3

Typesetting and origination by Tempus Publishing Limited
Printed in Great Britain by Midway Colour Print, Wiltshire

This book is dedicated to Gillian, a lady who has acquired the patience of Job to cope with our erratic and often chaotic lifestyle, something she has done unswervingly over the years.

Acknowledgments

I would like to thank the following organizations, colleagues and friends to whom I am indebted for providing me with valuable information regarding certain dates, names and venues that with the passing of time have slipped my mind:

Sue Robbins (*Gloucestershire Echo*), Becky Jarvis and Catherine Felix (Cirencester Hospital), Julie Brookes (RAF Innsworth), Debbie Young (Westonbirt School) and Gwen Fitch. Staff members of Grant Thornton, Gloucester Cathedral, Tewkesbury Abbey, The Meningitis Trust, Save The Children Fund. The Gloucestershire Regiments Museum, Bruce Stephens, Lord Apsley, Jean Flower, Nigel Dimmer, Paul Felix and Bernard Parkin. There are also numerous others to whom I am indebted for contributing in some small way, with facts and figures that are a vital ingredient in publications such as these.

Introduction

My first photographs of royalty in Gloucestershire were taken in the bitter snow-bound winter of 1963. Princess Margaret arrived in the county for a private weekend visit with friends at Dowdeswell, some three miles from Cheltenham. On Sunday morning the Princess, along with the Earl of Snowdon and her hosts, made the treacherous journey on foot to attend a service in the tiny village church.

At a discreet distance, a trio of frozen cameramen were on hand to record the occasion - myself among them. Later that day I received a call from two Press Association staffers who, although in the area, missed the royal church pictures due to the weather. They wanted my photographs and offered to collect the prints.

To say those were early days in my photographic career is no exaggeration. My start- up savings had been quickly swallowed up on petrol, film stock and chemicals - a proper darkroom would have to wait for much-needed income. I somehow managed to produce prints by jamming myself into a small airing cupboard which, despite the winter, was overpoweringly hot. As there was no running water, I had to transfer the prints to the bathroom using an array of bowls and saucepans before washing them under the tap! The Fleet Street hacks arrived in the middle of my printing capers and I was embarrassed to catch them grimacing to each other regarding my primitive set up. Suffice to say I eventually made the prints and they left, no doubt having a good chuckle on their way back to the office. God knows what they would have thought of my car - a basic Ford Popular with no heater, used daily on assignments in the frozen Cotswolds during the worst winter since 1946! I did have one crumb of comfort, suspended over the dashboard from the rear view mirror, a paraffin lamp. Each day I set out with the glowing lantern swinging across my vision and each night I returned reeking like an oil field! In fact the vicious winter was my saving grace - I received numerous assignments from ATV and BBC to film the atrocious weather conditions and that old Ford car never once let me down.

As I became more established during the 1960s and '70s, I was given increasingly more assignments for the monthly glossy magazine *Gloucester and Avon Life*, filling their social pages with photographs of the great and the good attending various balls and charity functions in the fine houses sprinkled throughout the county. Often a member of the Royal Family would be invited to support the worthy cause, their very presence guaranteed to swell the list of guests eager to rub shoulders with a member of the House of Windsor. From the outset I felt I had to at least look the part for these glittering occasions - a visit to Burtons the tailors made me the proud owner of an evening suit - it seemed by wearing the correct attire and using discretion in my picture taking, the powers that be accepted me as a 'safe' bet and the invitations began to fall regularly through the letter box. There were constant visits to the great Gloucestershire party venues: Berkeley Castle, Chavenage House, Badminton, Sudeley Castle, Stanway House and many other splendid homes in Gloucestershire where the rich and the famous congregated in all their finery.

As a spin-off from the party scene I found that I was being increasingly recommended by the police and various dignitaries to be official photographer whenever members of the Royal Family made visits to companies and organizations in the region. I found myself and my camera in factories, office blocks, charity shops and theatres across the region, picturing plaque unveilings, royal walkabouts, factory tours, tree plantings and stage productions - I was convinced that the £20 dinner jacket had been a great investment!

It is difficult now to believe that forty years have passed since I first pictured Princess Margaret and Lord Snowdon in that wild winter of 1963. In the decades since then I have photographed virtually every member of the Royal Family, only Sarah Ferguson and Prince Harry have eluded my lens.

Photography has opened doors to functions and events that as a young Hereford lad I could never have dreamt of. It has allowed me to cover royal tours in the Isle of Man and Belgium, to be presented on two occasions to Princess Margaret and Lord Snowdon, to dine with Prince Charles at a private function and have the honour of being official photographer to royal visits in the county on numerous occasions.

Am I a Royalist? Not avidly but I do believe that the monarchy is a wonderful insurance policy for the stability of our nation. Despite the ups and downs experienced by the House of Windsor in the past few years, I cannot think of any other system that could replace the Royal family, do as much good, and remain as benign.

I would like to think that I can repay, in some small way, the people of Cheltenham in particular and Gloucestershire in general, for their help, assistance and generosity over the past forty years. With this in mind I wish to donate half of the royalties from this book to The Gloucestershire Prostate Cancer (Bachytherapy Unit) Trust. The Trust was launched in July 2001 with the aim of raising the initial operational costs of a specialist unit for Cheltenham General Hospital for the benefit of NHS patients suffering from prostate cancer. In just over twelve months, supporters of the Trust have raised an amazing £100,000, the result being that the unit can now be established in Cheltenham. Further funds are now required to supply and run the unit with vital materials until such time as the NHS takes the unit under its wing.

Michael Charity
February 2003

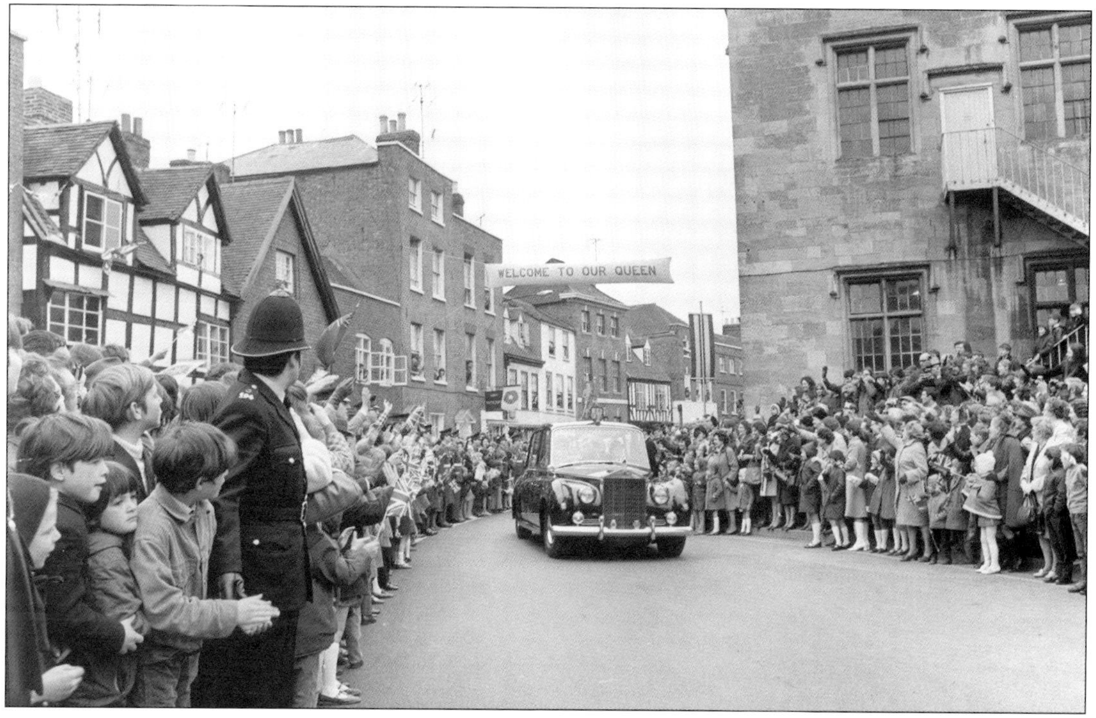

Welcome for a Monarch
Crowds greet Her Royal Highness Queen Elizabeth II and the Duke of Edinburgh, arriving by royal car in Tewkesbury in 1970 to take part in the Maundy Thursday service at Tewkesbury Abbey. This ancient ceremony, where parishioners within the diocese are rewarded for their good works with a purse of specially-minted coins presented by the Monarch, was the first occasion of its kind to take place in Tewkesbury Abbey. The service was given by the vicar of Tewkesbury Abbey, Canon Cosmo Pouncey, in the year that also marked the 850th anniversary of the founding of the great church.

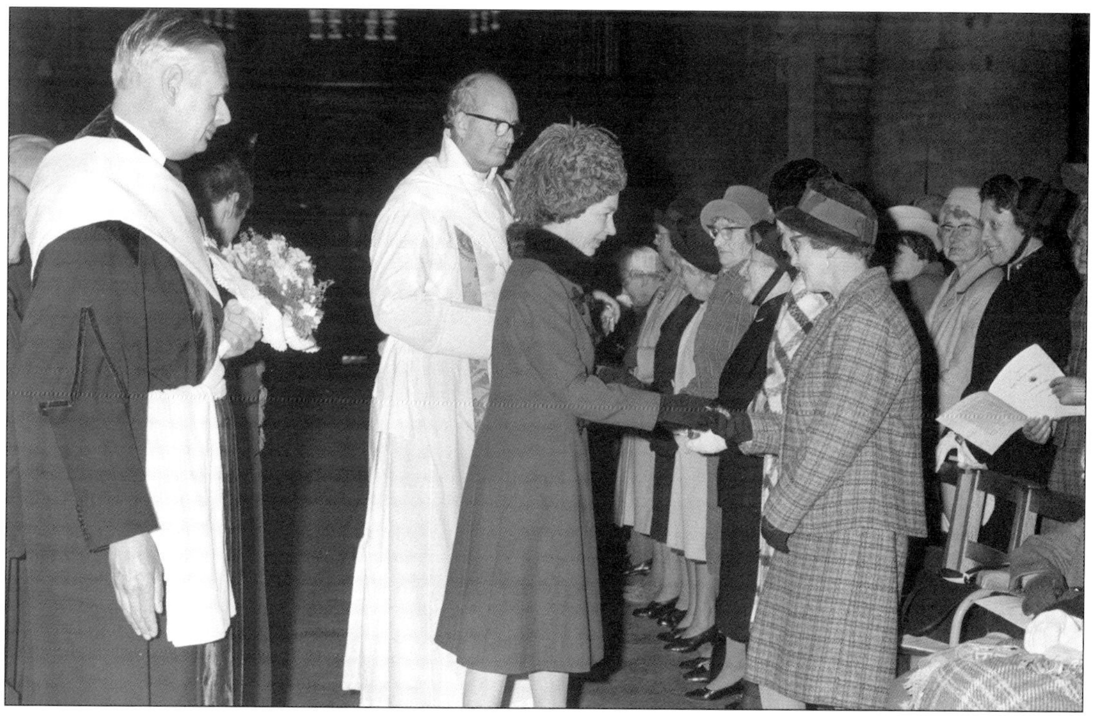

The Royal Purse
Her Majesty the Queen seen during the service, handing purses of Maundy money to deserving recipients inside the abbey.

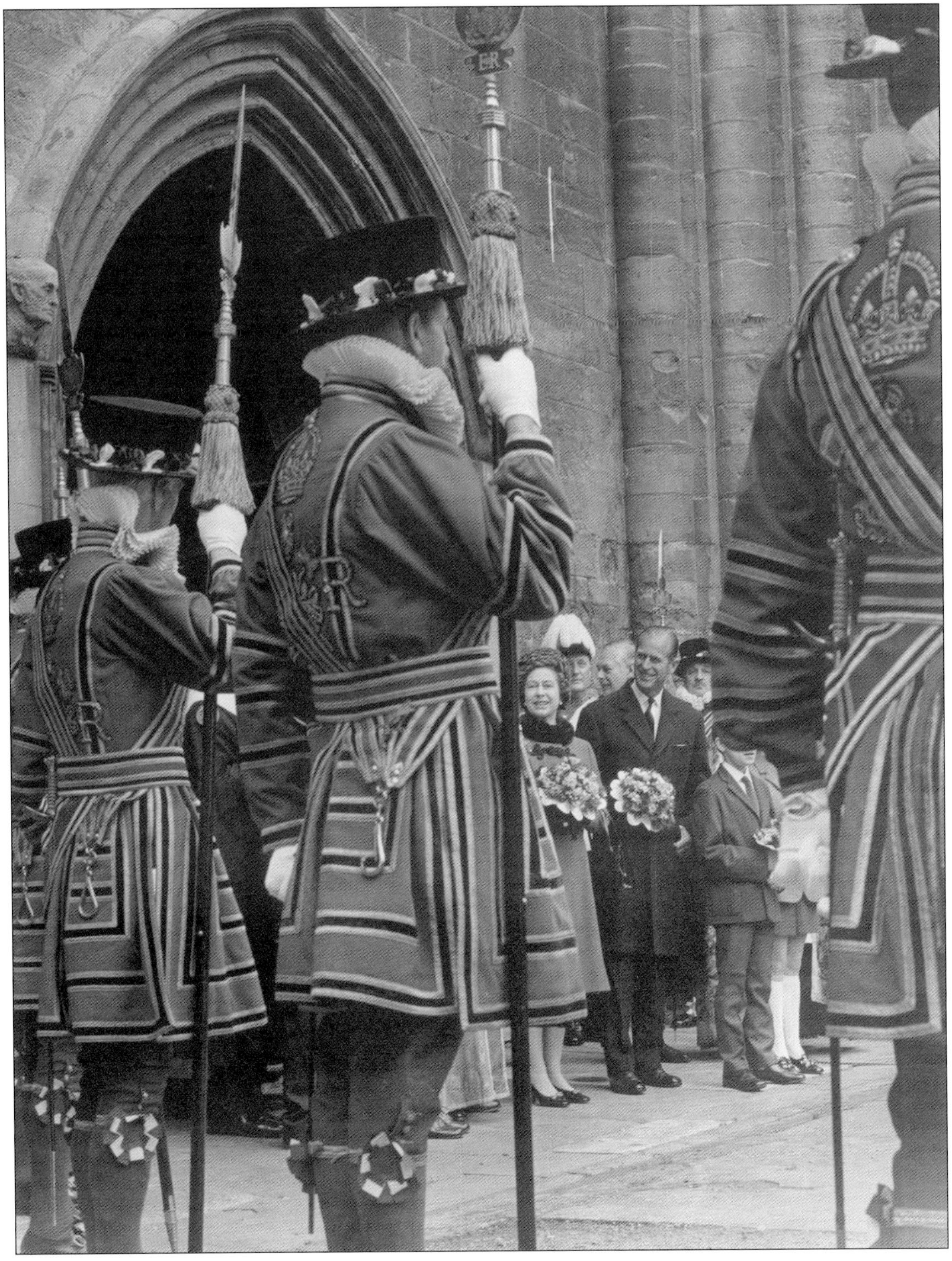

Royal Beefeaters
Beefeaters form a colourful Guard of Honour for the Queen and Duke outside Tewkesbury Abbey after the historic Maundy service.
Photo: Gillian Charity

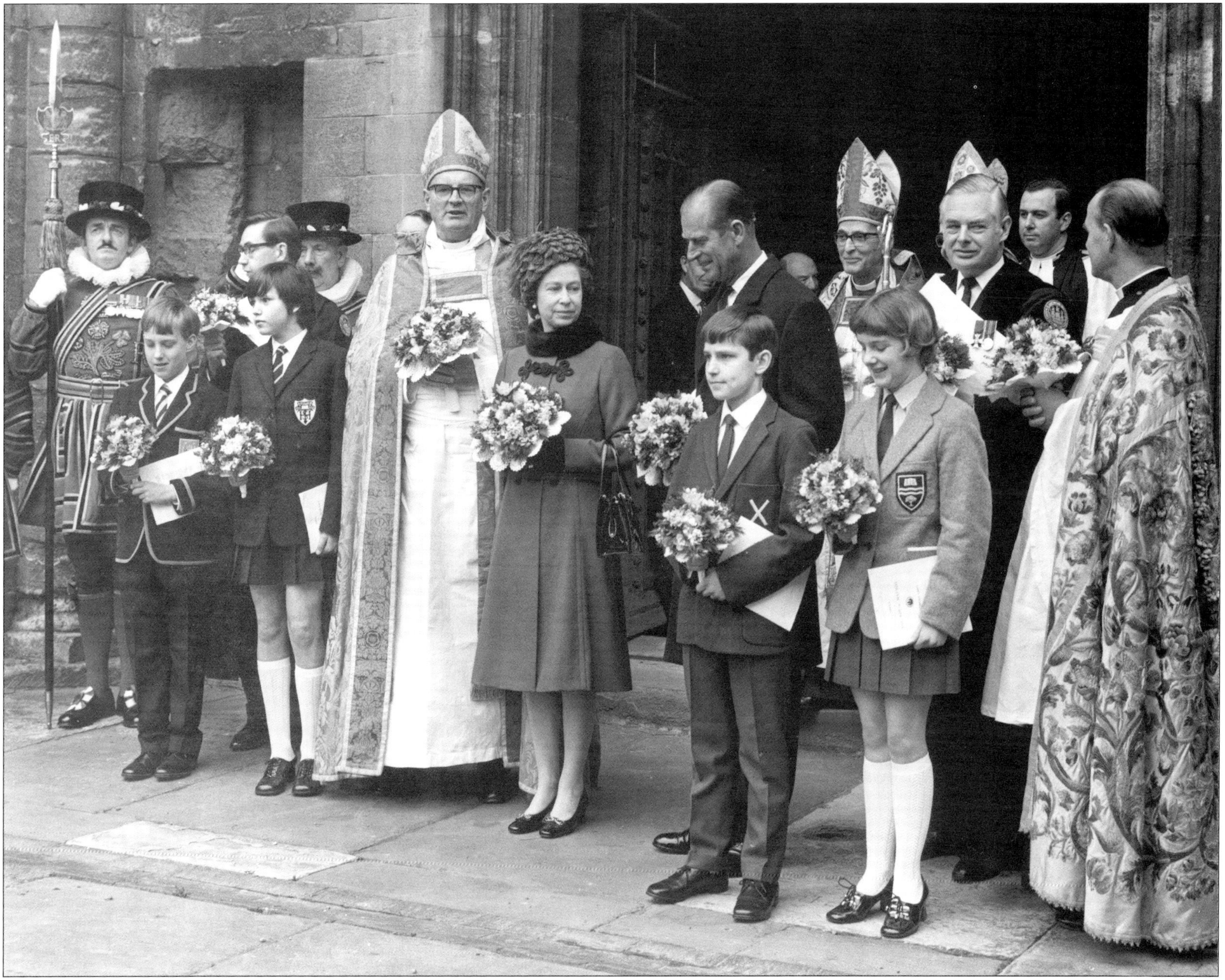

One for the Royal Album
Her Majesty the Queen and the Duke of Edinburgh along with church dignitaries and Beefeaters pose for photographers outside Tewkesbury Abbey.

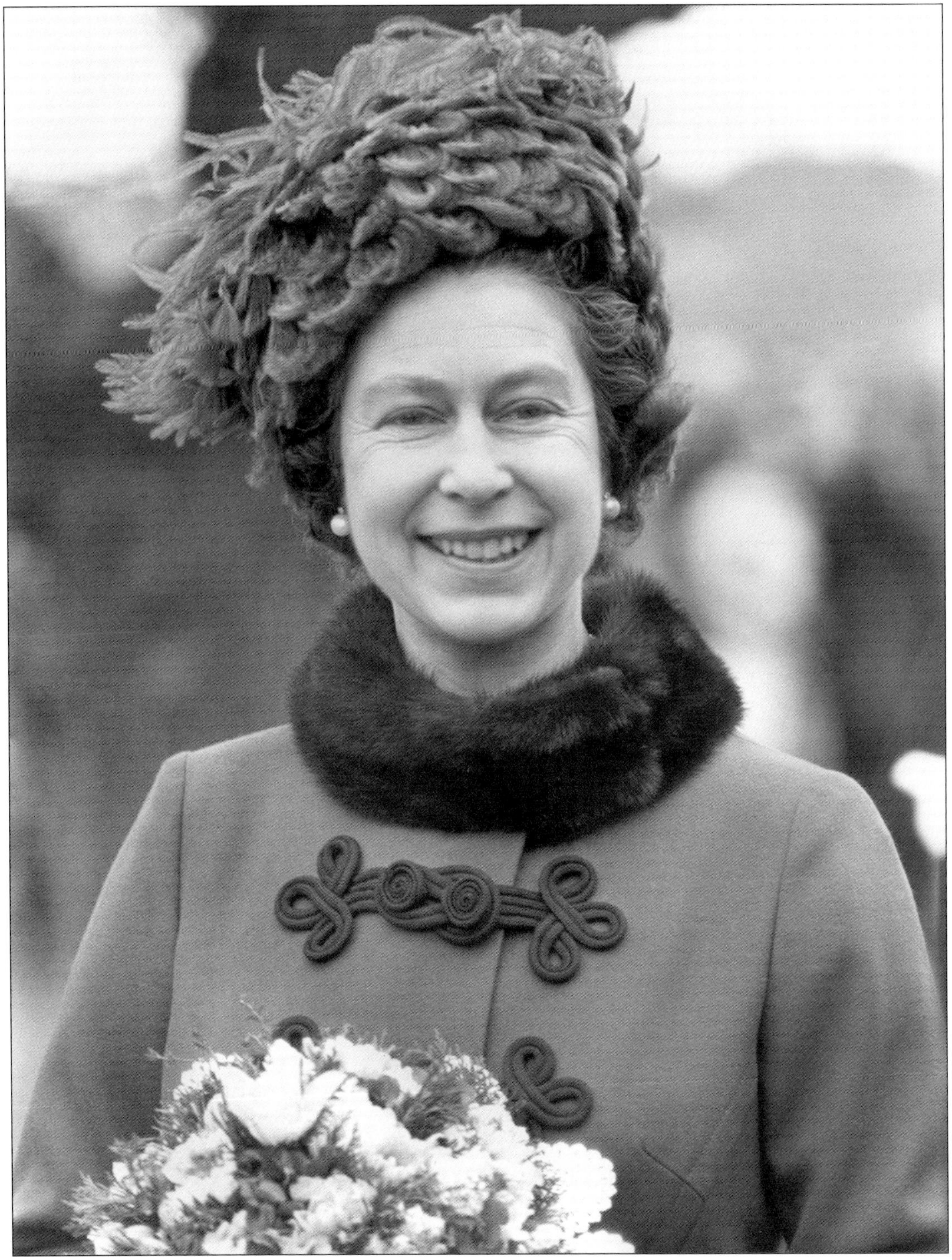

A Right Royal Smile
A radiant and happy-looking Queen Elizabeth acknowledges the camera during her Tewkesbury walkabout in 1970.

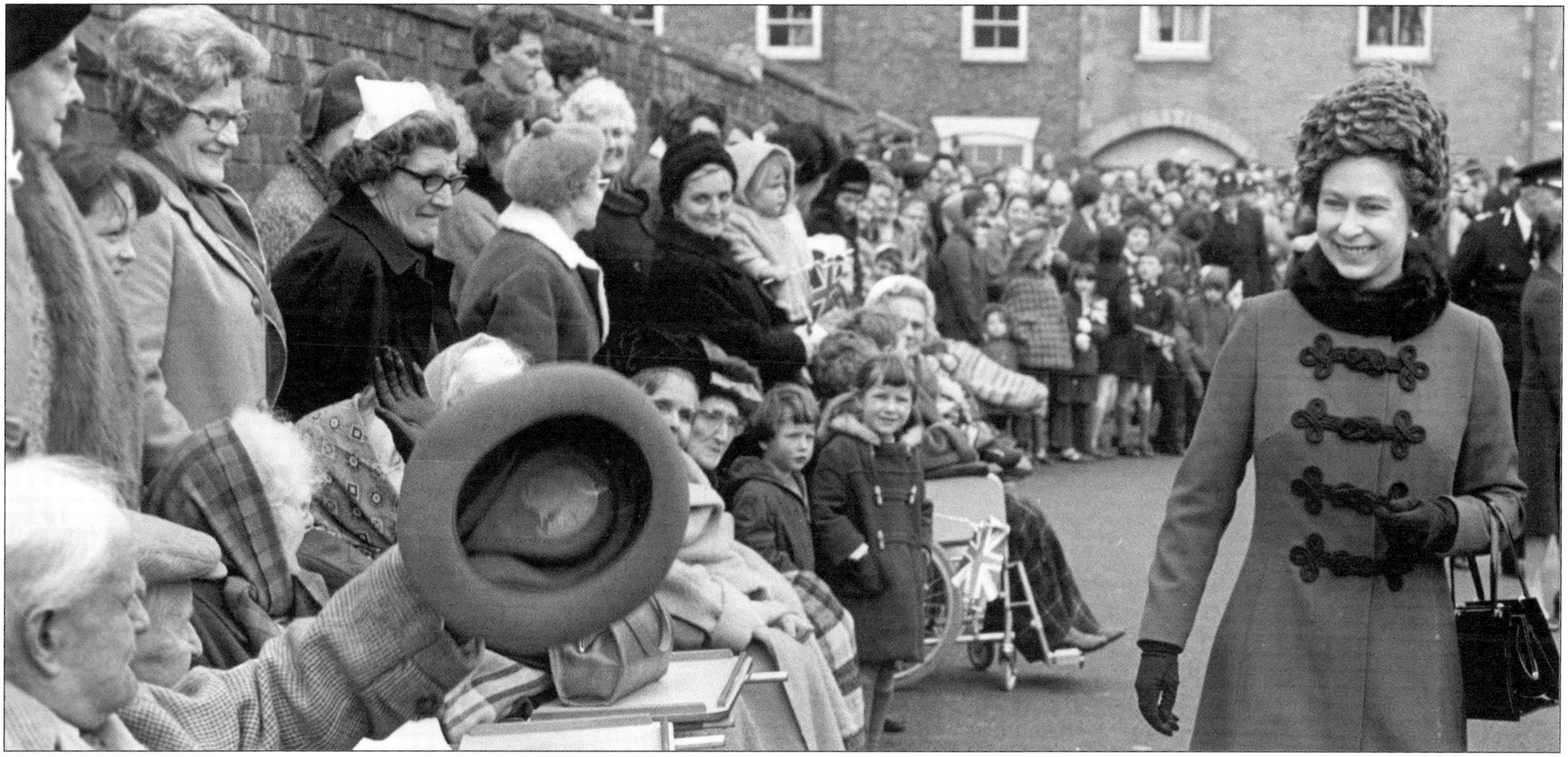

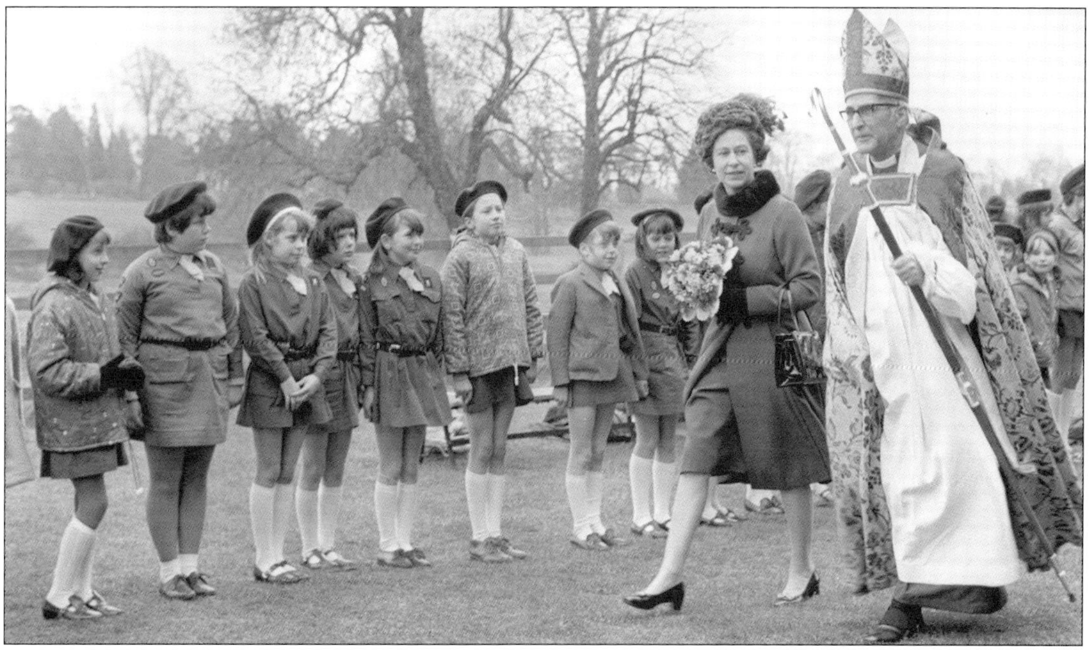

God Bless You Ma'am
Her Majesty goes walkabout to meet the residents of Tewkesbury after the Abbey's Maundy service.

To Serve the Queen…
Tewkesbury Brownies and Girl Guides on their best behaviour during the royal visit.

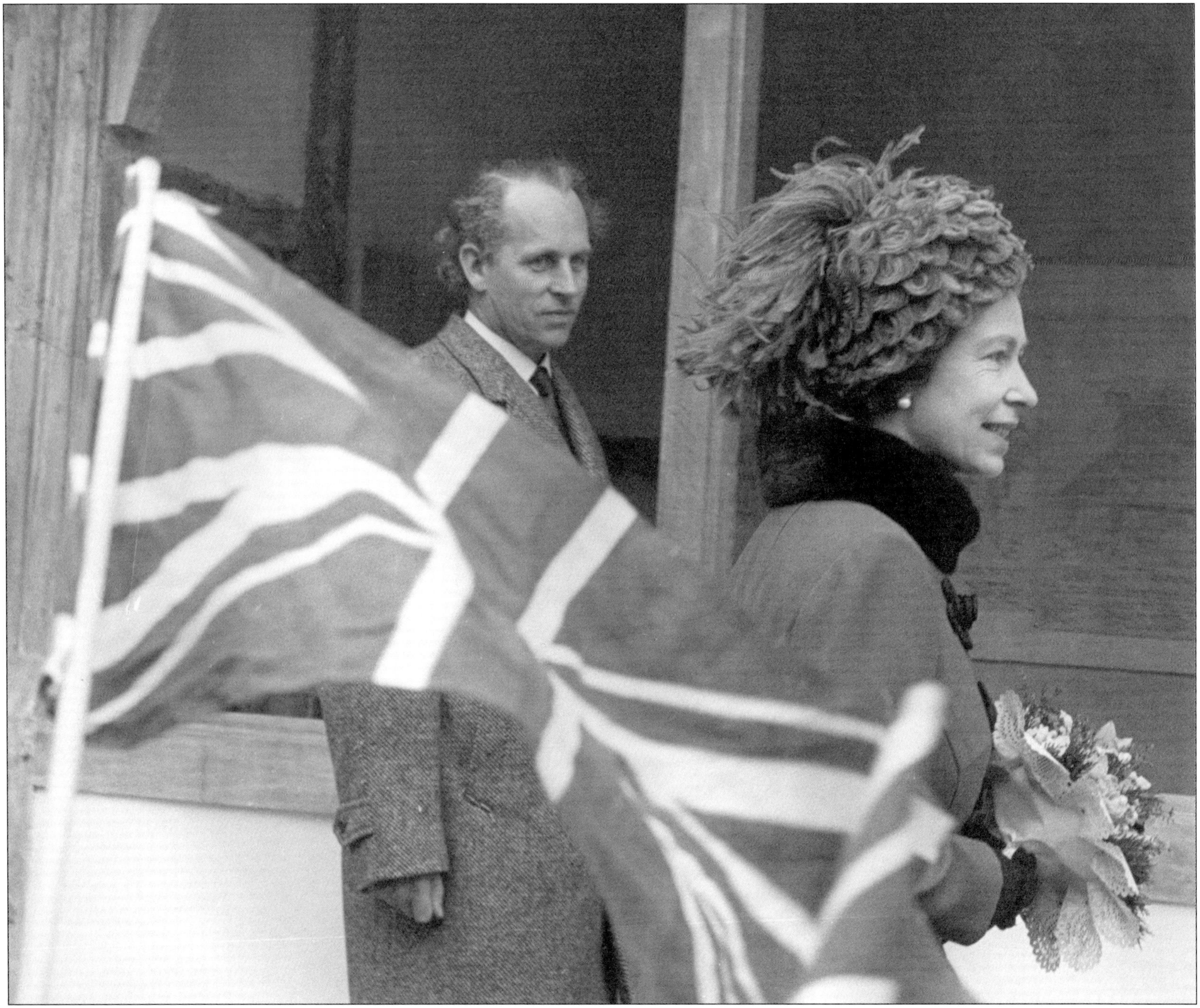

Queen and Country
Her Majesty sets a steady pace on her Tewkesbury walkabout.

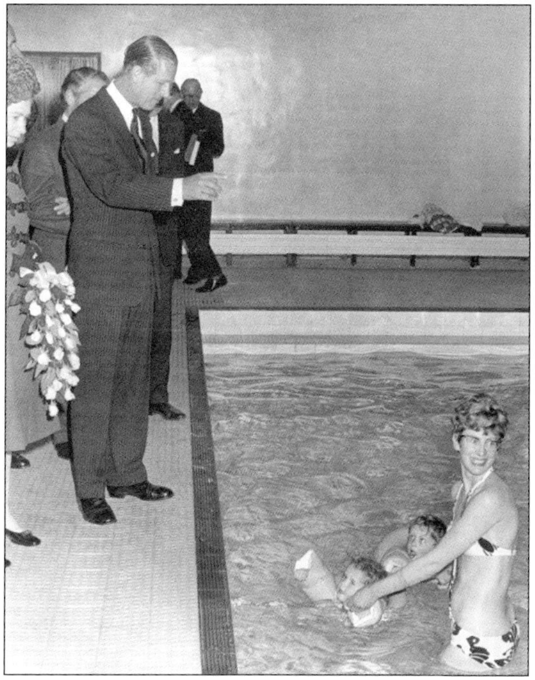

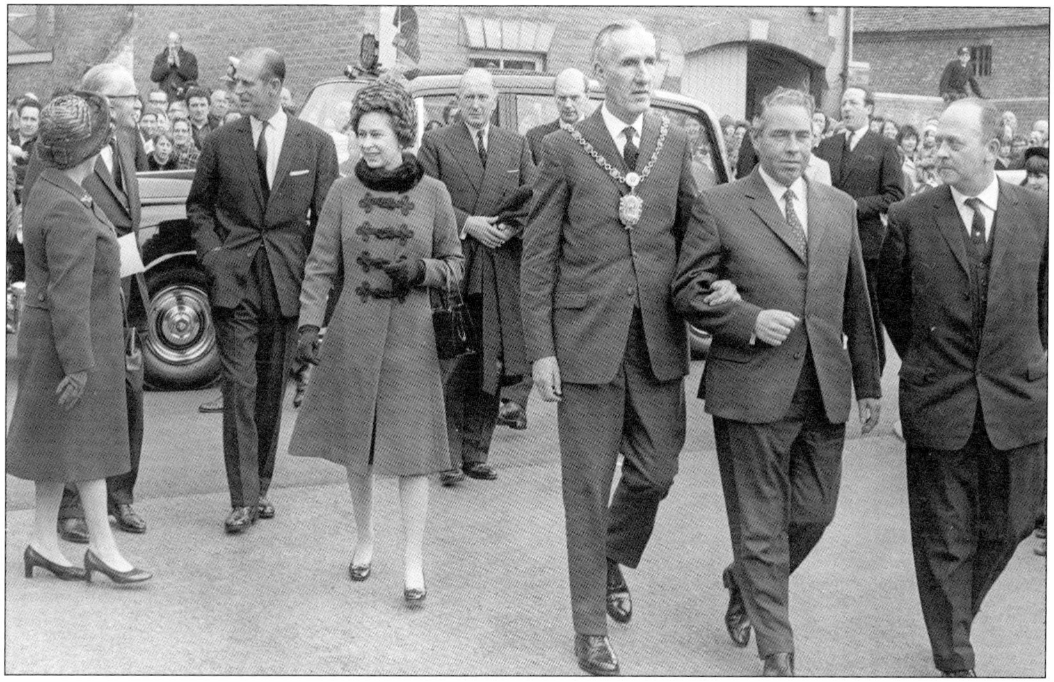

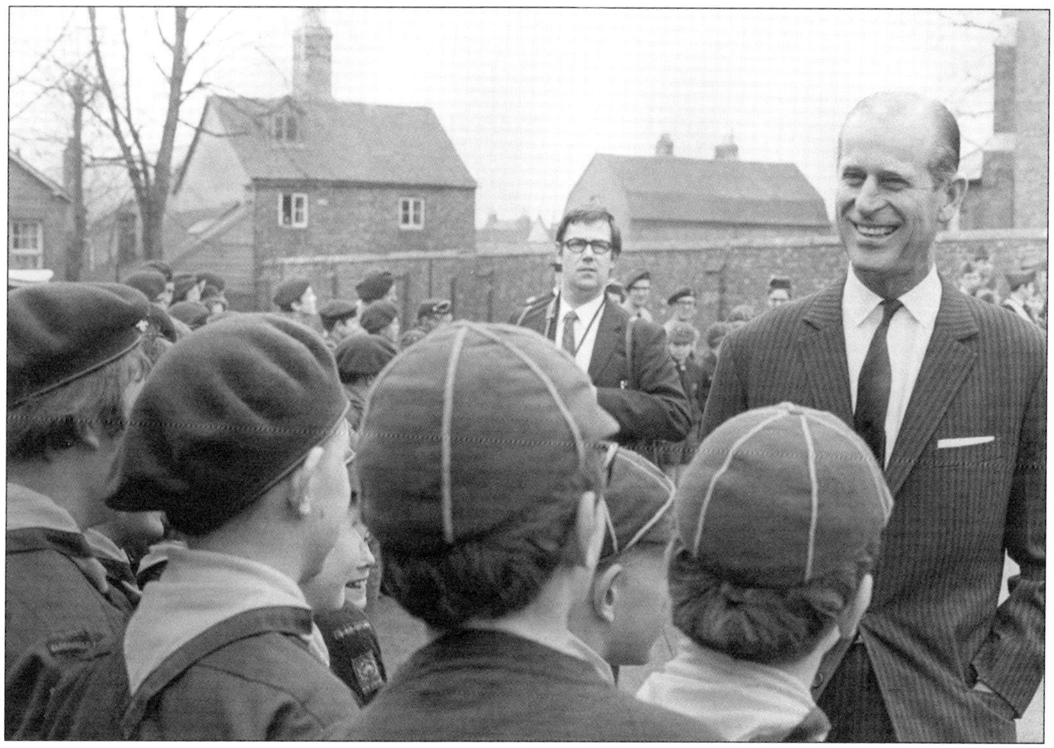

Come on in – the Water's Lovely!
After the abbey service and town tour, the Queen and the Duke of Edinburgh call in on the local Mother and Baby swimming lessons at Tewkesbury's pool – the Duke didn't get his feet wet!

Chain of Office
The Queen and the Duke of Edinburgh are preceded during their royal visit by Tewkesbury's blind mayor Mr Webber, who was being guided by a colleague on the royal tour.

Dib Dib Dib!
HRH Prince Philip has a friendly chat with Tewkesbury Cub and Scout Troops. Hovering in the background waiting for a photo opportunity is local cameraman, Ken Upton.

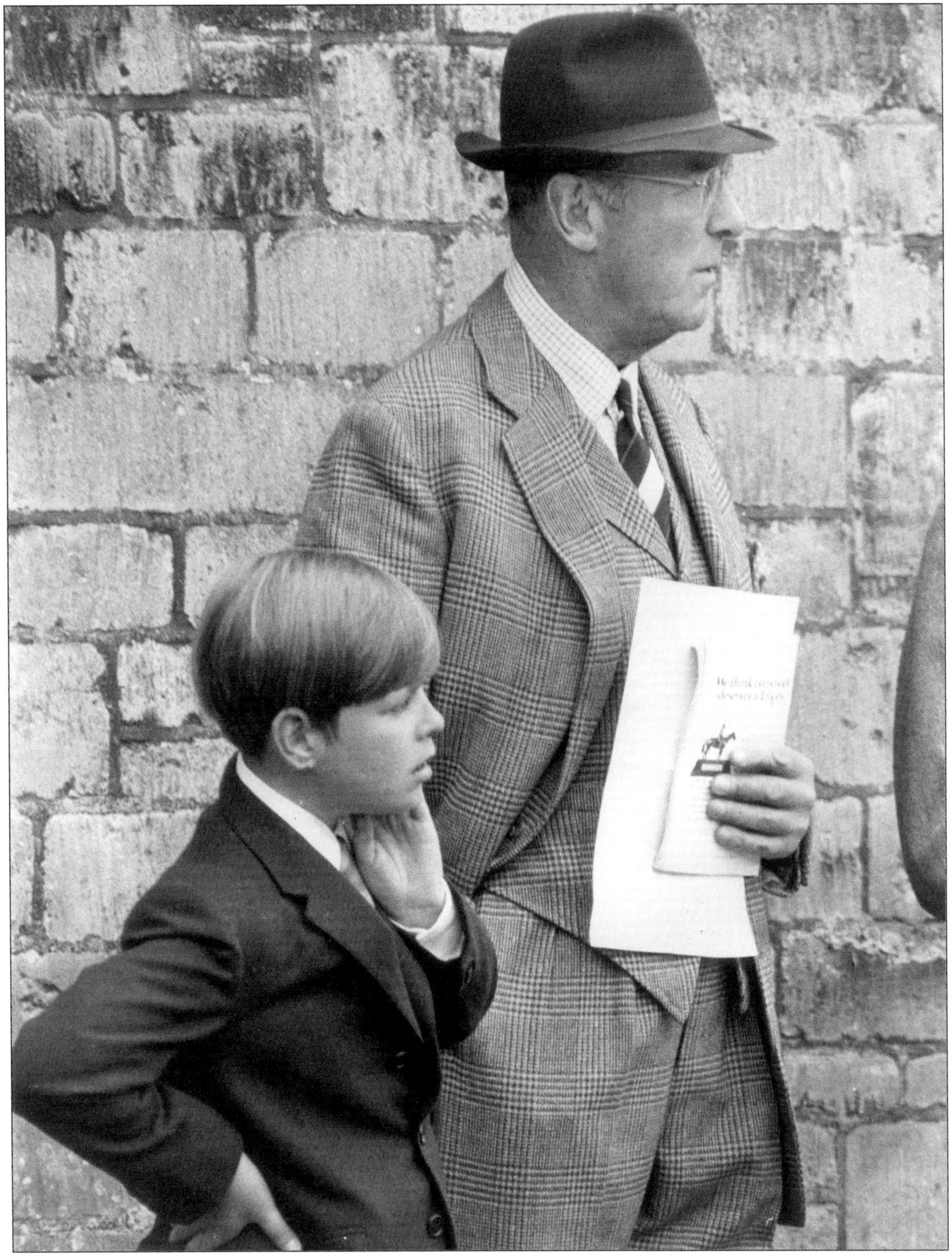

Beaufort Country
The now world-famous Badminton Horse Trials, held every spring at Badminton House, the estate of the Duke and Duchess of Beaufort, became an annual pilgrimage for members of the Royal family during the early 1960s. The relaxed, informal surroundings provided a pleasant weekend break for the royal horse lovers and their children. During those early days, they were seldom bothered by the press presence, which amounted to just a handful of photographers and journalists hovering discreetly in the background. Pictured here is a young Prince Andrew, in the company of the Duke of Beaufort, during the traditional vet's inspection held prior to the cross-country event.

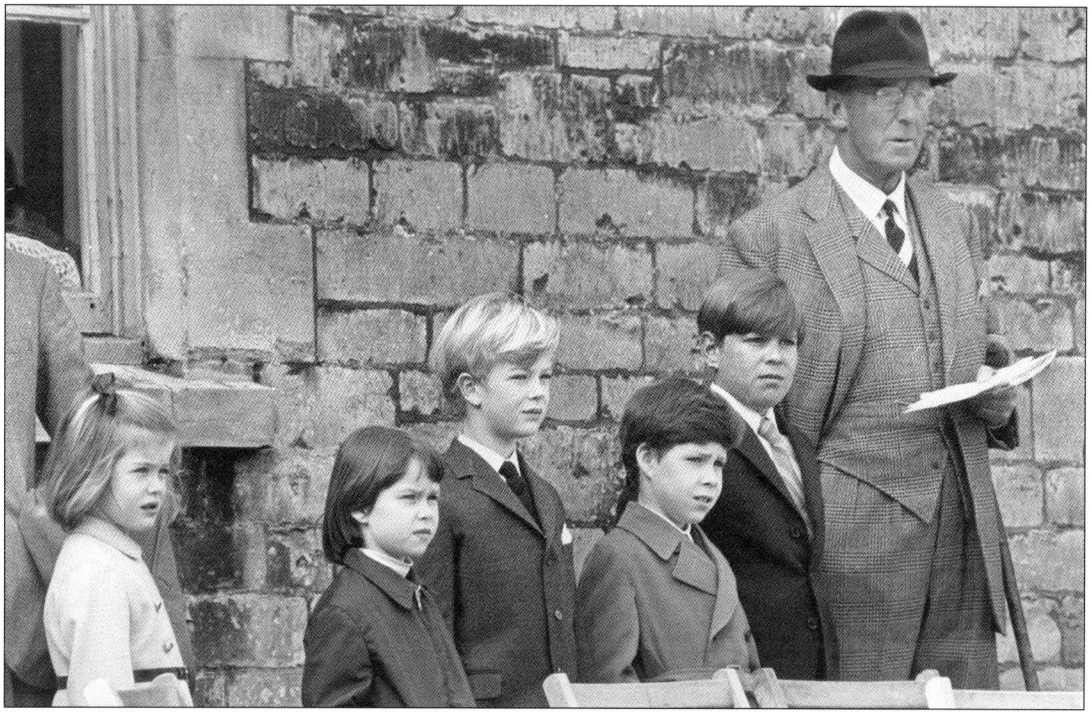

The Master
The children of the Duke and Duchess of Kent, Princess Margaret and Lord Armstrong Jones' offspring, Viscount Linley and Lady Helen Windsor, with Prince Andrew, watch fascinated as as the Duke of Beaufort, fondly known in horse circles as 'The Master', guides them though the morning's veterinary procedures.

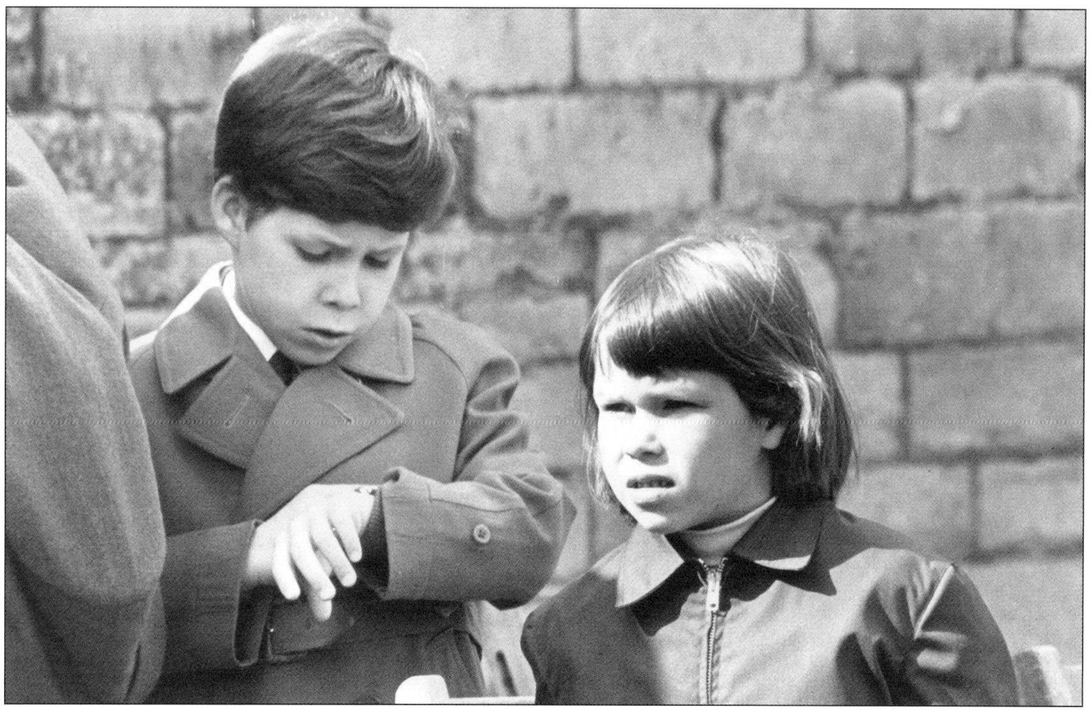

Royal Watch
Viscount Linley, obviously proud of his watch, manfully checks the time as his young sister, Lady Helen Windsor, keeps her eye on the horses.

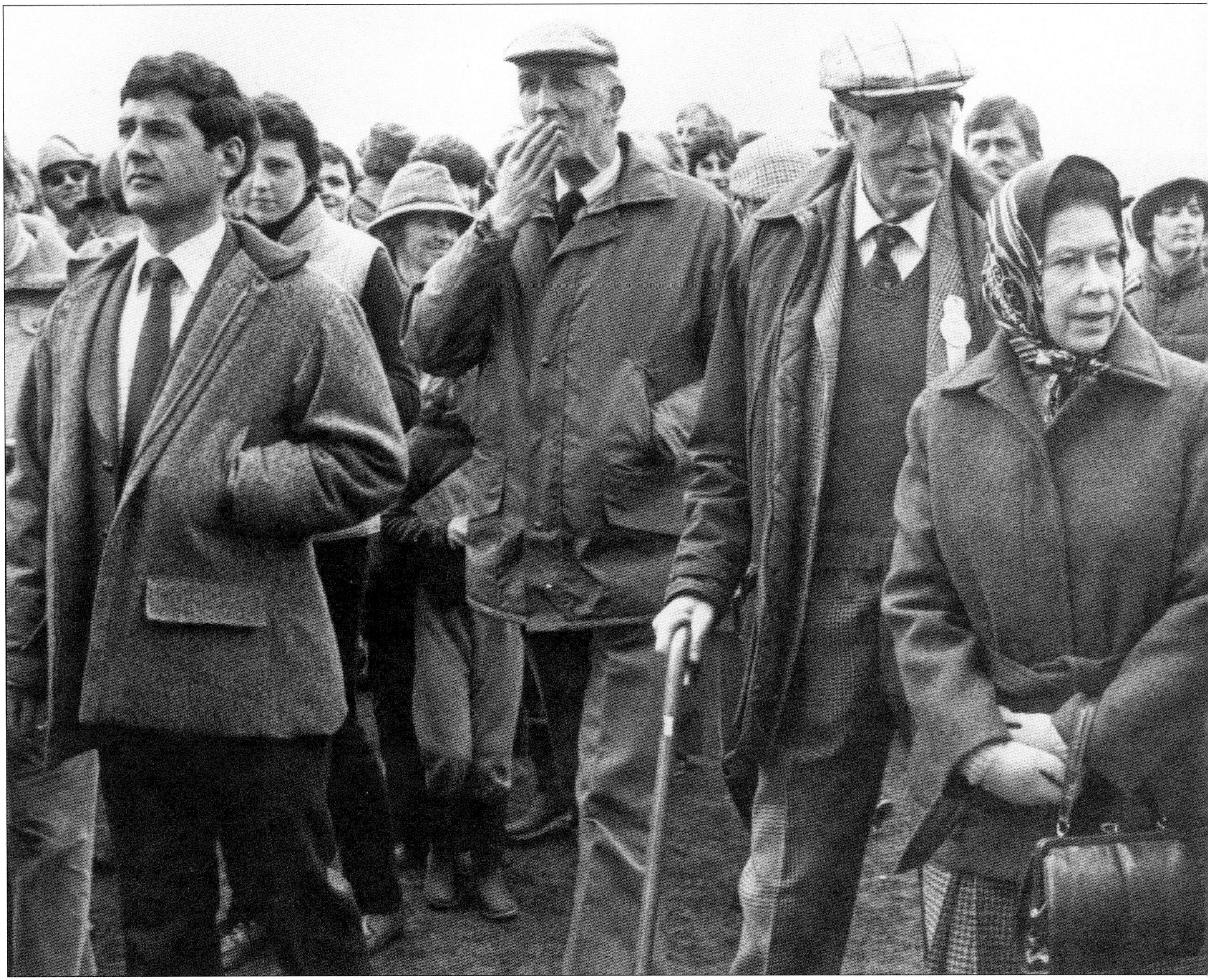

Village Life
Another year, another Badminton. The Queen with the Duke of Beaufort (standing behind) and Sir John Miller (on her left), stroll through the tented 'village' that boasted a Whitbread 'pub', restaurants, snack bars and shops selling all things equine.

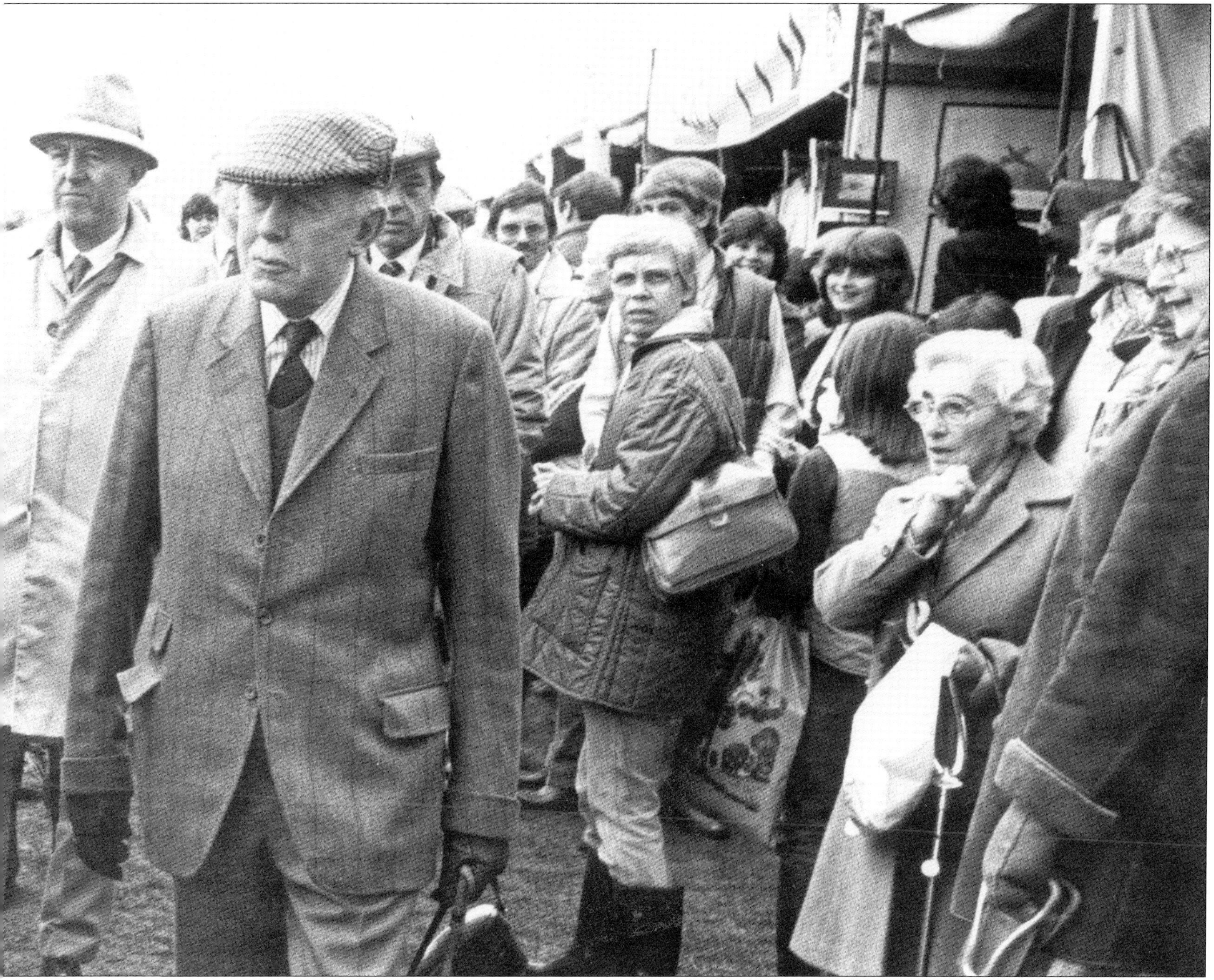

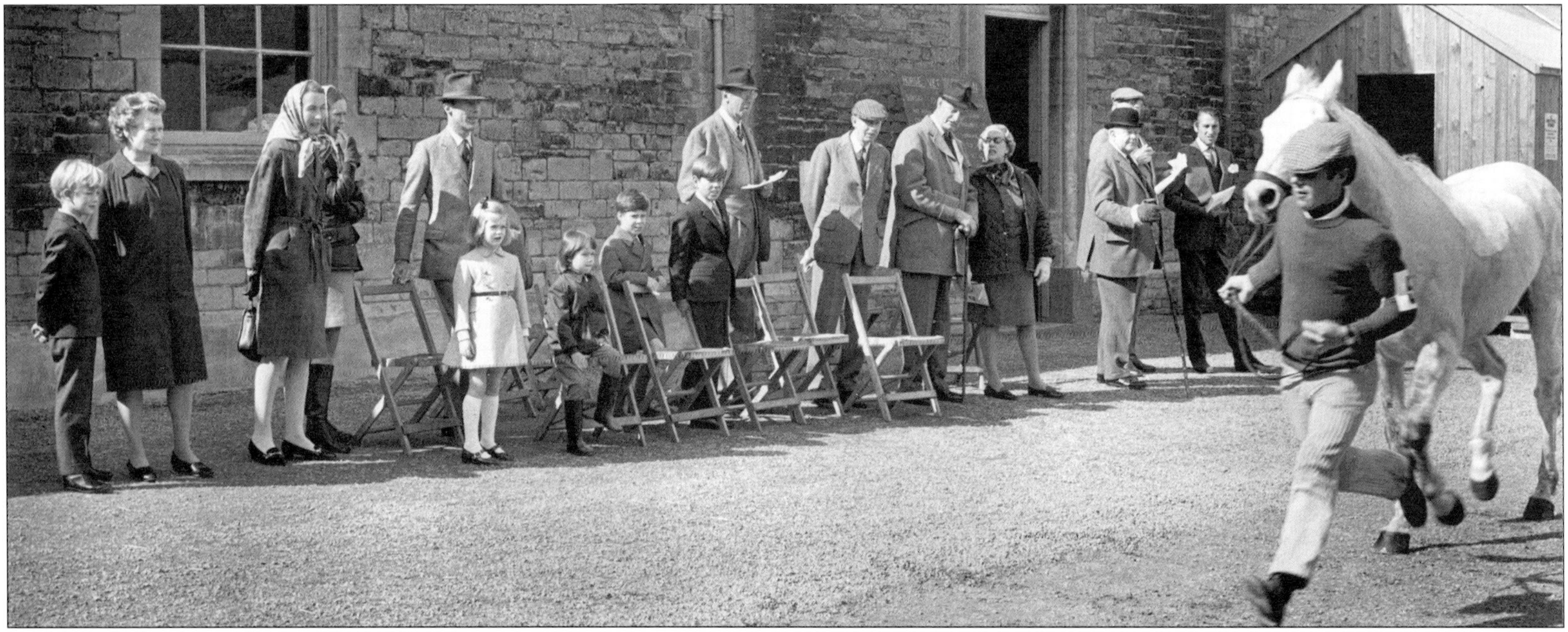

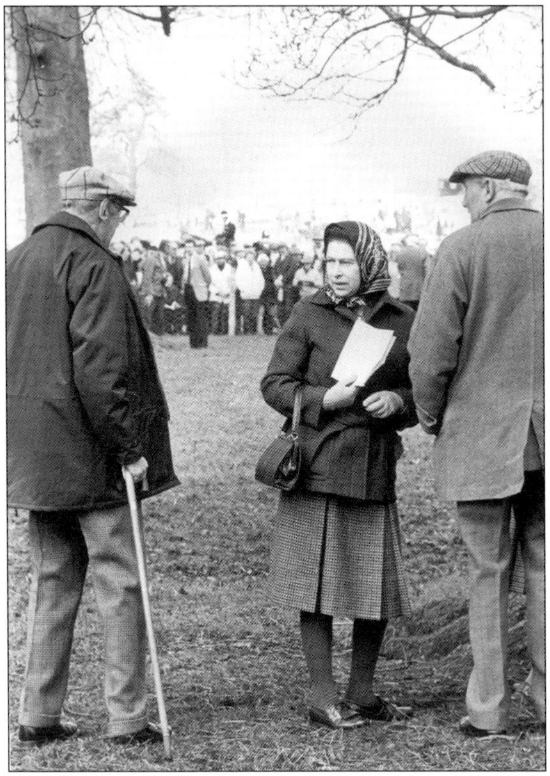

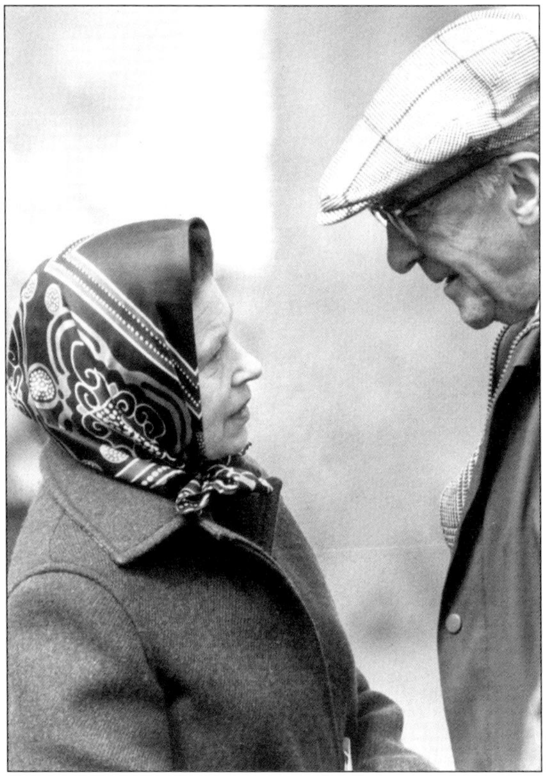

A Princely Posse
With a seemingly professional interest, the young Royals cast their eyes over the equestrian scene during the Badminton vet's inspection. Once the animals were checked and judged fit for the gruelling cross-country event, everyone retired for a hearty breakfast at the great house. This included the press party – all four of us – courtesy of 'The Master'.

Laid Back Royals
The Queen seemed at her most relaxed wandering around the Badminton course in those early eventing days, seen here in conversation with the Duke of Beaufort. The informal mix of visitors, riders and royalty in the estate grounds created a delightful atmosphere that unfortunately did not last as media interest grew.

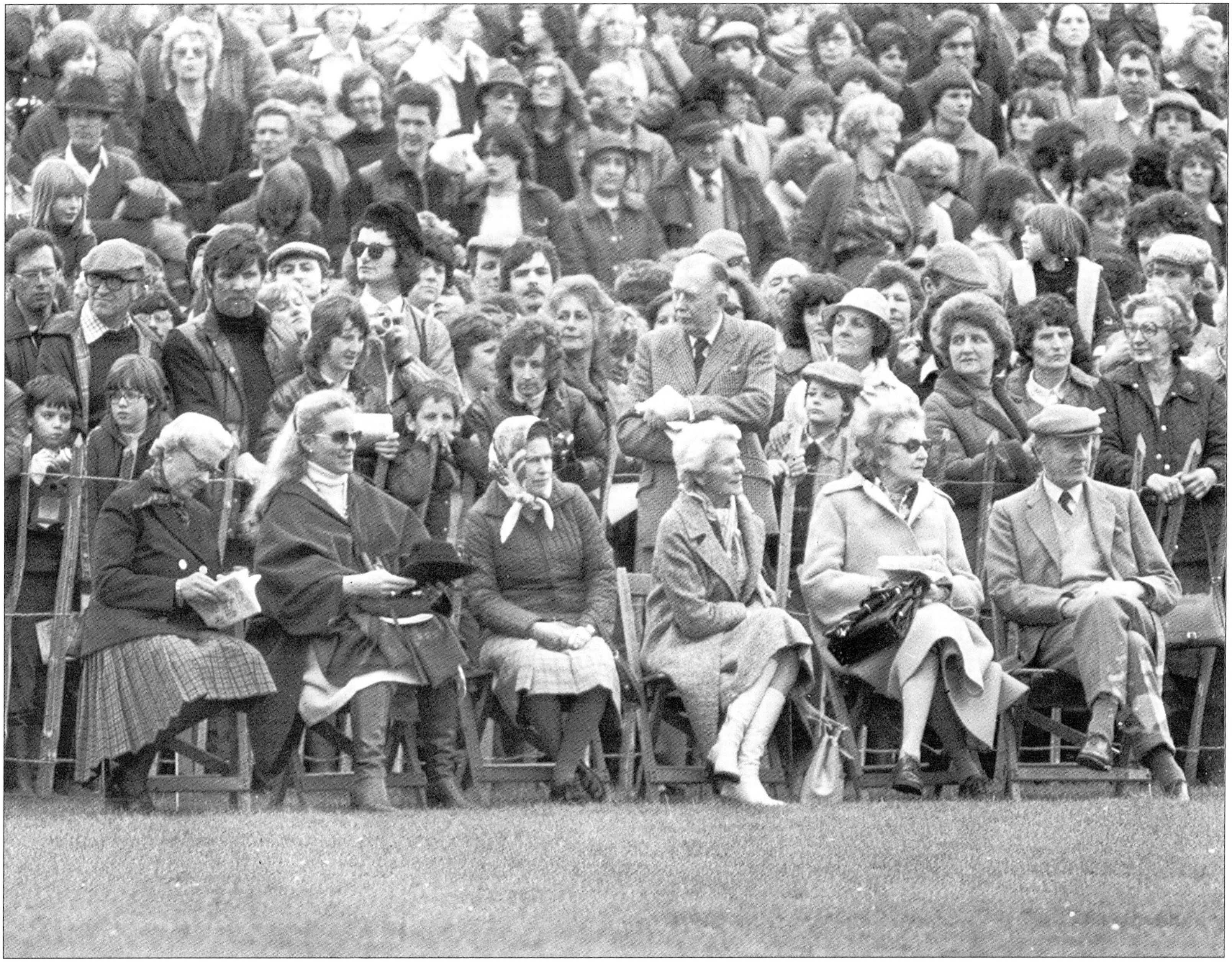

Standing Room Only
An enthralled Queen Elizabeth among quite a few of her subjects, and alongside Princess Michael of Kent during a Badminton cross-country event at Badminton Horse Trials in the 1970s.

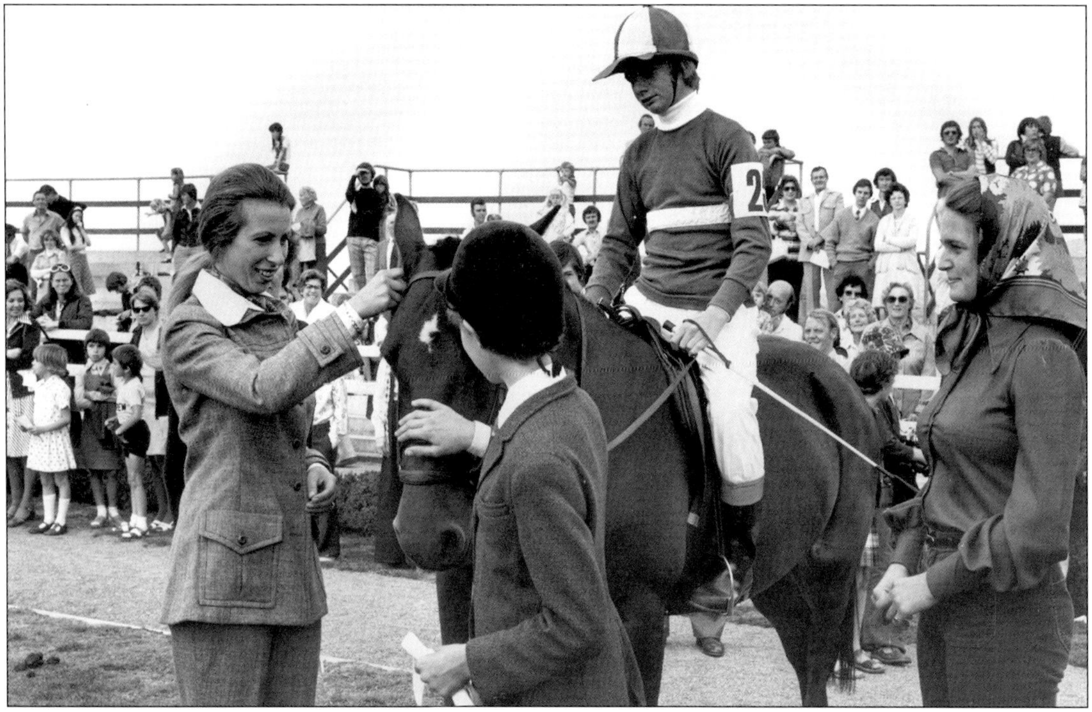

The Queen's Daughter
Princess Anne attends a Riding for the Disabled charity event, held at Cheltenham Racecourse in the late 1960s. The young Princess was obviously delighted to lend her support to the occasion, an association that she has kept up over many years.

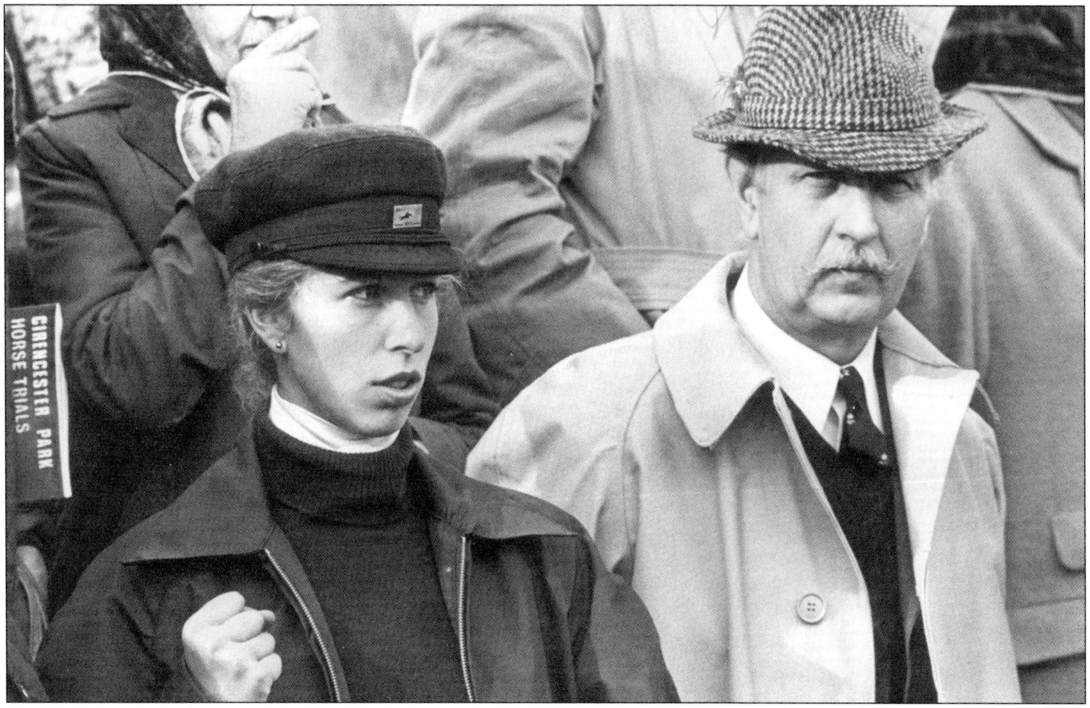

Get Ahead – Get a Hat!
A stylish Princess Anne, sporting a natty line in headwear, spurs on fellow competitors during horse trials held at Cirencester Park in the early 1970s. Standing beside her, and keeping a beady eye on my photographic activities is Gloucestershire Constabulary Royal Protection Officer Don Deakin.

Opposite: *Horses and Riders*
Passing comments between riders at Cirencester Park Horse Trials.

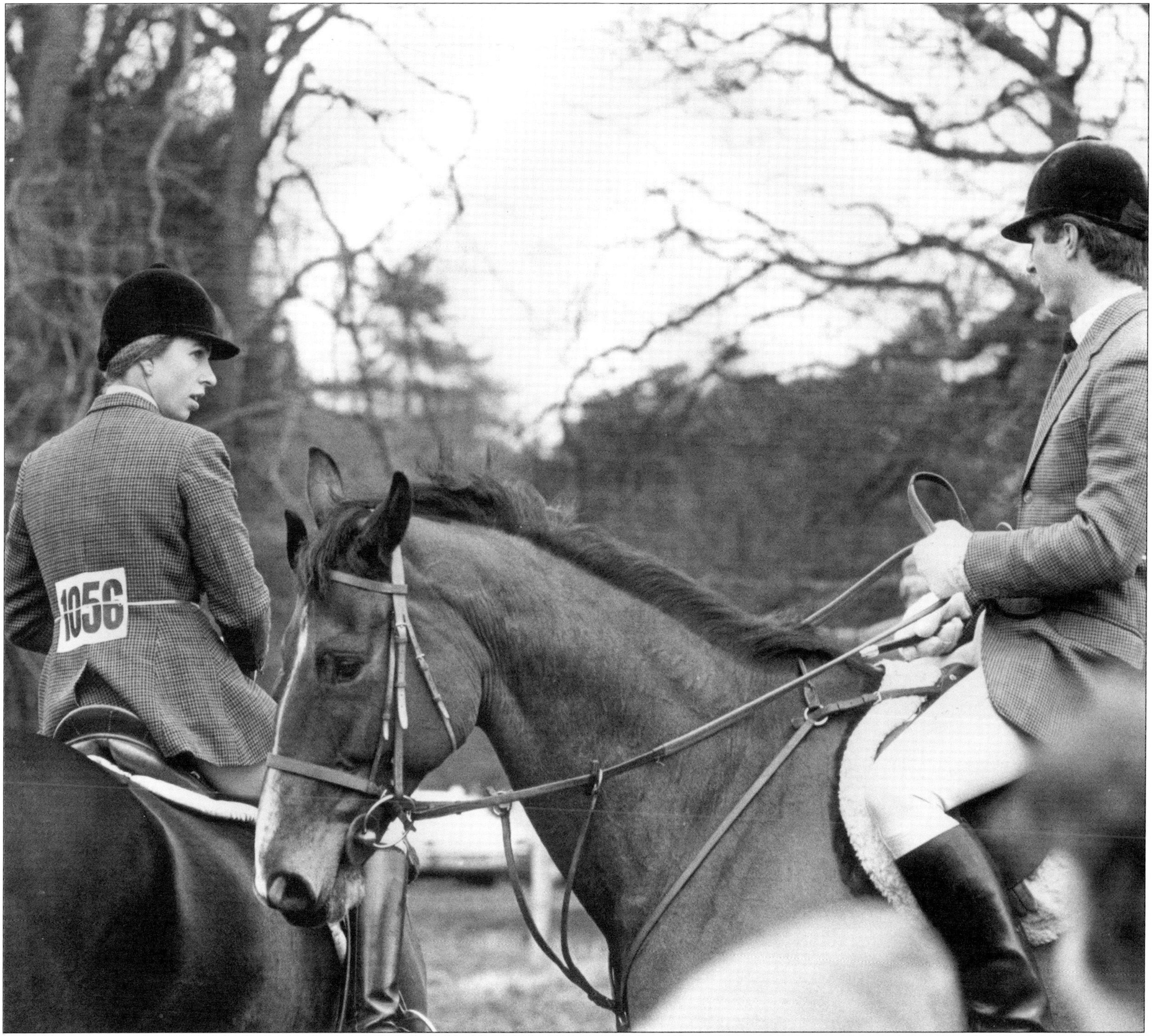
1056

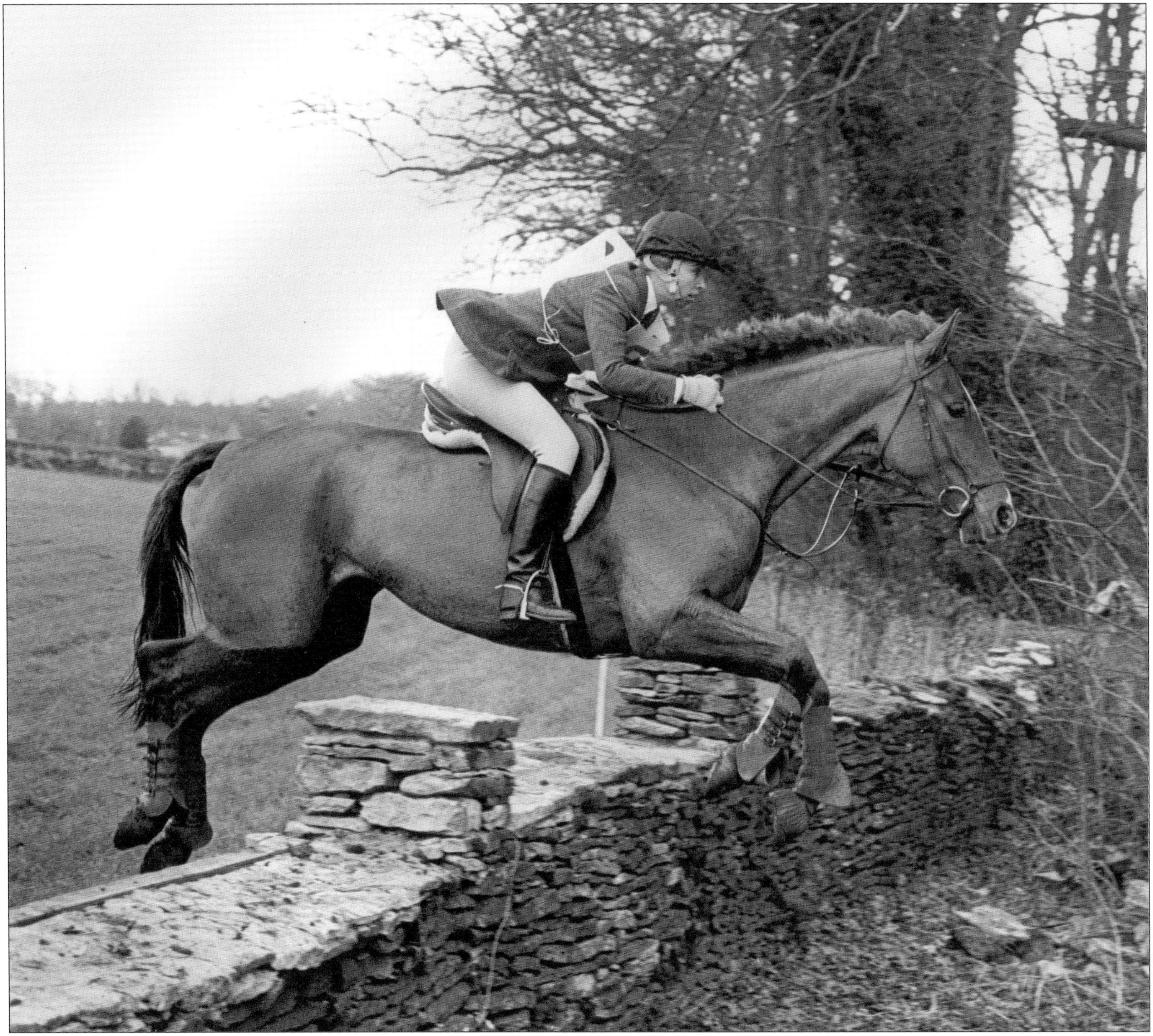

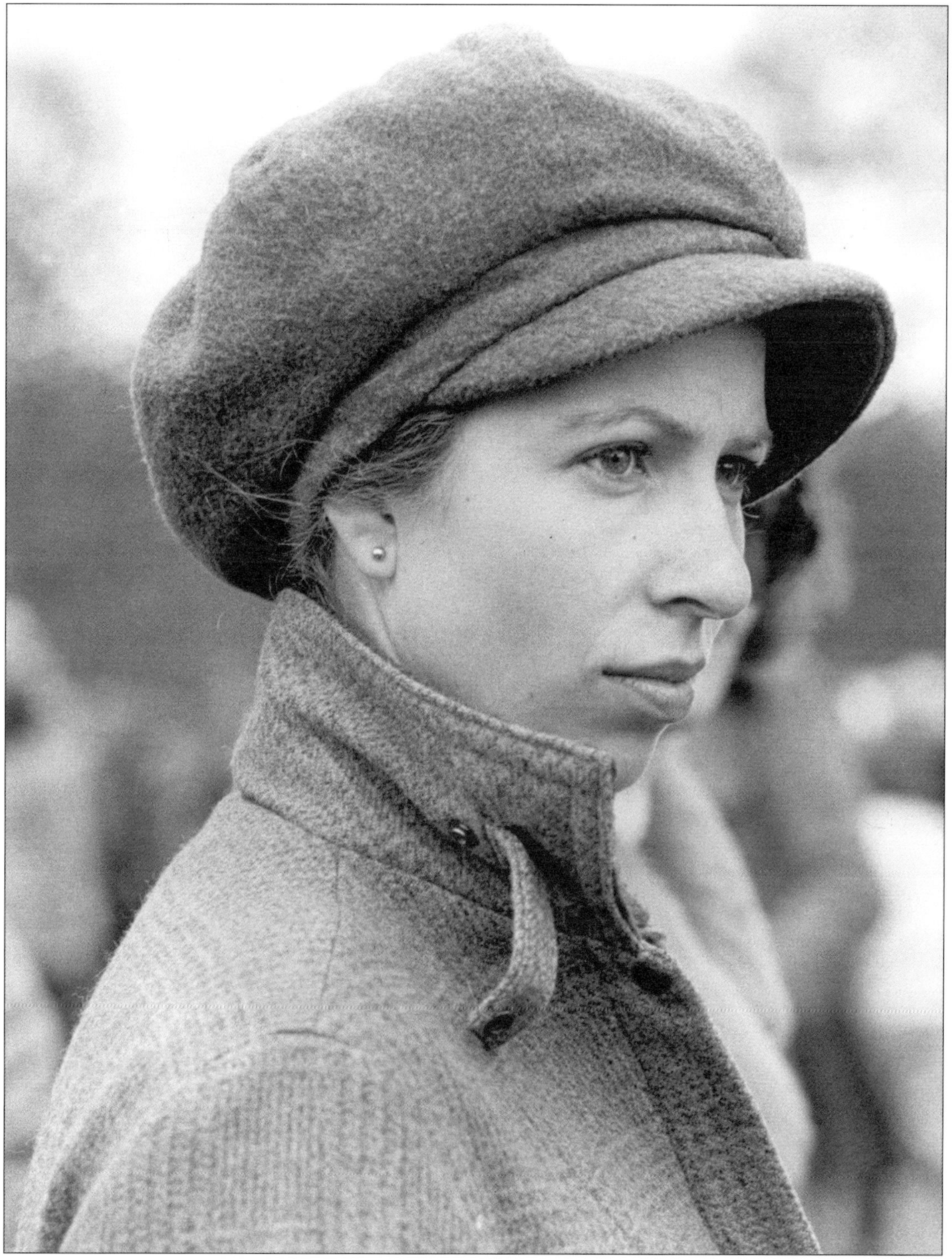

Opposite: *Leaping Ahead*
Princess Anne's eventing skills came to the fore during a cross-country event at Cirencester Park during the 1970s.

A head for hats
Badminton during the 1970s. The Princess' penchant for fashionable hats made her an instant attraction for the cameras.

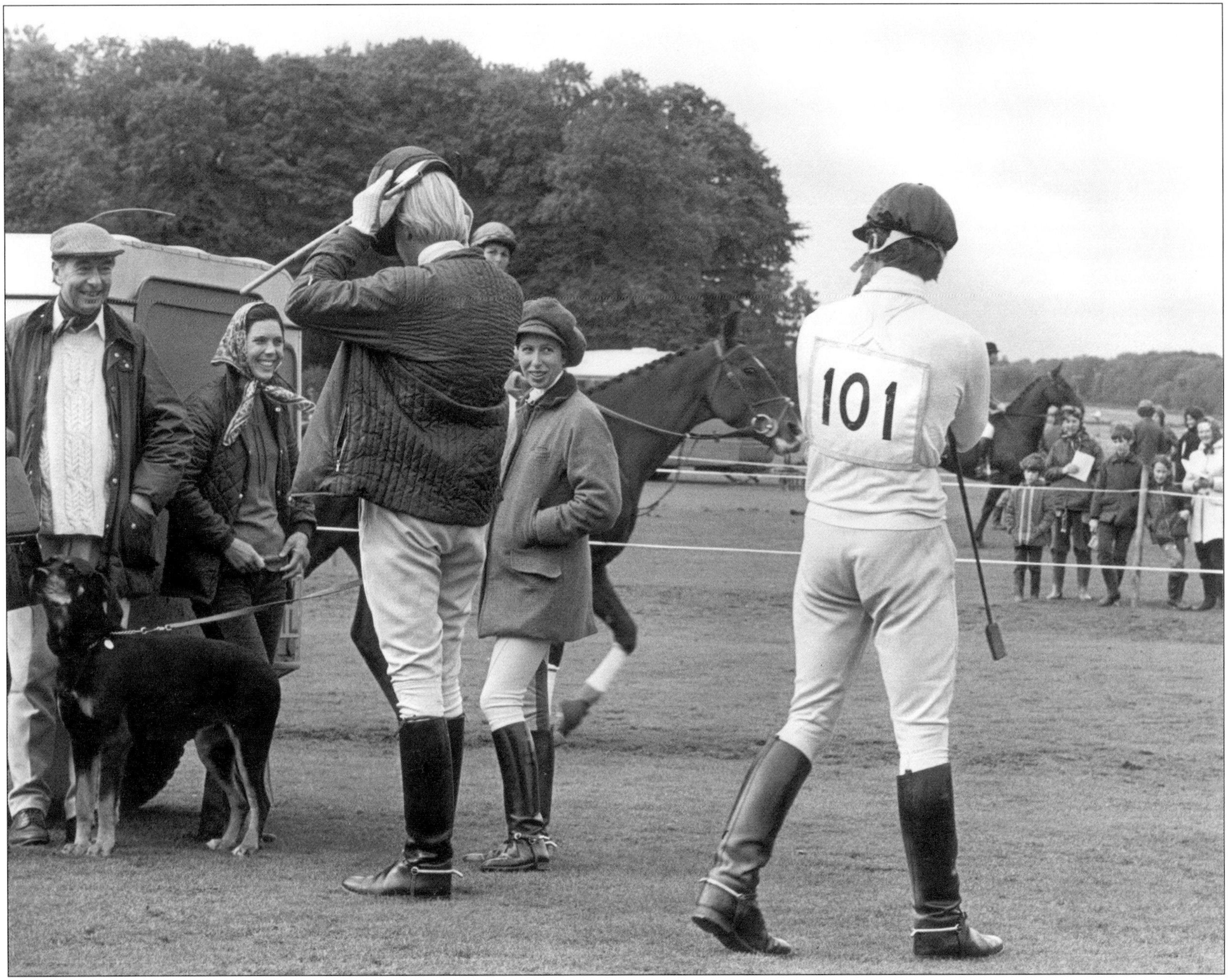

The Eyes Have It
It was through her love of horses and eventing that Princess Anne met her husband-to-be. This smiling glance from the Princess to a passing Captain Mark Phillips says everything. On the extreme left is her future father-in-law, Peter Phillips.

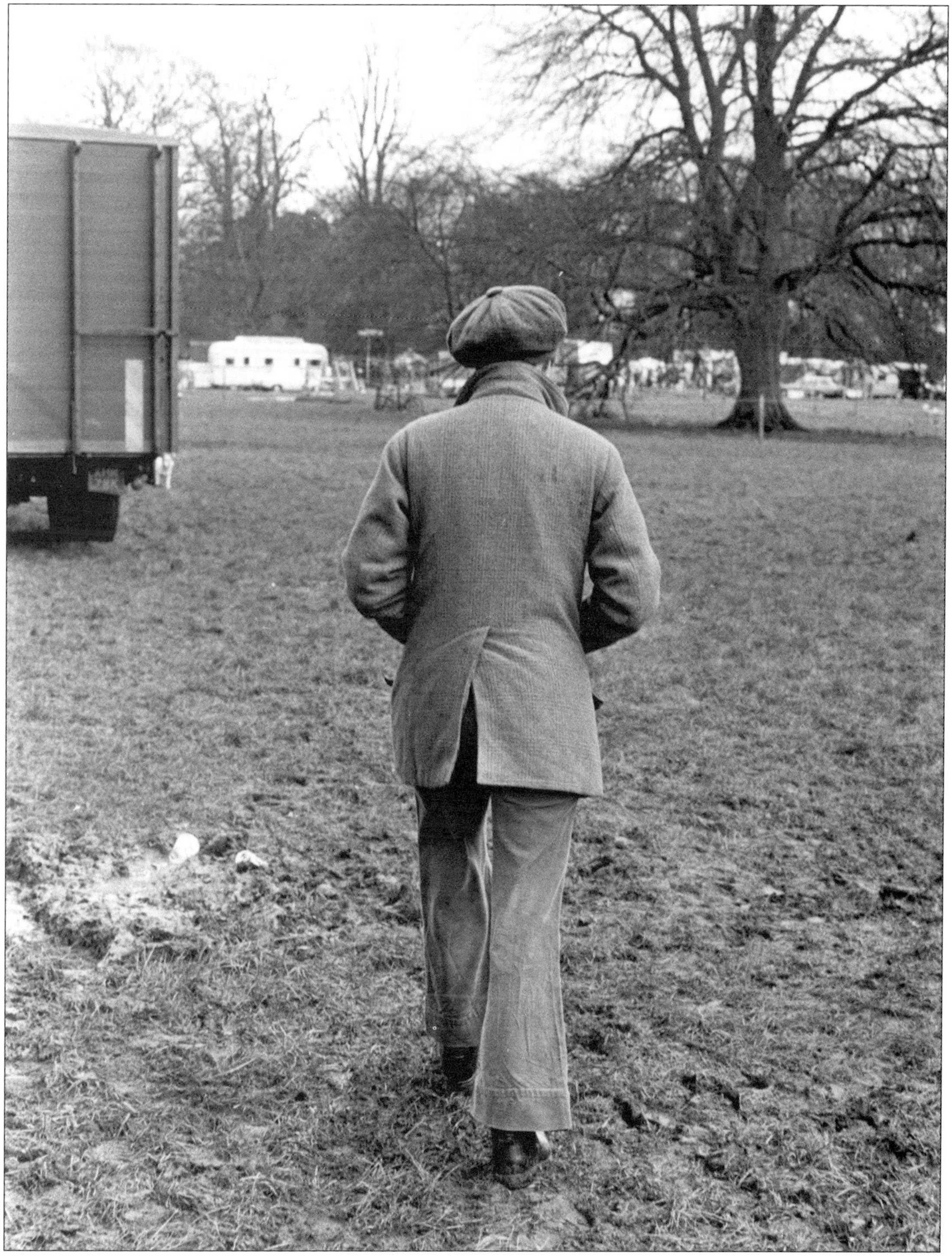

Meet the Family
With the Badminton Horse Trials over for another year, Princess Anne makes her way from the estate – possibly pondering on equestrian events or perhaps with affairs of the heart on her mind? When the media rumours started flying that she was to become engaged to Captain Mark Phillips, I made a chance visit to the Phillips' household in Great Somerford, in the hope of photographing the family and their home for possible syndication. After a gentle knock on the door I was greeted by a frosty Mrs Phillips, who stated 'There is no truth in these rumours and certainly no engagement in the offing – you are wasting your time.' I must have looked rather crestfallen, for suddenly she softened a little and commented, 'I'll say this. You are the only one of the press who has had the decency to call at the house. All the others have lurked behind walls and hung off trees, trying to get any pictures they can. In view of your good manners, should there be any announcement – and I am not saying there will be – give me a call, and we'll see what we can do.' Some two weeks later, I was invited into the Phillips' family home, given a large gin and tonic, and subsequently obtained an exclusive set of pictures that graced the next issue of *Woman's Own* magazine. The lady kept her word!

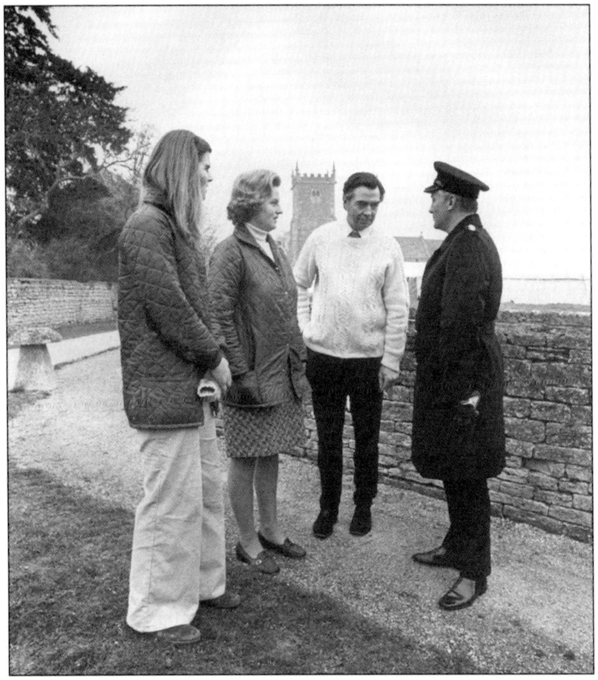

Wedding Bells
Wednesday 17 November 1973 was the day chosen for the wedding of Princess Anne and Captain Mark Phillips – the venue – Westminster Abbey. In the village of Great Somerford in Wiltshire, just over the Gloucestershire border, Mr and Mrs Peter Phillips (Princess Anne's future parents-in-law) with their daughter Sarah, discuss police arrangements for local celebrations on the big day.

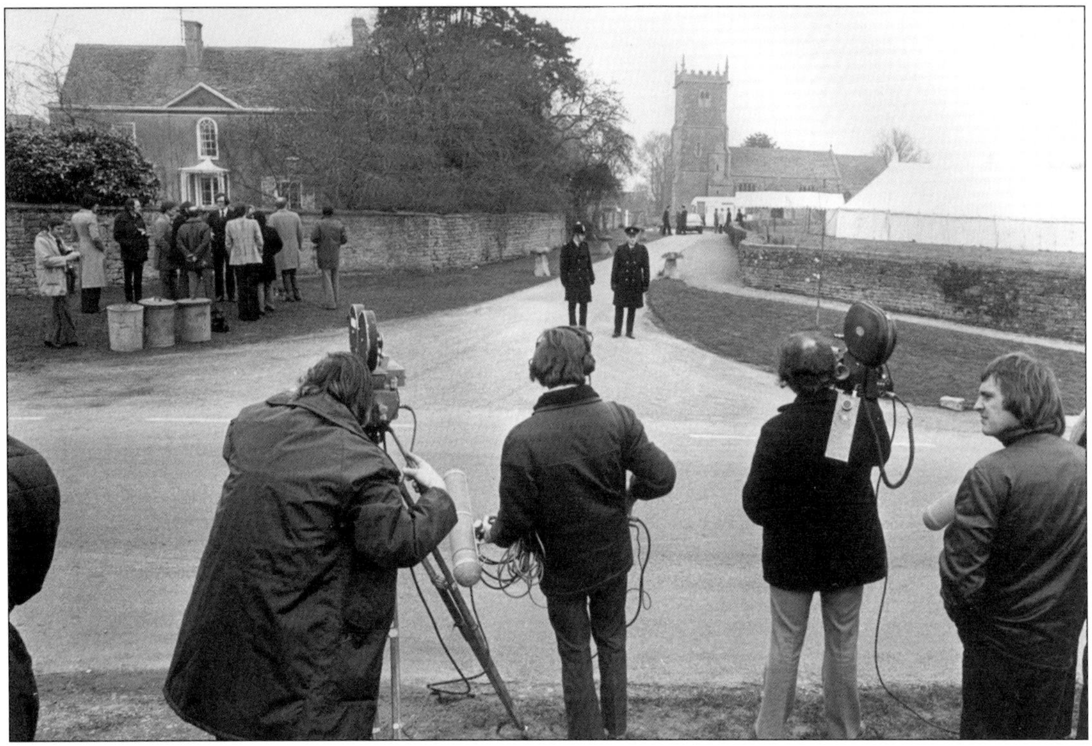

Wedding Pictures
The media arrive in Great Somerford to record the royal wedding celebrations. A large marquee had been erected on land adjacent to the Phillips' home to accommodate guests, for what must have been one of the biggest events in the history of this tiny village.

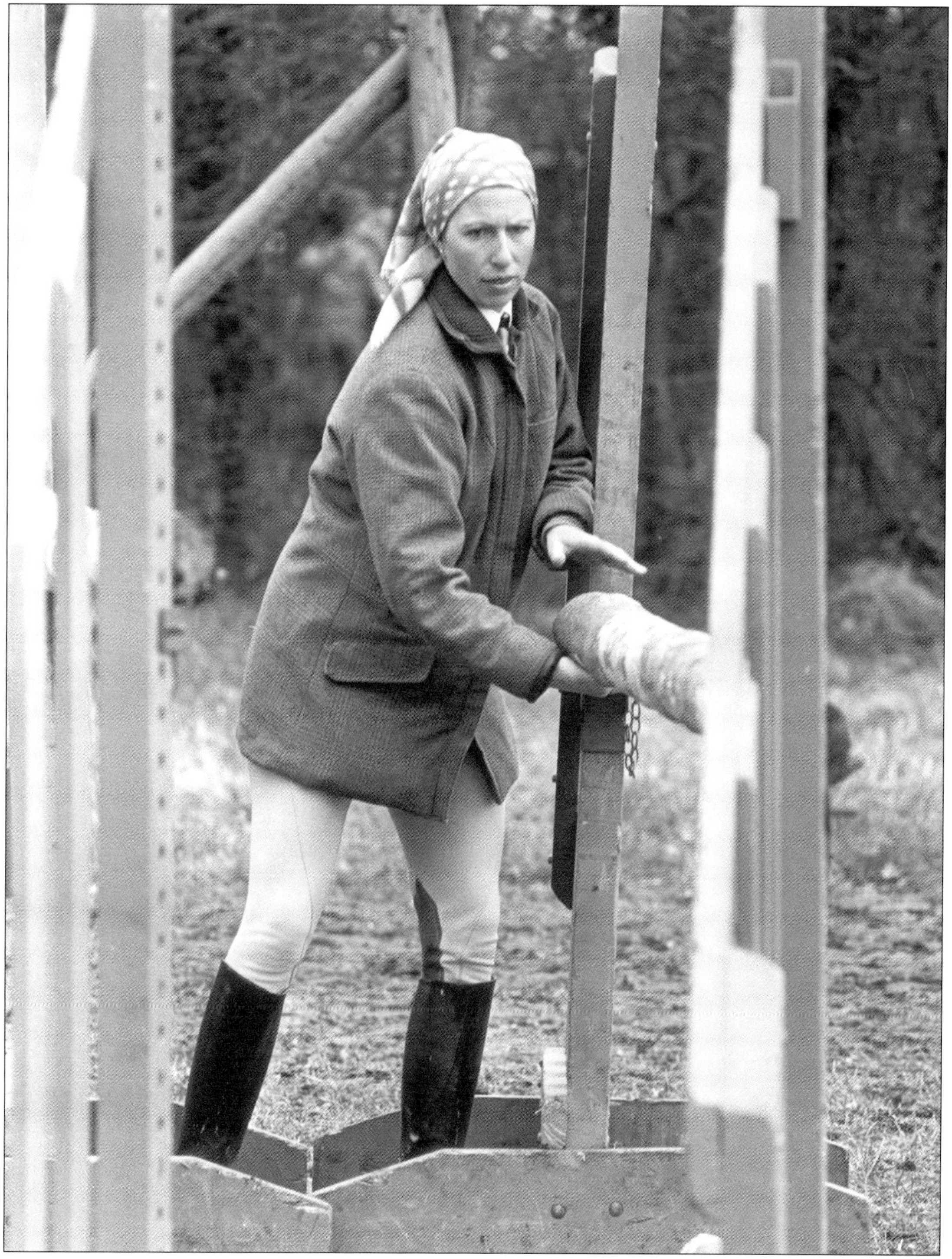

Down to Earth Royal
Cirencester Park, home of the Bathurst family, was a popular venue for equestrian events during the 1970s and '80s. Here, an informally dressed Princess Anne shows she is not afraid to get her hands dirty, as she helps assemble a course jump.

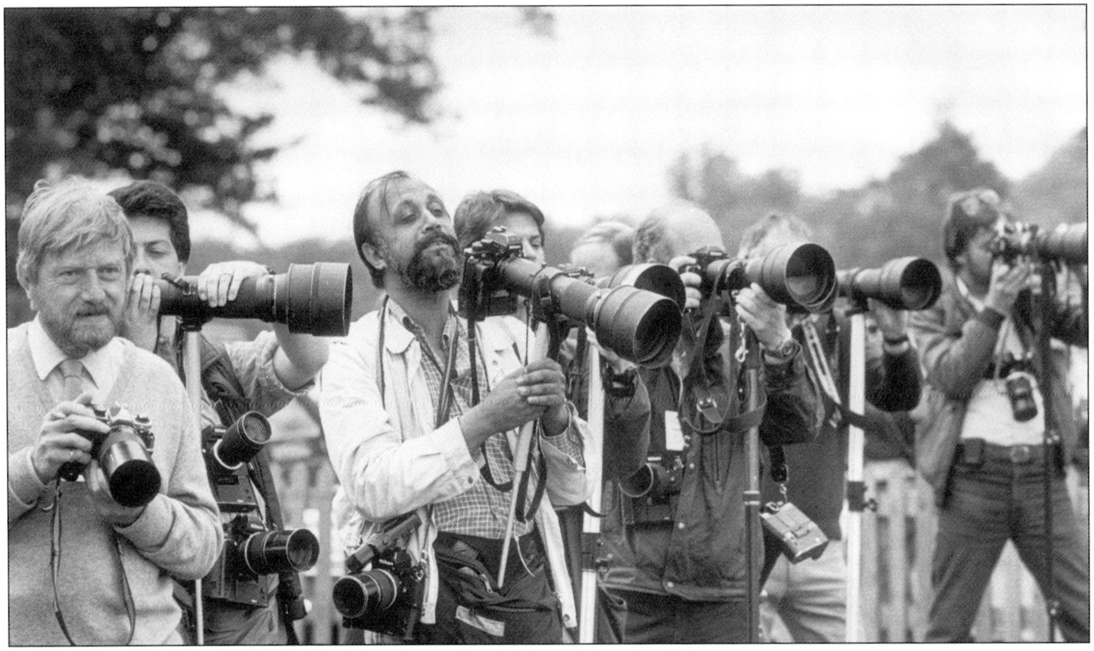

Happy Snappers
A dignified, well-behaved group of national and local photographers line up for the prize-giving ceremony after a polo match at Cirencester Park, during the 1970s. On the left is my old colleague, Richard Sturdy from the *Gloucestershire Echo*, mixing with the 'big boys' from Fleet Street.

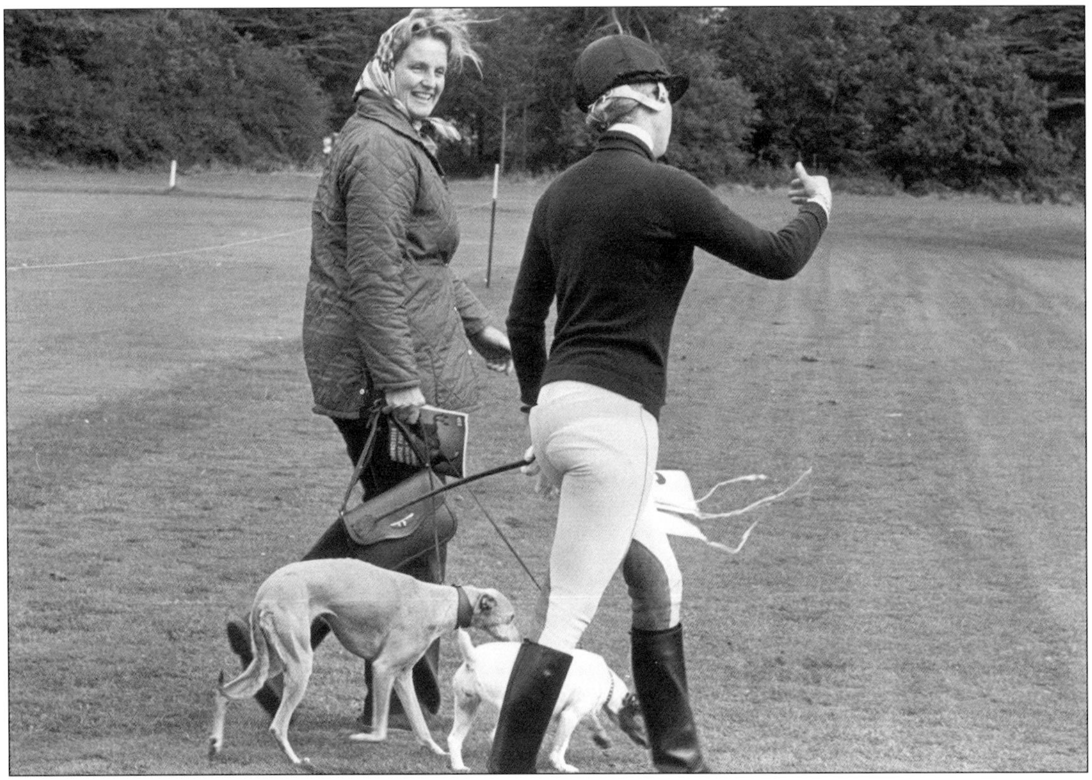

And the Dogs Came Too…
Mrs Peter Phillips with her daughter-in-law Princess Anne strolling through Cirencester Park as they walk the course, whilst at the same time giving the dogs some exercise.

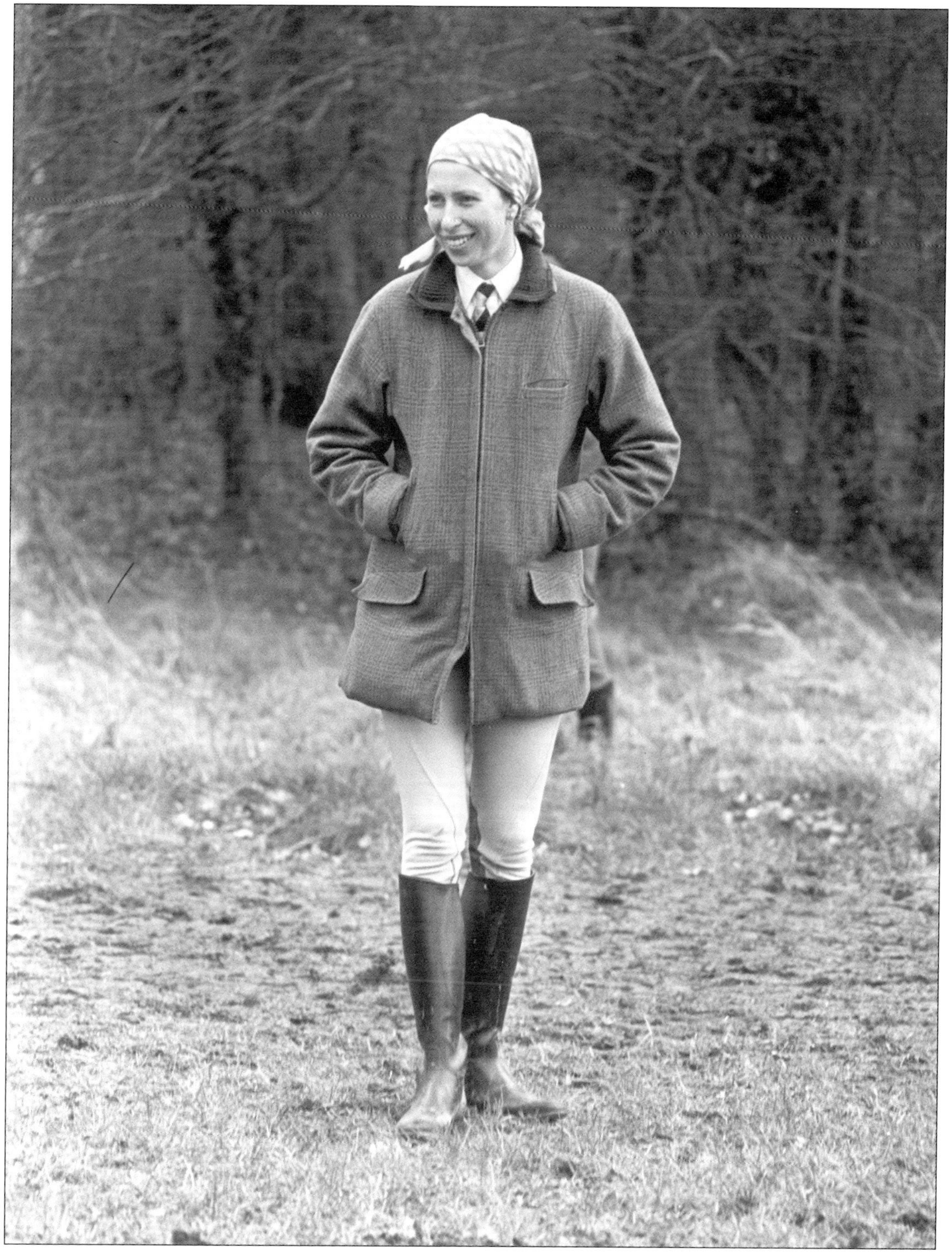

Smiling Royal
Princess Anne, never happier than when involved with horses, in a jolly frame of mind at Cirencester Park.

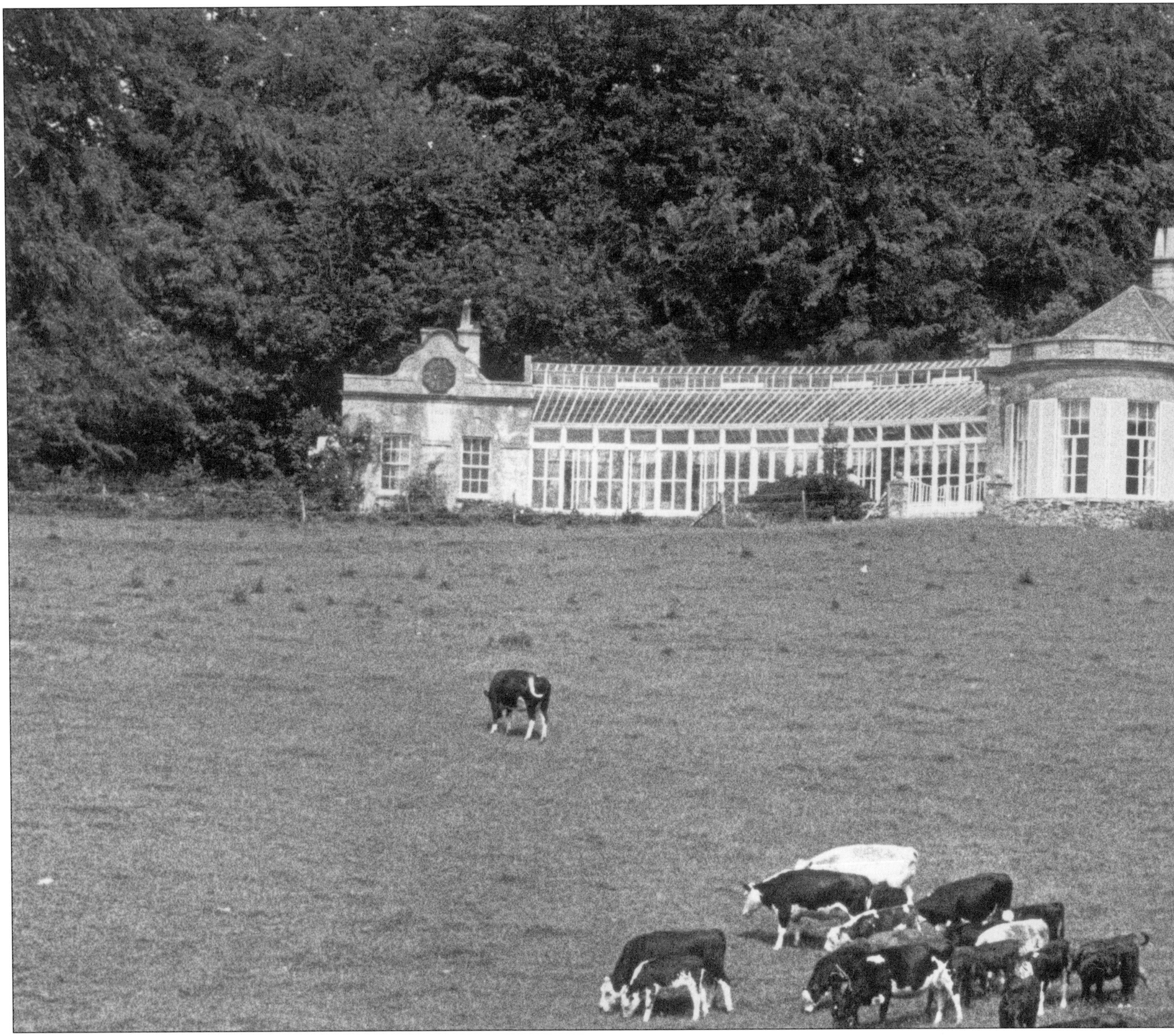

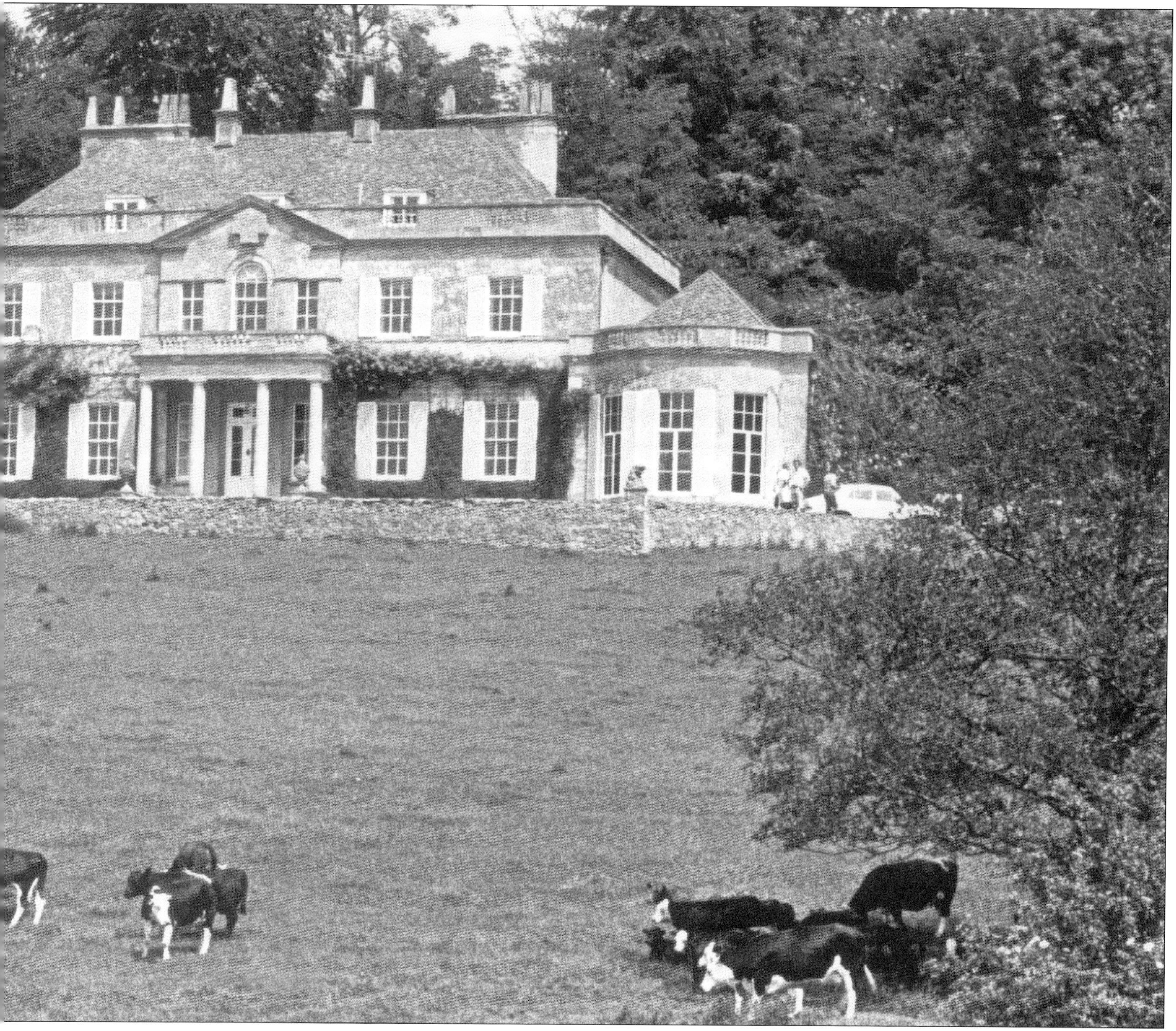

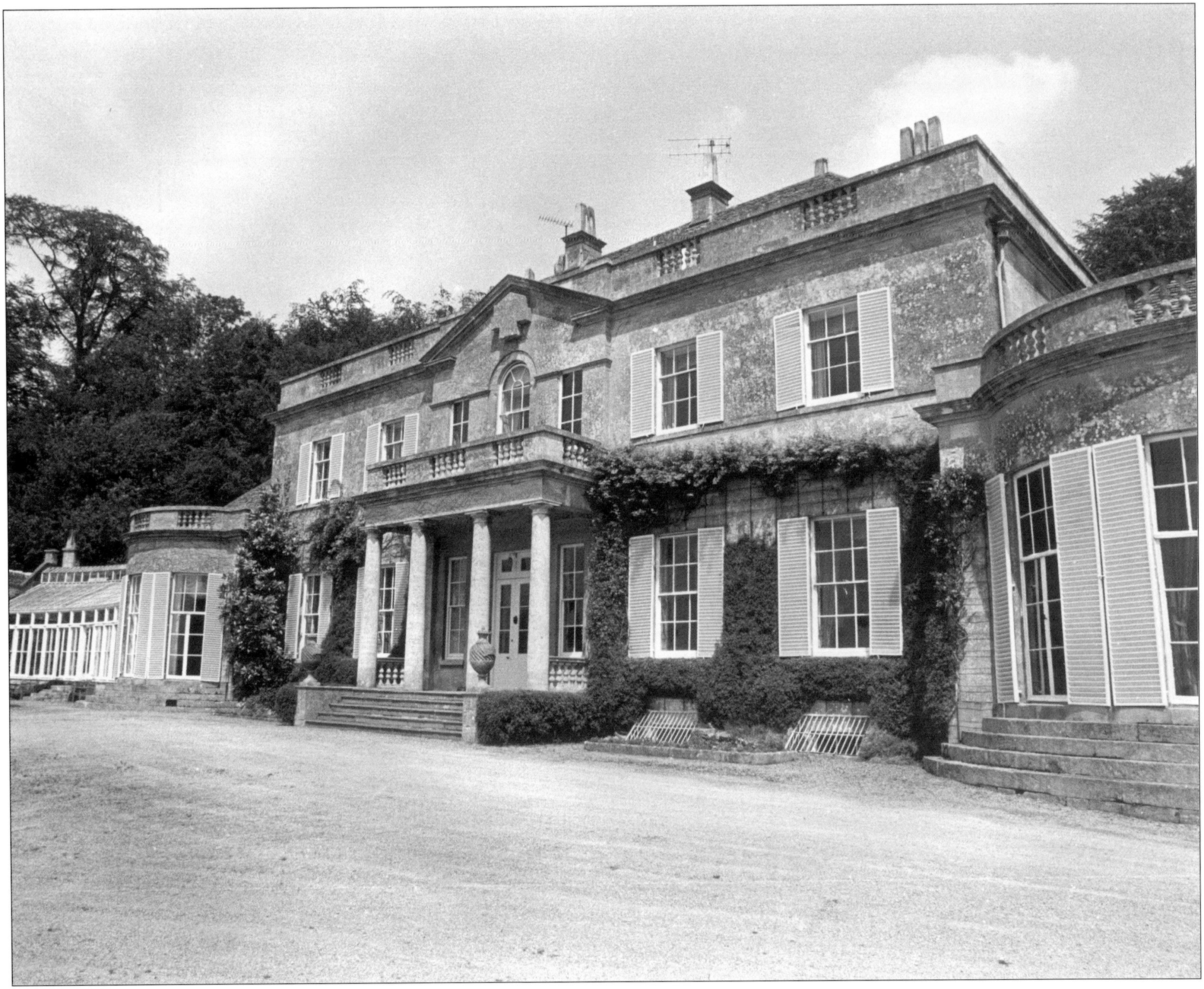

Previous page and left: *Royal Residence*
Cattle peacefully graze in front of Princess Anne and Captain Mark Phillips' future home, Gatcombe Park. The house was brought by the Queen as a wedding present for the royal couple.

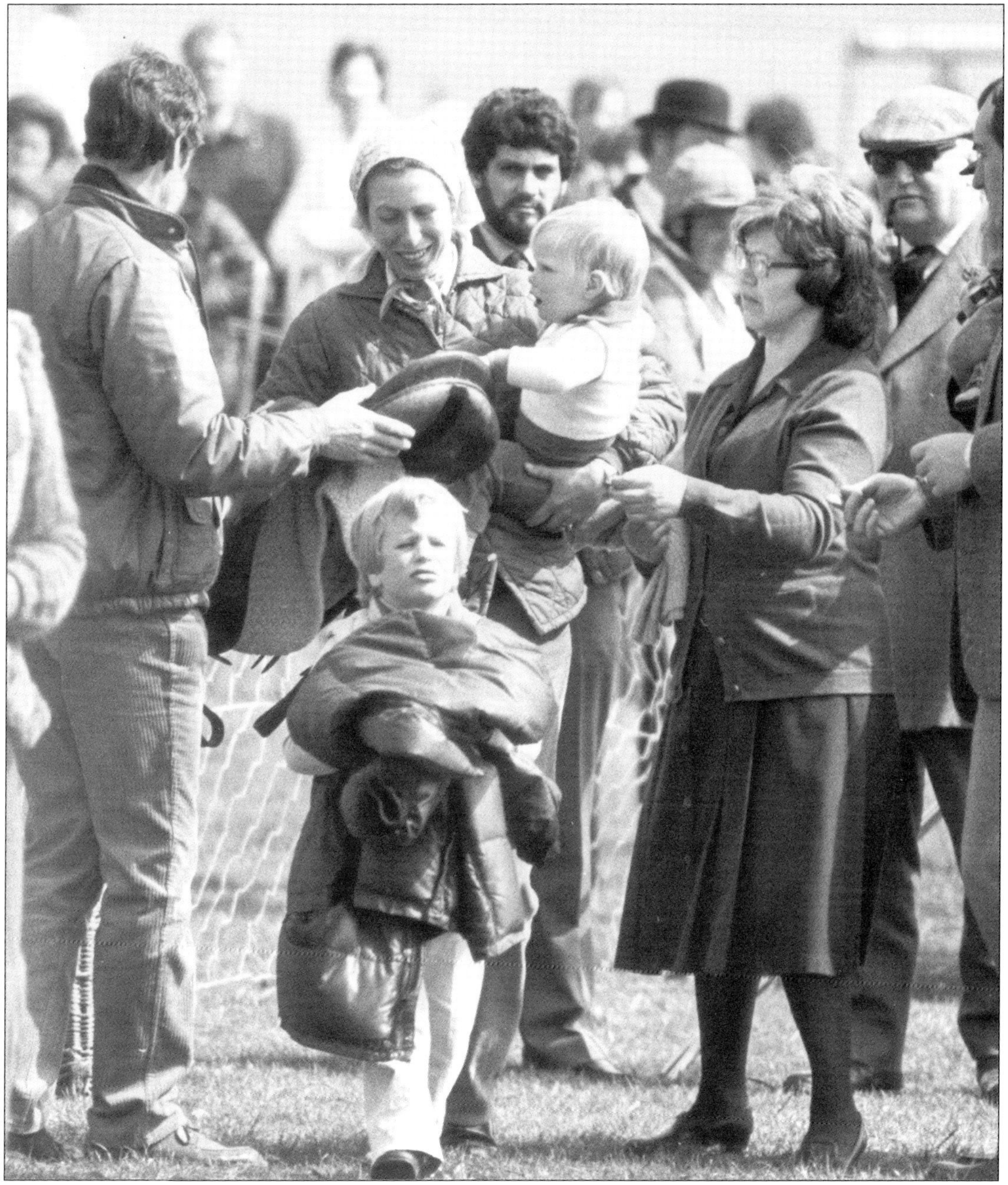

Changing Times
Princess Anne busy with baby Zara and her son Peter – his arms full of coats – as they stroll around Badminton at the 1983 horse trials. By now the media involvement at the annual event was, to say the least, becoming overwhelming. The young royals and their offspring had been a photo opportunity waiting to happen. The equestrian aspect of Badminton was becoming of minor newspaper interest – it was the younger royals who were now the target of the journalists' camera lenses. The occasion here was the last time I covered Badminton. I arrived at the Press Tent to find that over 300 assorted members of the media had registered for press passes, quite a few of whom looked as though they may never have seen the inside of a newspaper office or peered through a lens! We were shuffled about the place in a fleet of Land Rovers like a flock of unruly sheep and dropped at various vantage points to record the royals. All of this activity upset the paying enthusiasts in the crowd who were frequently heard voicing their feelings, a far cry from those early, pleasant Badminton days of the 1960s!

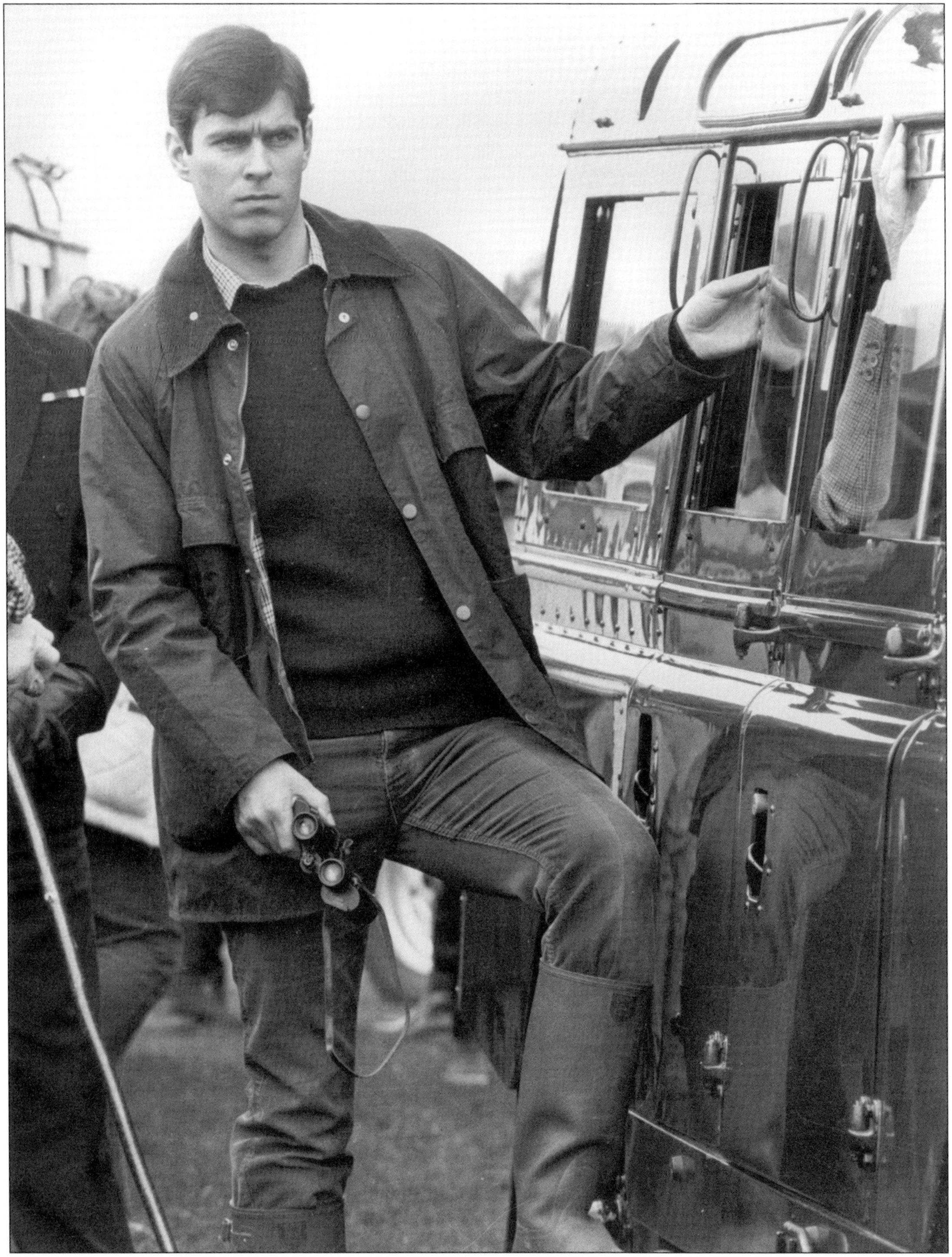

Land Roving Prince
Prince Andrew is seen here at the 1983 Badminton Horse Trials. The royal visitors, along with the press corps, had the benefit of a fleet of Land Rovers for reaching vantage points on the cross-country course.

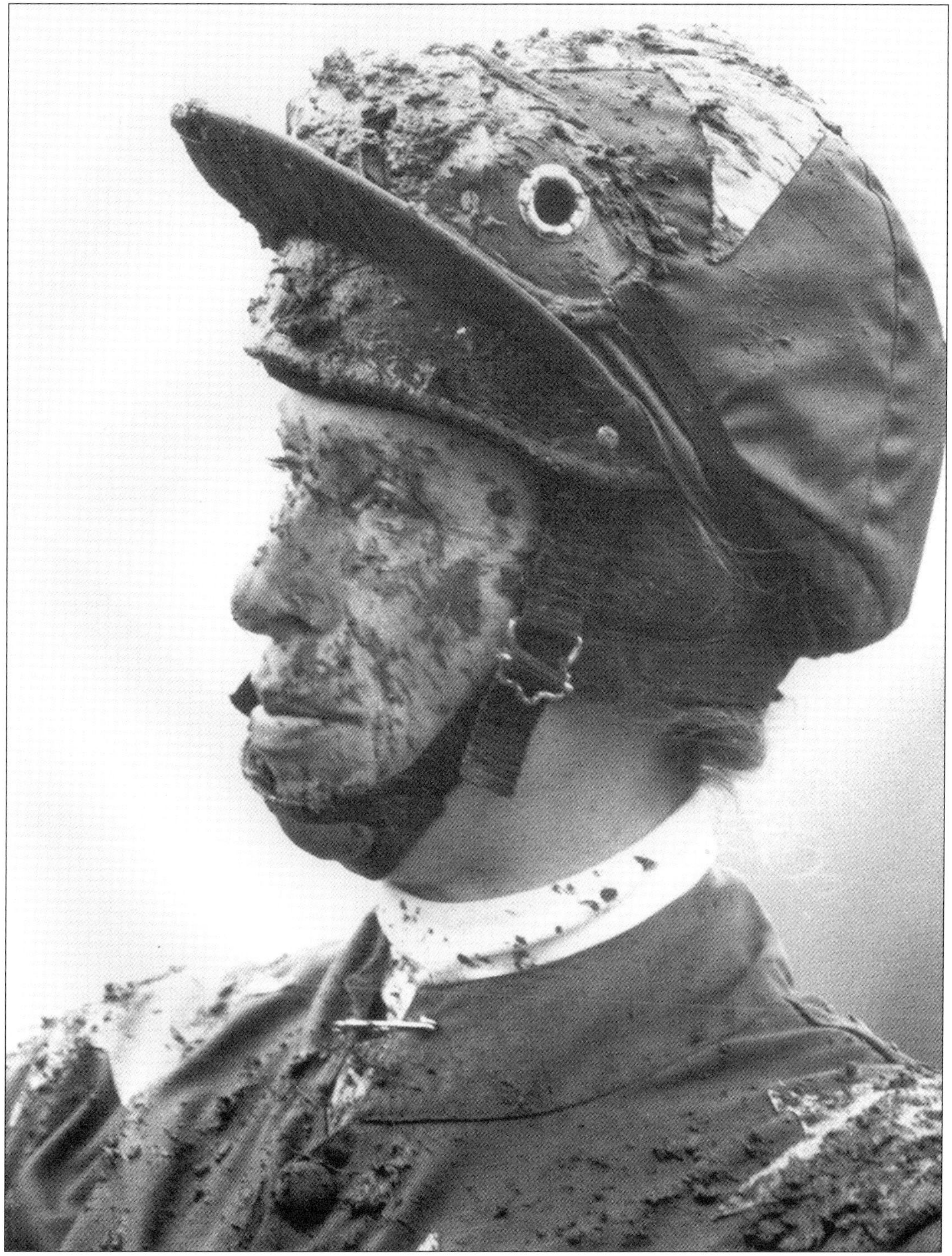

Racing Colours of a Muddier Shade
The weather was not kind to Princess Anne when she took her first ride at Cheltenham's Prestbury Park. The Princess was taking part in a special evening meeting in 1983, but as the riders were given the 'Off' there was a torrential downpour. My fellow photographer Richard Sturdy – much wiser than me regarding horse racing – quickly interpreted the situation and started running for the finishing post, calling out that as the Princess was last in the running order, she was bound to be caked with mud from the hooves of the forward mounts. He was right; through sheer luck of positioning, my picture made the front page of the *Times*. However, the credit for this photograph really belongs to Richard.

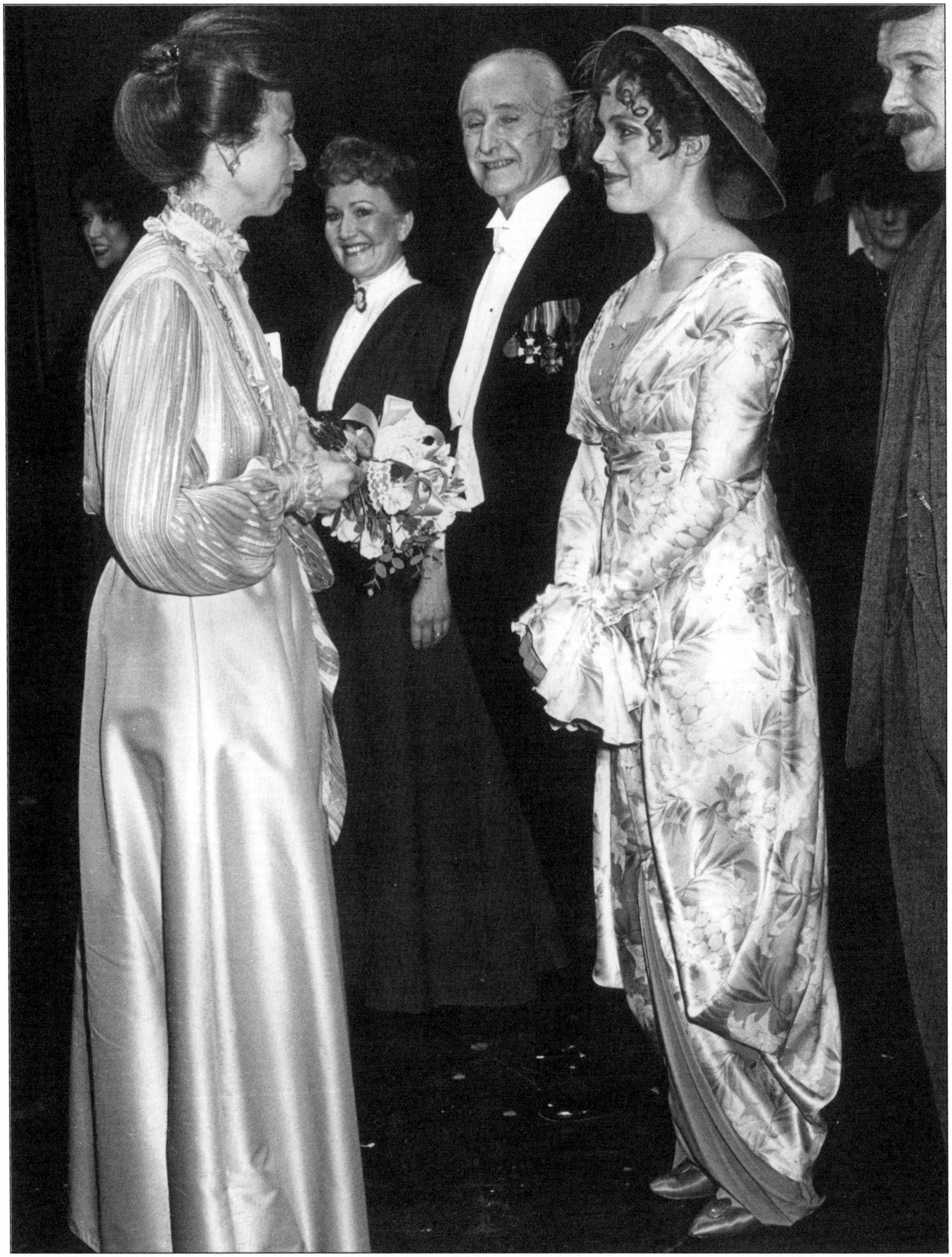

Stage Struck
The relaunch of Gloucestershire's only full-time theatre took place in 1986 when Princess Anne and Captain Mark Phillips attended a glittering gala performance of *My Fair Lady* at Cheltenham's Everyman Theatre in Regent Street. After the show, the Princess, patron of the theatre, went backstage to meet the cast. She is seen here in conversation with 'Eliza', played by Jacqueline Dankworth, the daughter of bandleader Johnny Dankworth and the singer Cleo Laine.

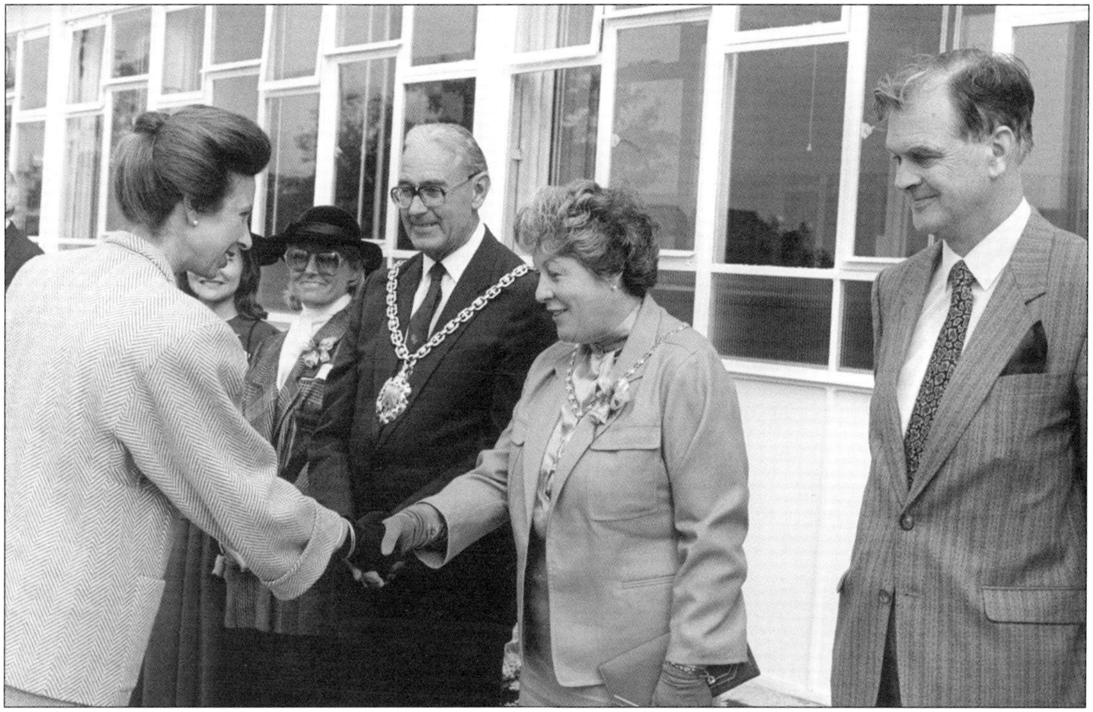

Birthday Party
When Cheltenham's Indelex factory celebrated its twenty-fifth anniversary in 1986, Princess Anne was guest of honour to mark the occasion. The Princess is seen here being greeted by Cheltenham's Mayor and Mayoress, Councillor and Mrs Don Perry, and the Town Clerk, Brian Wynn.

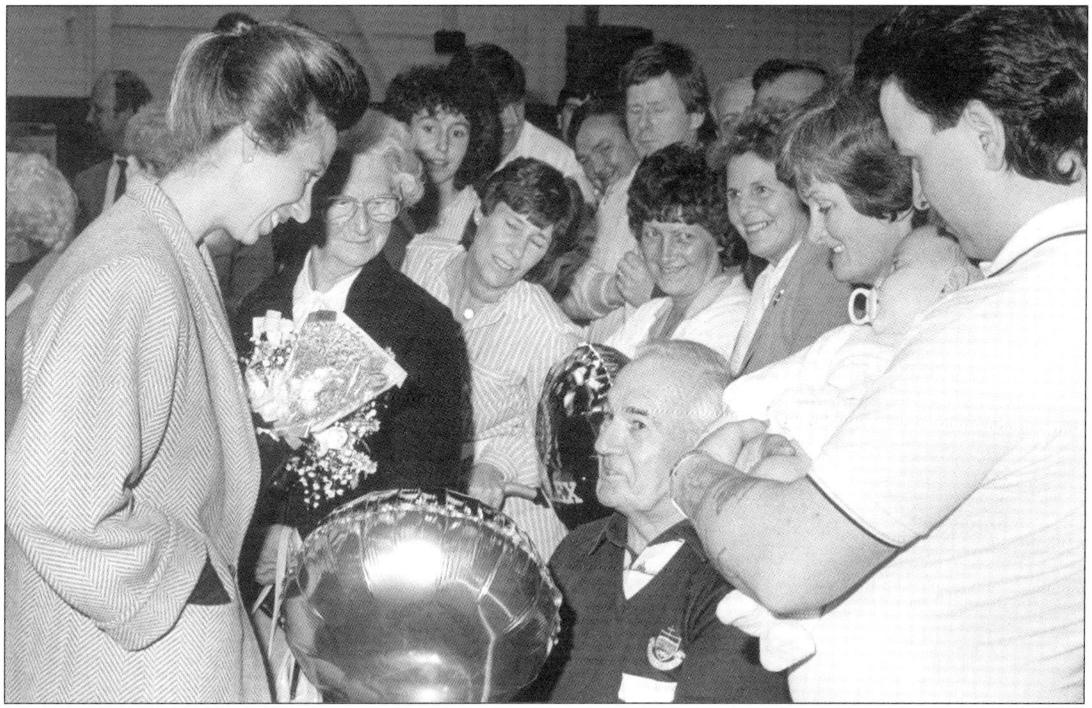

Workers Playtime
After touring the Indelex factory, off Cheltenham's Tewkesbury Road, the Princess met with a delighted group of retired and current members of the workforce during her day-long visit.

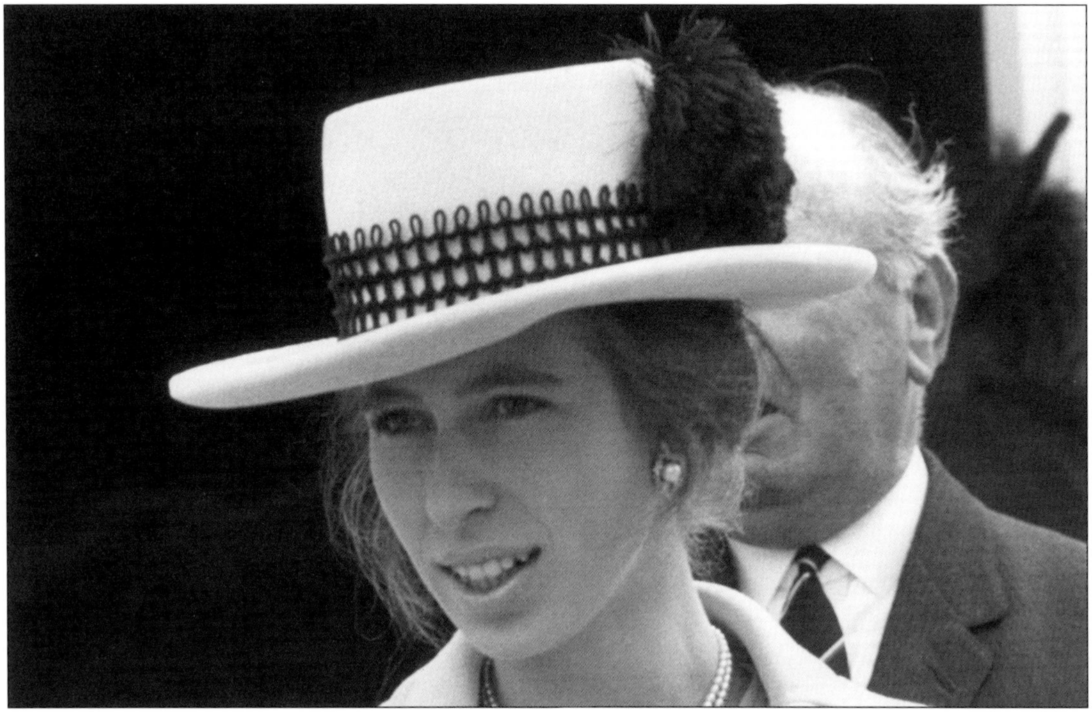

Another Day, Another Hat
Princess Anne in American ranch-style headwear.

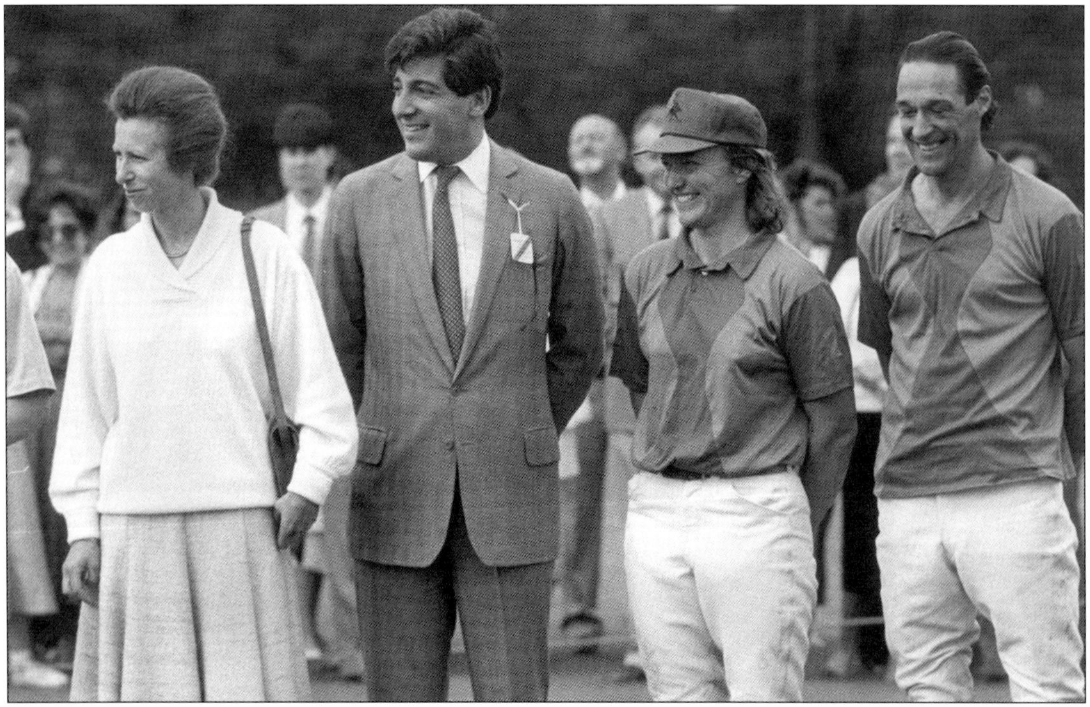

Polo Princess
Princess Anne enjoys a joke during the prize-giving at one of the many polo games held at Cirencester Park. On the right of the picture are Claire and Simon Tomlinson, both well-known polo players, who now have their own polo ground, The Beaufort Polo Club at Westonbirt in South Gloucestershire.

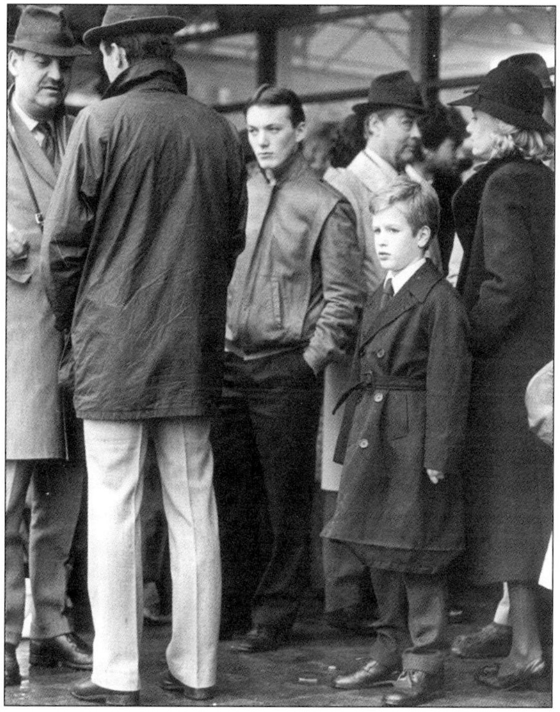

Watching and Waiting
Master Peter waits patiently during a Cheltenham Gold Cup meeting while his father Captain Mark Phillips (back to camera) seen talks with Piers Bengough, a director of the Cheltenham Racecourse Company.

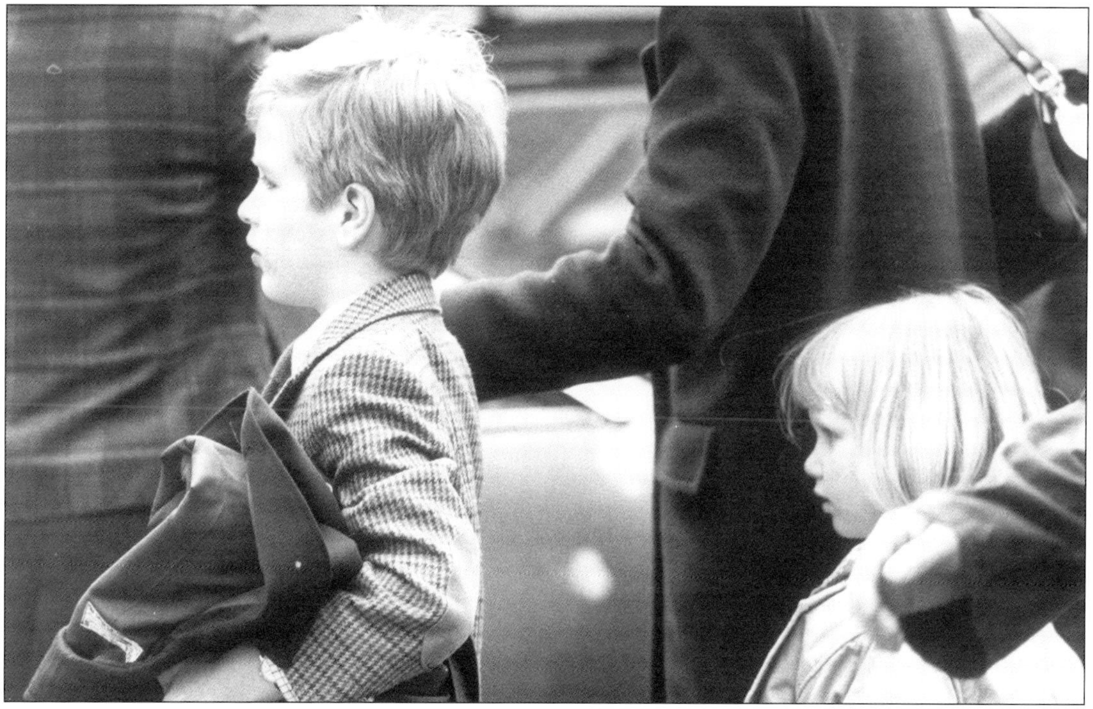

Young Racing Royals
Peter Phillips and his sister Zara arrive for Cheltenham's Gold Cup meeting at Prestbury Park, both looking a little overwhelmed by the occasion.

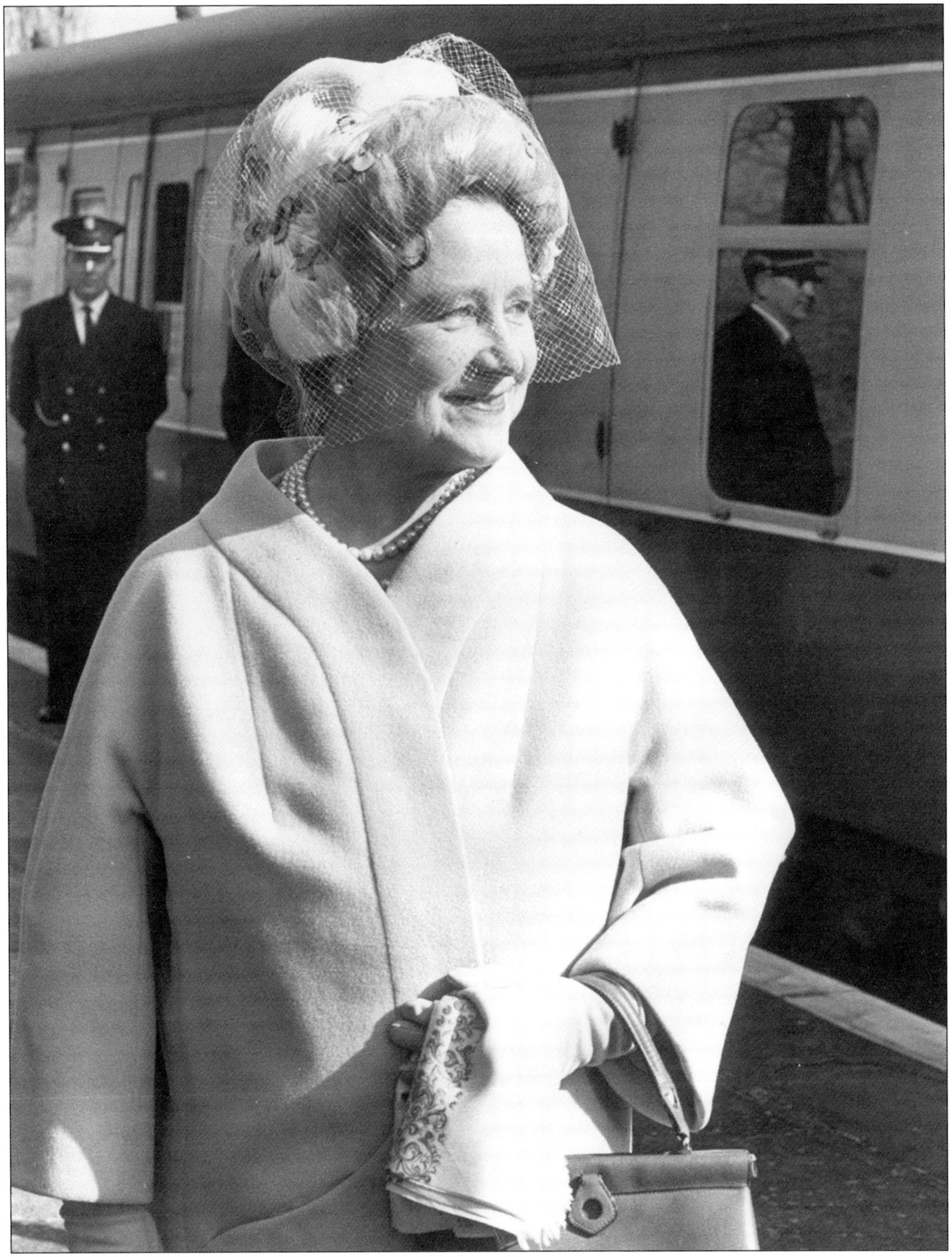

Royal Train
My first ever photograph of the Queen Mother was taken at Cheltenham railway station as she alighted from the train that brought her to the 1964 Gold Cup meeting. In later years, the Queen Mother made her annual pilgrimage to the famous March meeting by royal car.

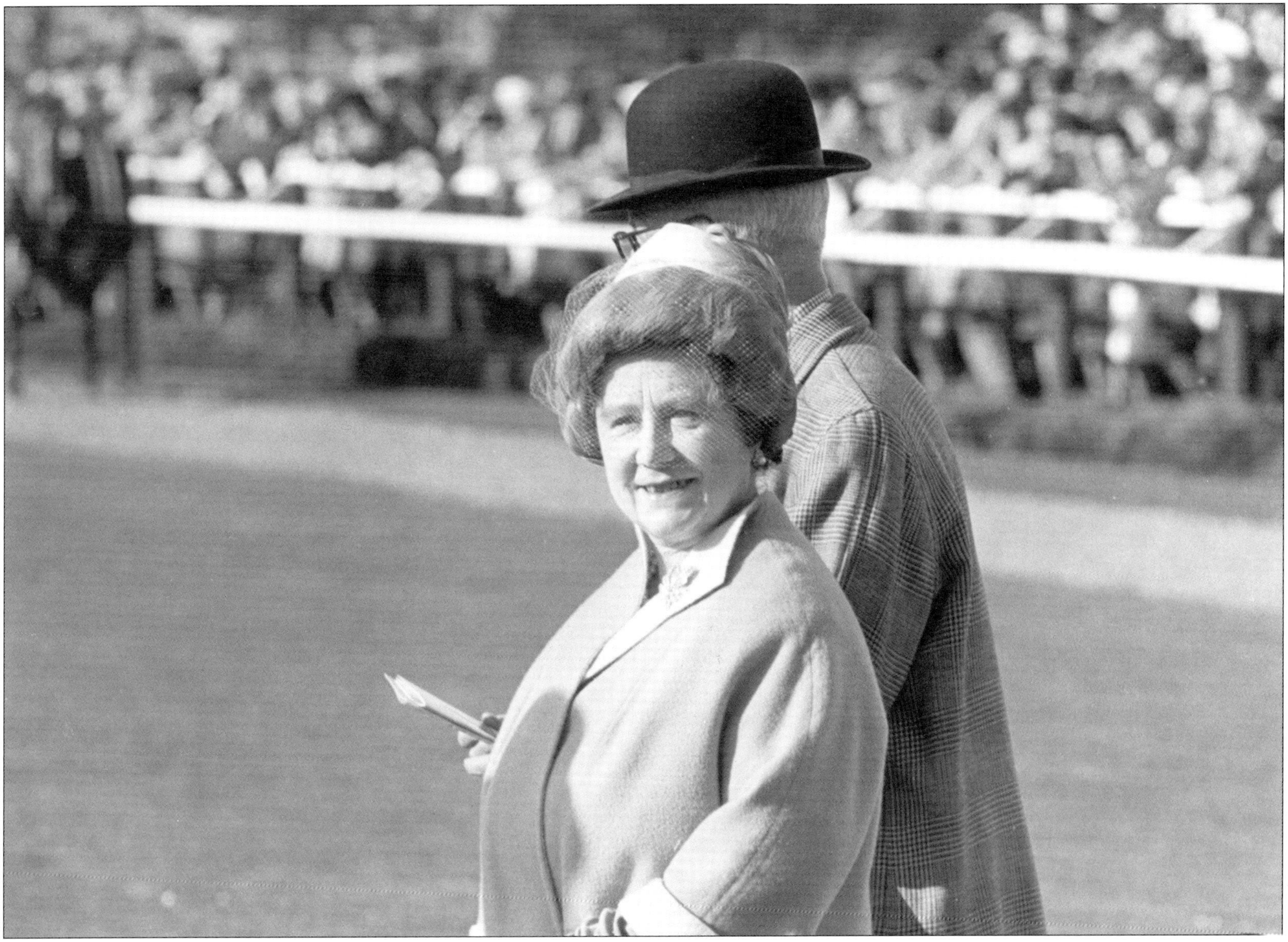

An Eye for Form
The Queen Mother casts a knowledgeable glance around the Parade Ring at a Gold Cup meeting in the 1960s. Horseracing was a major part of her life; she loved the world of the turf, and took a great interest in all aspects of it. When making a stable visit to check out the twelve or so mounts she owned, she always made a point of chatting with the stable lad regarding the condition of the horses, realising that he would know most about the horses in his charge. Her horse Game Spirit came third in the 1974 Gold Cup, but her most famed mount was Devon Lock who, on the point of winning the Grand National, literally collapsed on the run into the finishing post! When Dick Francis later told her how sorry he was that it happened, she replied, 'Don't worry, Dick. That's horseracing!'

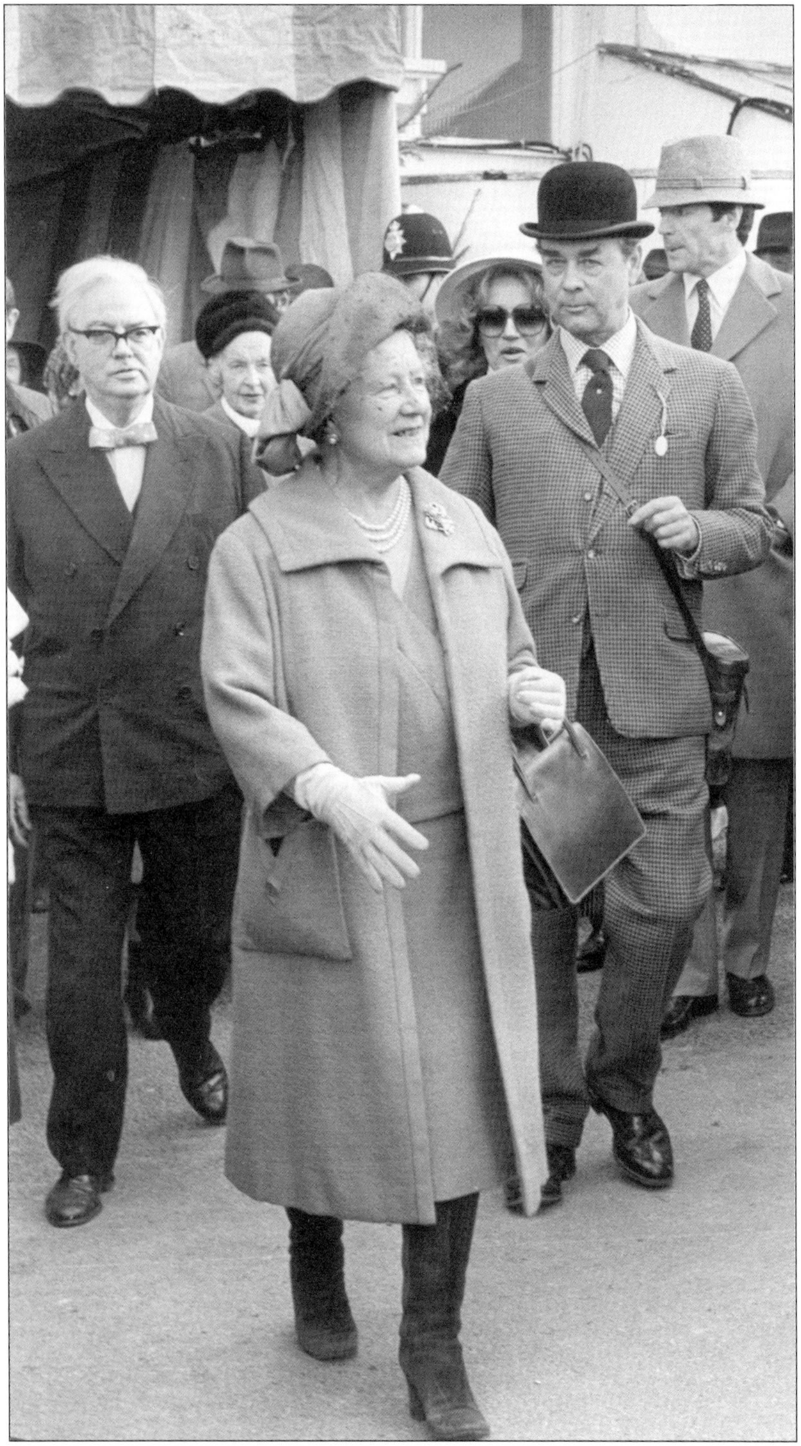

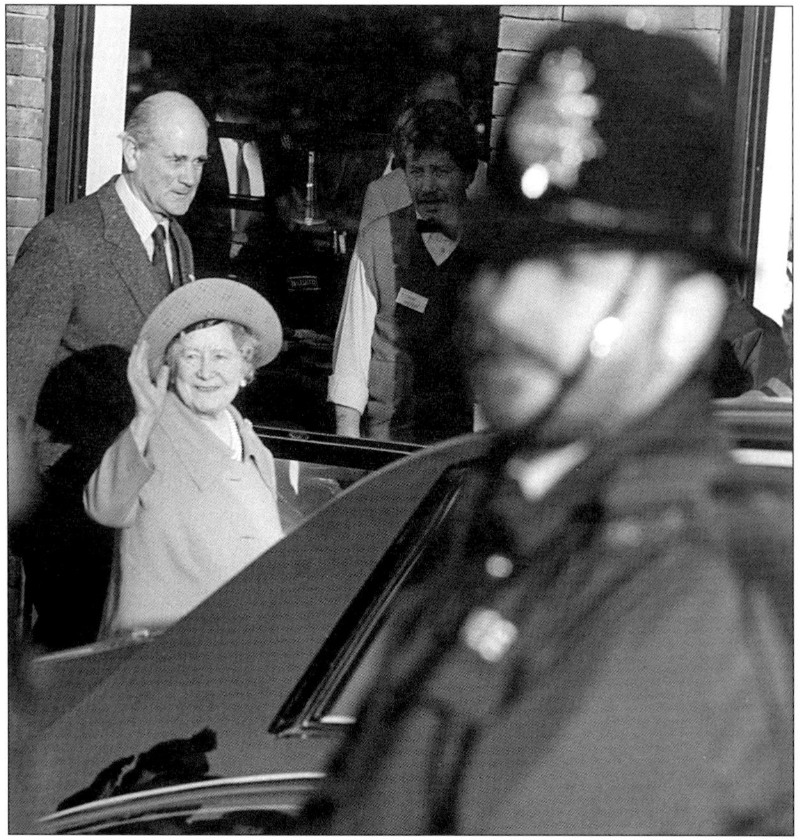

Prestbury's Favourite
The Queen Mother, rarely missed Cheltenham Gold Cup week, makes her way from the Royal Box to the Parade Ring. Behind her and sporting his trademark bow tie is Woodrow Wyatt, with Lord Willoughby de Broke.

Regal Wave
The Queen Mother waves to the crowd as she leaves a Gold Cup meeting at Cheltenham. With her is Colonel Martin Gibbs, Lord Lieutenant of Gloucestershire.

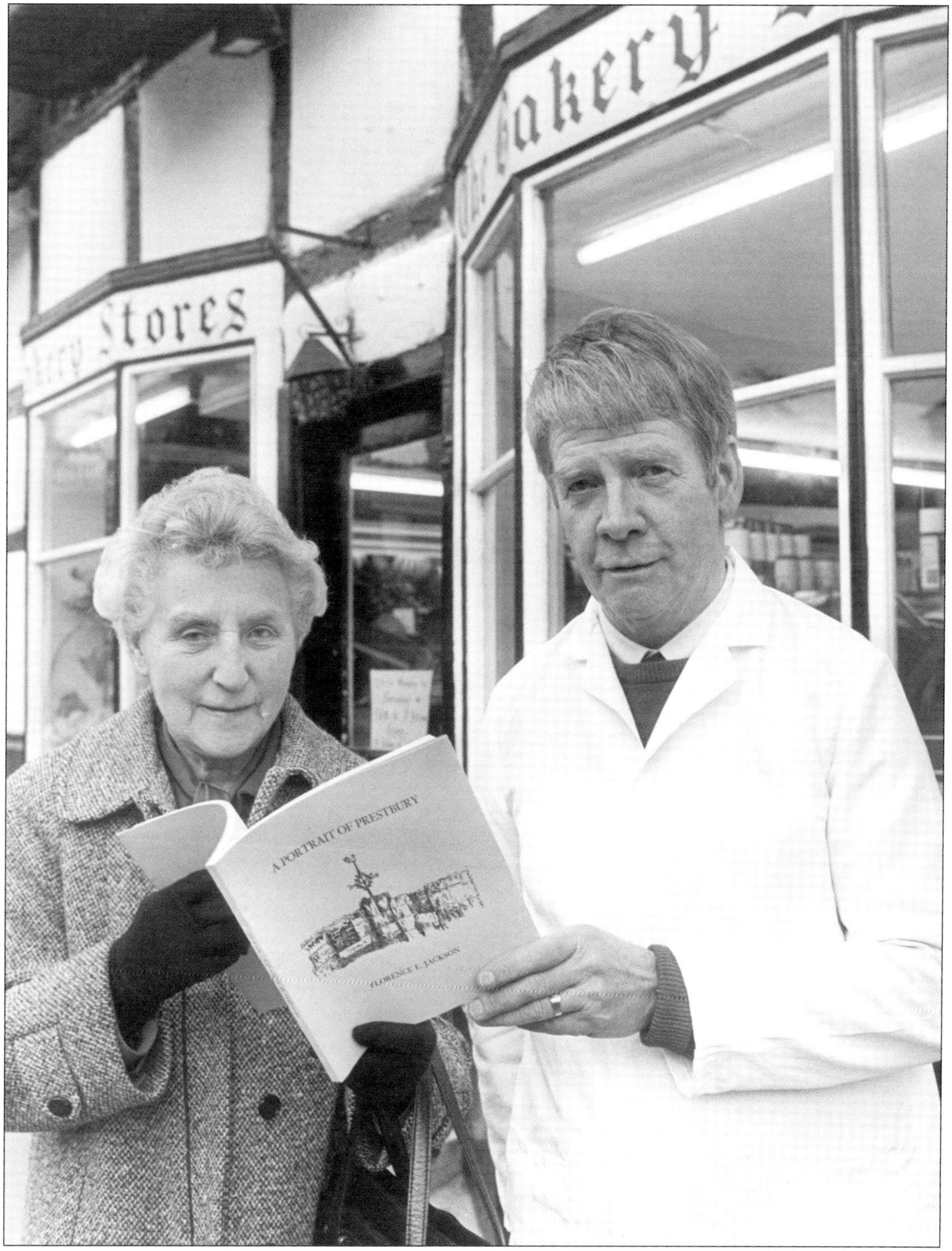

Chocolate Box
The route for the Queen Mother's visit to the Cheltenham Gold Cup always took the same course; from Birdlip down Leckhampton Hill, through the town centre and then, via Pittville, to Prestbury Park. An enterprising shopkeeper, Philip Delaney, owned a small store in the Leckhampton district, where, during the 1970s he managed to persuade the royal entourage to stop whilst he presented the Queen Mother with a box of chocolates. The occasion developed into an annual event, with crowds waiting to glimpse the Queen Mother. When Mr Delaney sold his store and teamed up with John Forgarty at Prestbury village stores, the Queen Mother altered her route to call at the new venue for her box of goodies! Very much a royal fan, John Forgarty continued the tradition into the 1990s, when it was deemed that the crowds awaiting the royal party caused unacceptable disruption in the small village, and the event ceased. Pictured here is Jon Fogarty, with Florence Jackson, and her book *A Portrait of Prestbury* that detailed these unique visits by the Queen Mother.

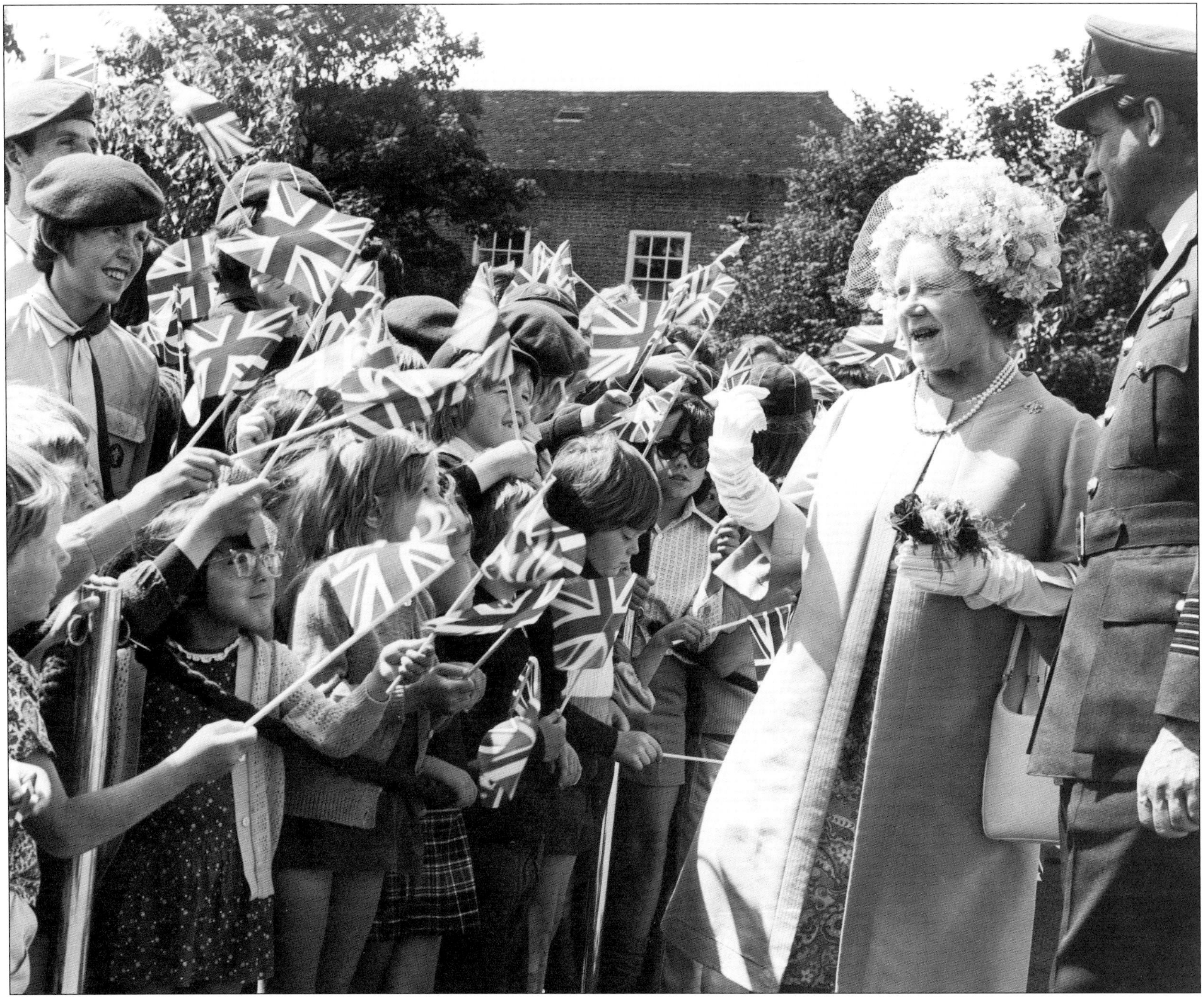

Royalty Air Force
The Queen Mother meeting children of serving airmen and officers at RAF Rissington, the former home of the famous Red Arrows acrobatic team. The station has since closed, the married quarters are private homes and the camp an industrial park.

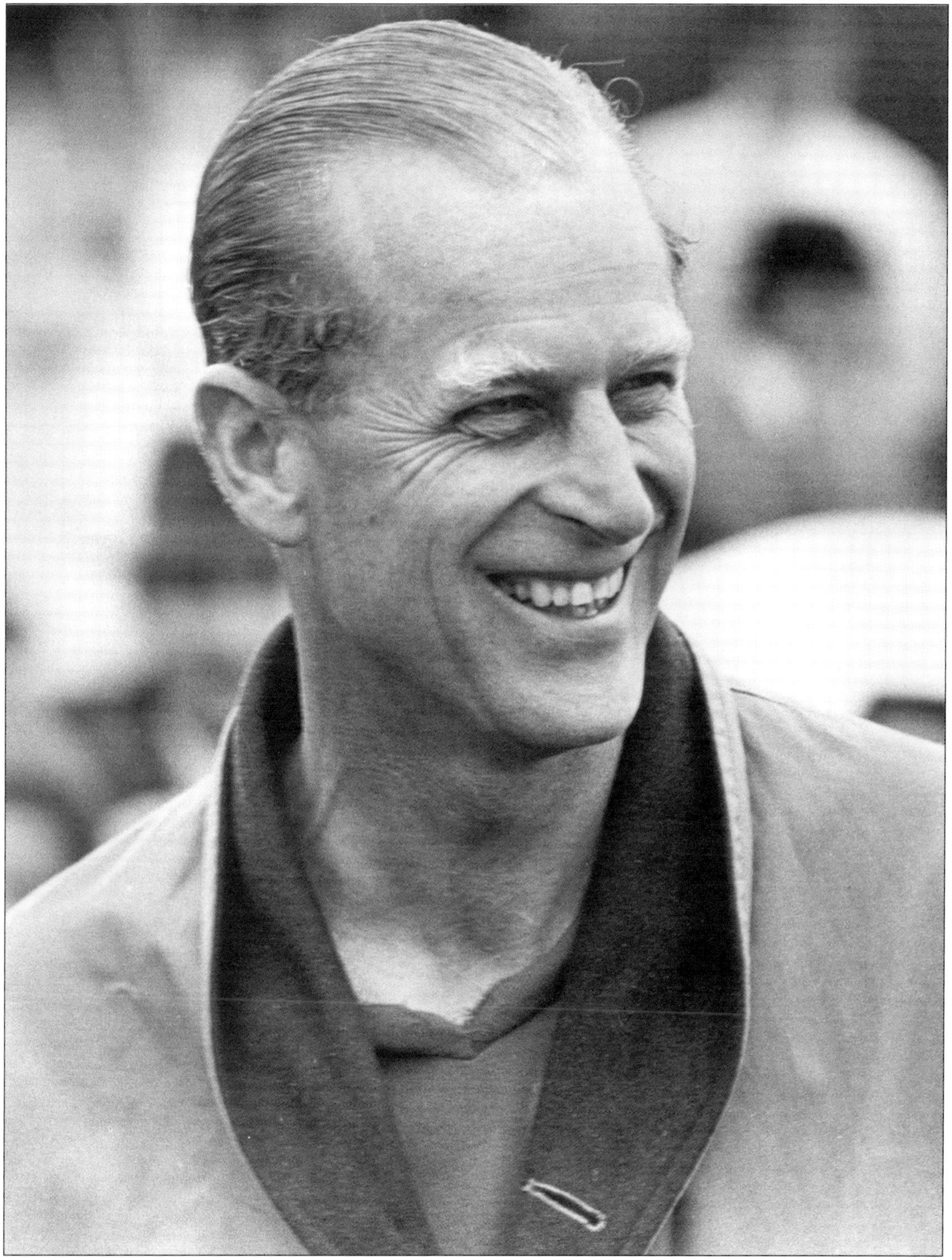

Duke of Hazard
A relaxed Prince Philip after tackling a particularly testing section of the National Carriage Driving event at Cirencester Park in 1973.

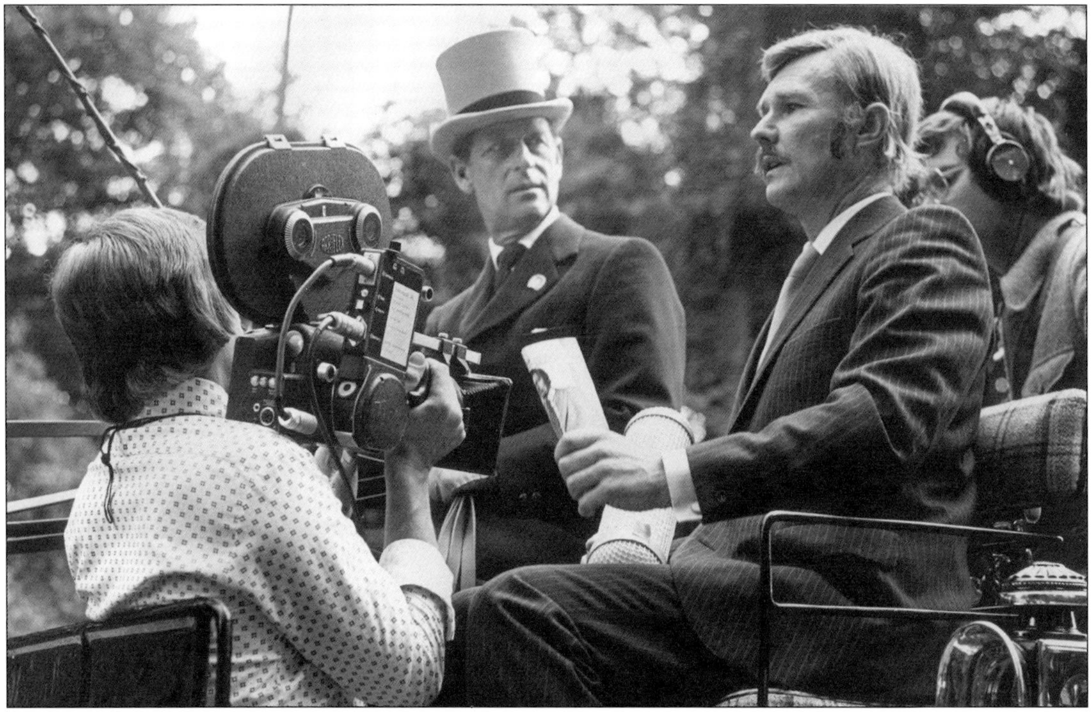

Your Carriage Awaits
Prince Philip, certainly not as relaxed as in the previous photograph, taking part in the National Horse Carriage Championships, held at Cirencester Park in 1973. His passengers were a television crew recording an interview for BBC Bristol's *Points West* programme. The cameraman is Ricky Calder, who trained with me at the Derek Evans Agency in Hereford, before joining Border Television.

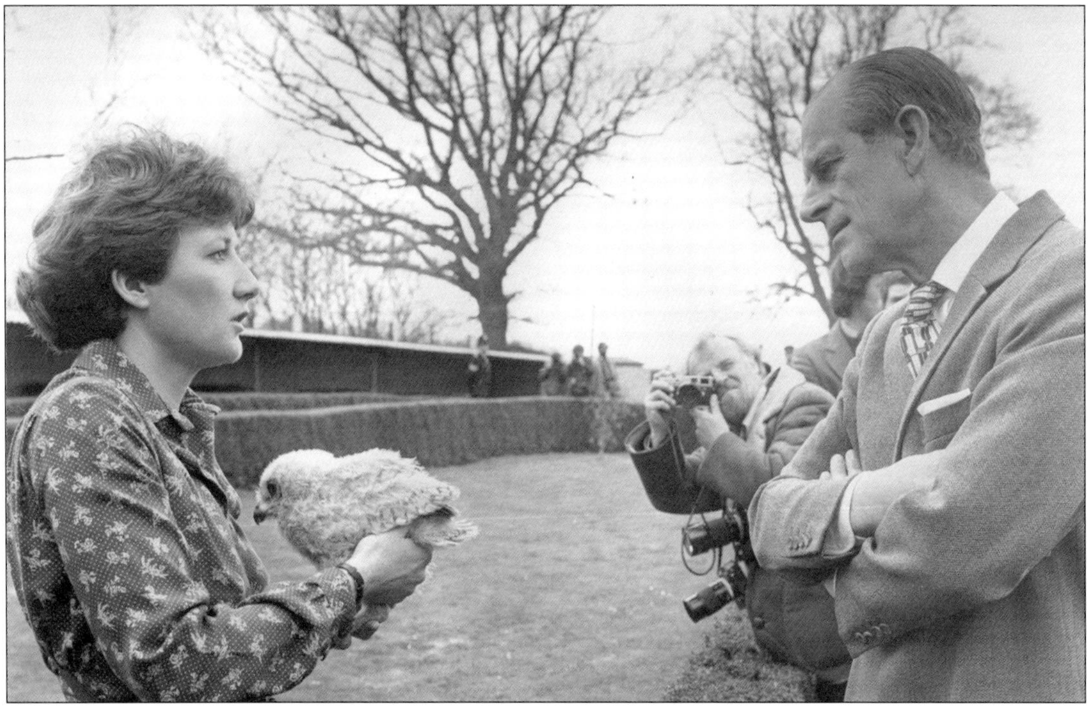

Birds Eye View
Phillip Glasier created the Newent Falconry Centre in the early 1960s and attracted many visitors to his collection of birds of prey. Among the first callers to descend on the centre was the Duke of Edinburgh, who flew in by helicopter, in the company of birdman Eric Hoskins, a famous wildlife photographer who had lost an eye in an owl attack some years earlier. The owner's daughter, Gemima, is seen here in discussion with a fascinated Prince Philip. When her father retired, Gemima took over the establishment and later the name changed to The National Birds of Prey Centre. Gemima received an MBE in 1999 for her services to bird conservation.

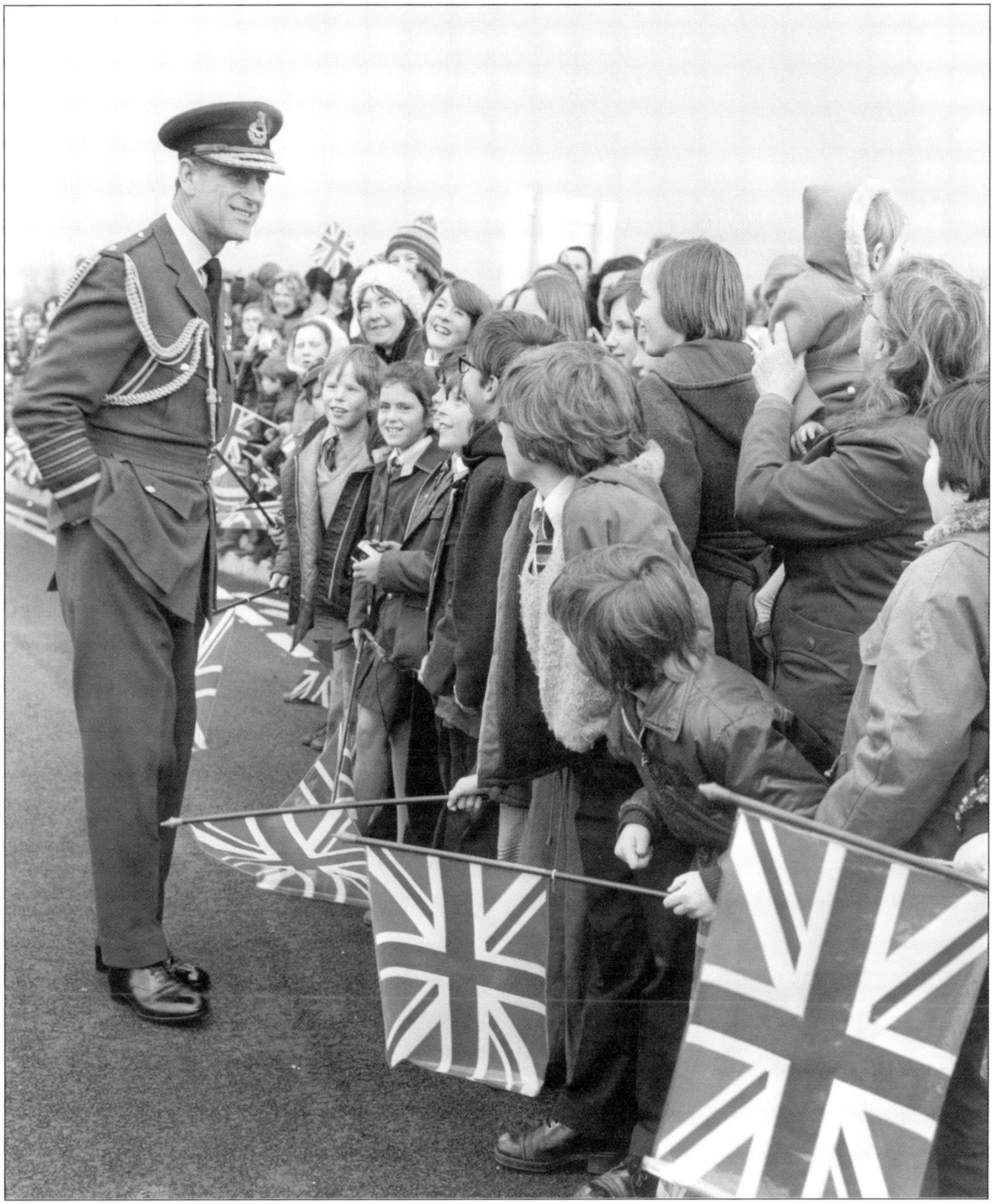

Boys in Blue
A group of children enjoy a meeting with Prince Philip in March 1976 during a visit to RAF Innsworth, the Royal Air Force administration centre near Gloucester.

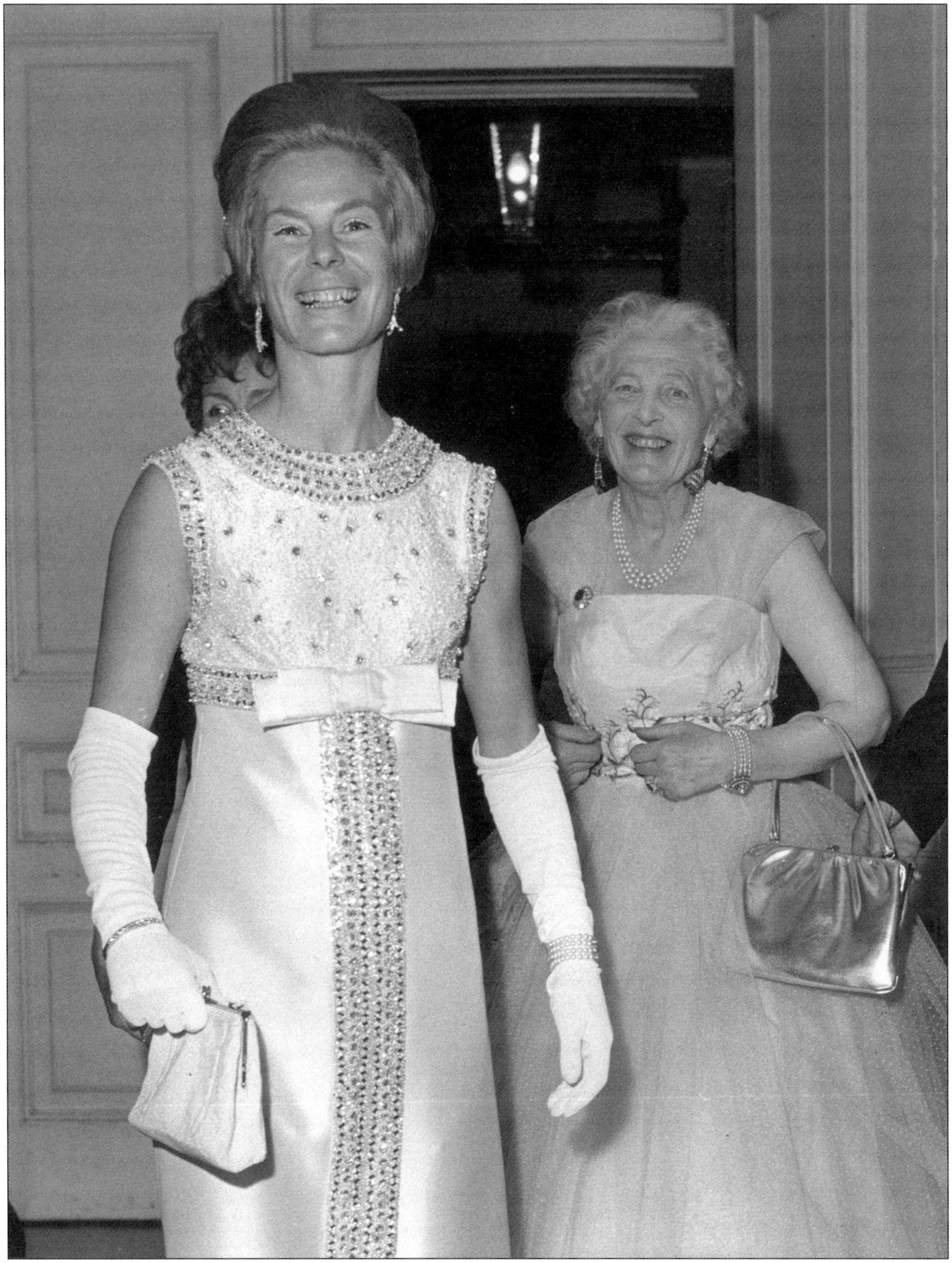

Royal Entrance
The Duchess of Kent and the Duchess of Beaufort arrive in the ballroom of Badminton House in 1973 for a ball held in aid of the National Star Centre in 1973.

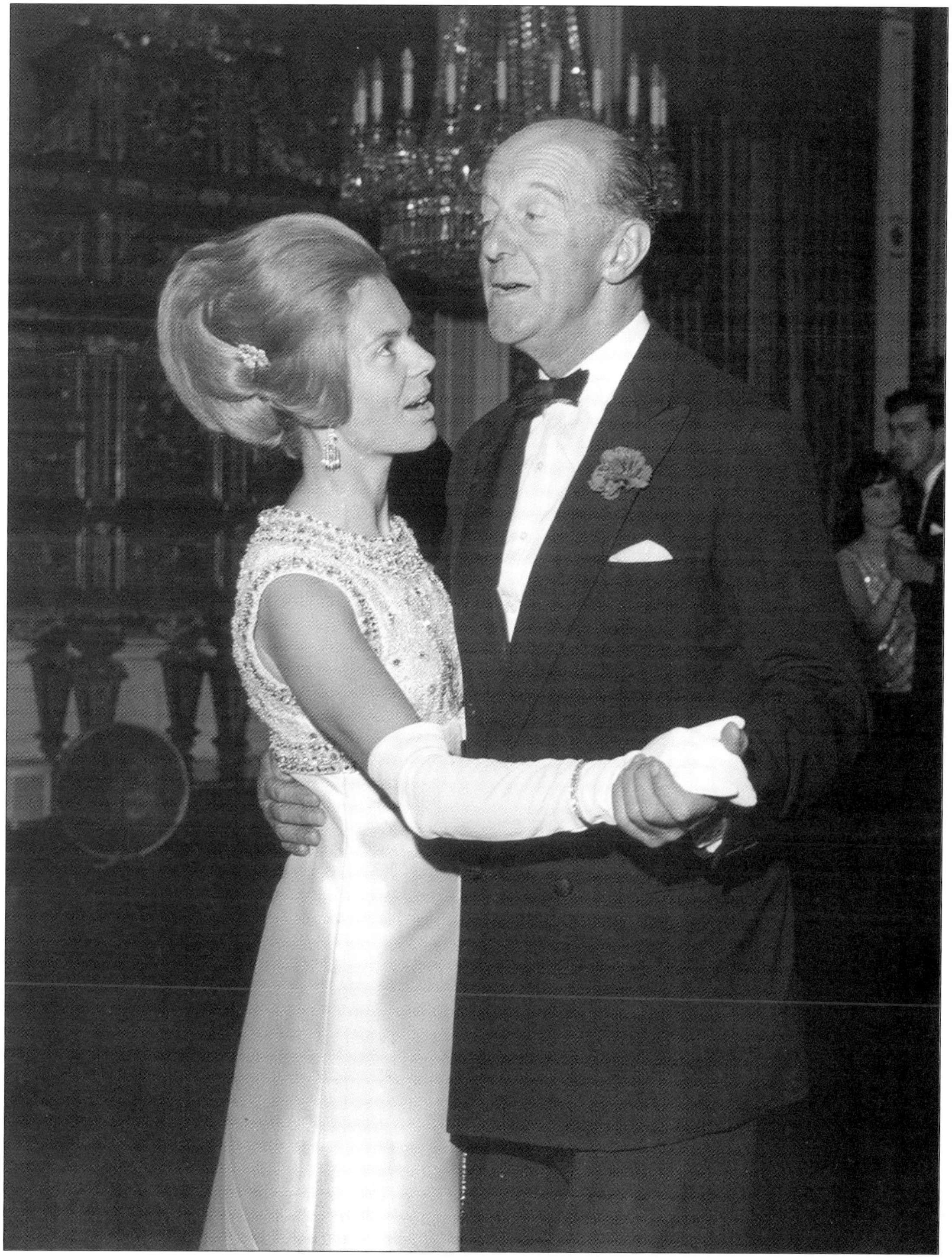

The Dancing Duke and Duchess
Besides hosting equestrian events on their estate, the Duke and Duchess of Beaufort often opened the door of their fine home for glittering charity fund-raising functions, many of which were graced by members of the Royal family. Here, the 'The Master' takes to the dance floor with the Duchess of Kent during a ball held at Badminton House in October 1973. Proceeds went to the National Star Centre at Ullenwood, of which the Duke was vice-president.

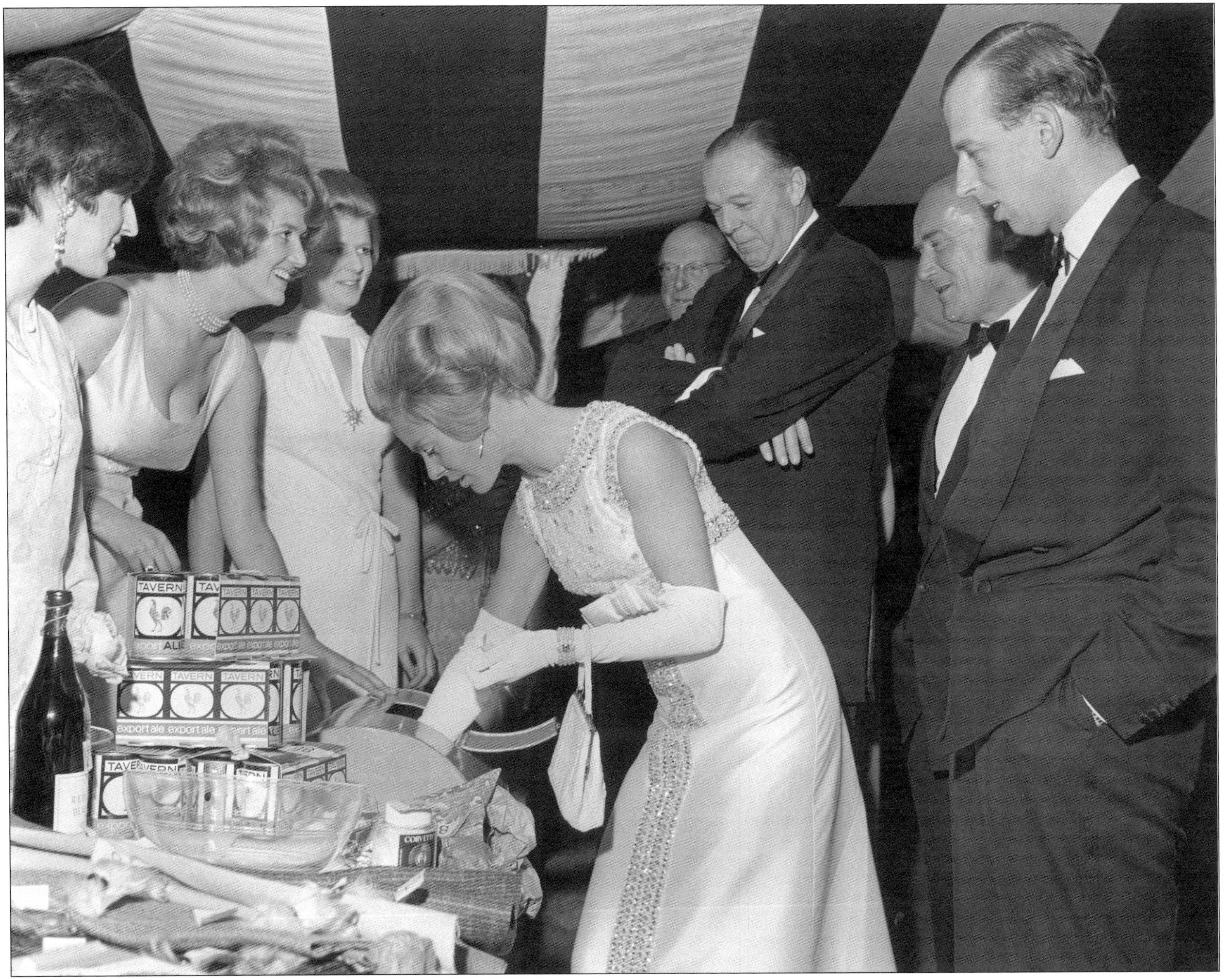

Lucky Dip
The Duke of Kent looks on as his wife draws a ticket from the tombola as part of an event to raise funds for the Star Centre for Youth Charity Ball held at Badminton House in 1973.

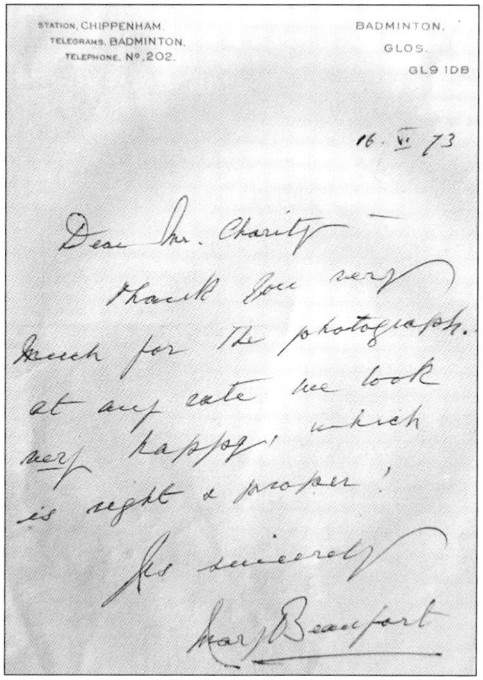

STATION, CHIPPENHAM.
TELEGRAMS, BADMINTON.
TELEPHONE, No 202.

BADMINTON,
GLOS.
GL9 1DB

16. VI 73

Dear Mr. Charity —
Thank you very much for the photograph. At any rate we look very happy! which is right & proper!

Yrs sincerely
Mary Beaufort

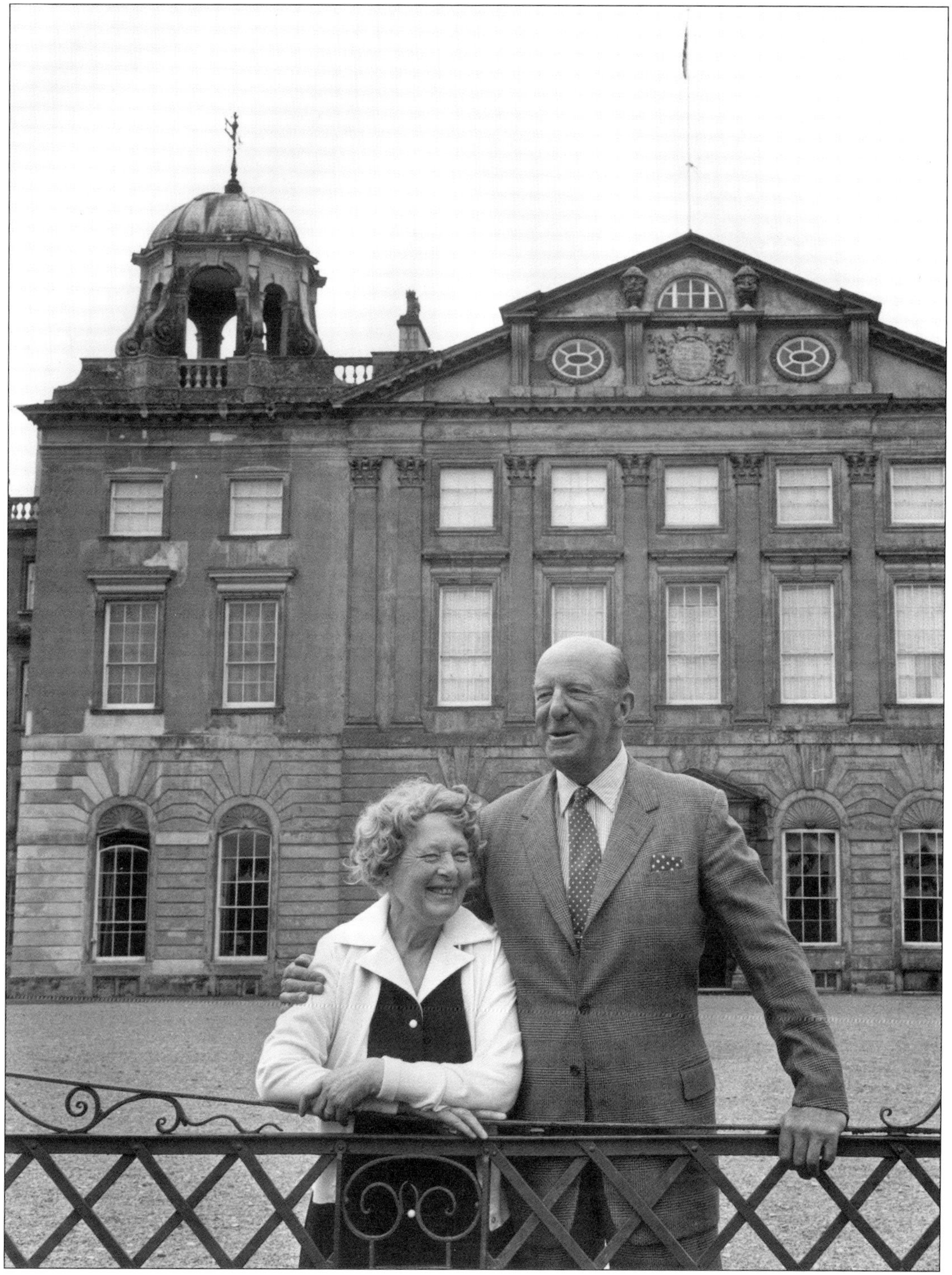

Golden Wedding
The 10th Duke of Beaufort with the Duchess outside Badminton House, their Gloucestershire home, on the morning of their Golden Wedding Anniversary in June 1973. The occasion was marked by a sixteen-guest dinner party at the house, which included five of their bridesmaids. The Duke and Duchess often requested copies of pictures from me and above is a letter from the Duchess which displays her wry sense of humour.

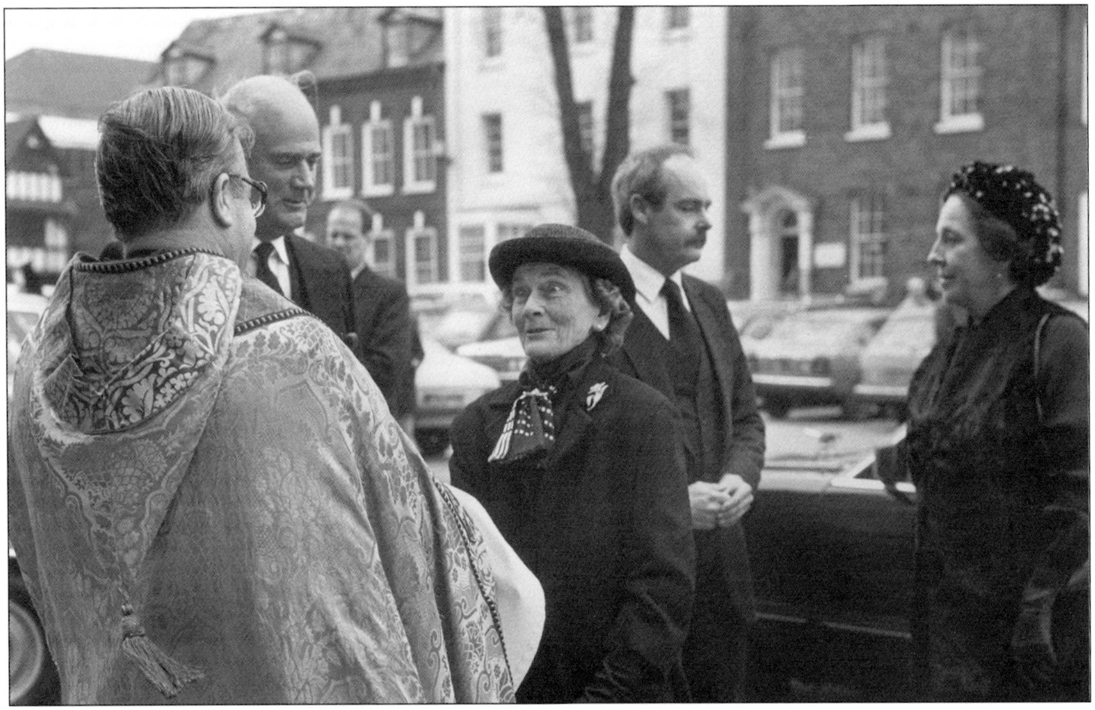

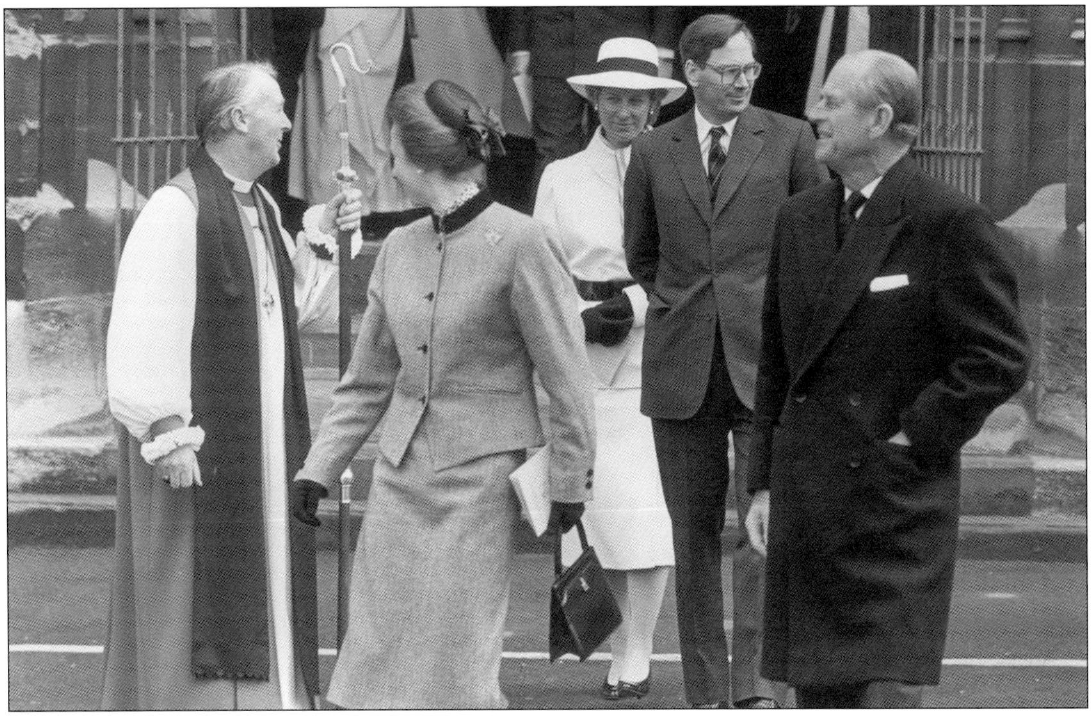

Congregation of Royals
Sadly, Henry, 10th Duke of Beaufort passed away in 1984. A measure of the esteem in which he was held by the Royal family was shown by their subsequent attendance on 14 April two years later at Gloucester Cathedral, for the dedication of a memorial in the Cathedral in his memory. This gathering of the royal clan was well documented by the media, who were taken by surprise to see so many members of the Royal family in the city. Here, the Bishop of Gloucester the Rt Revd John Yates, watches over a royal flock as they leave the cathedral after the service.

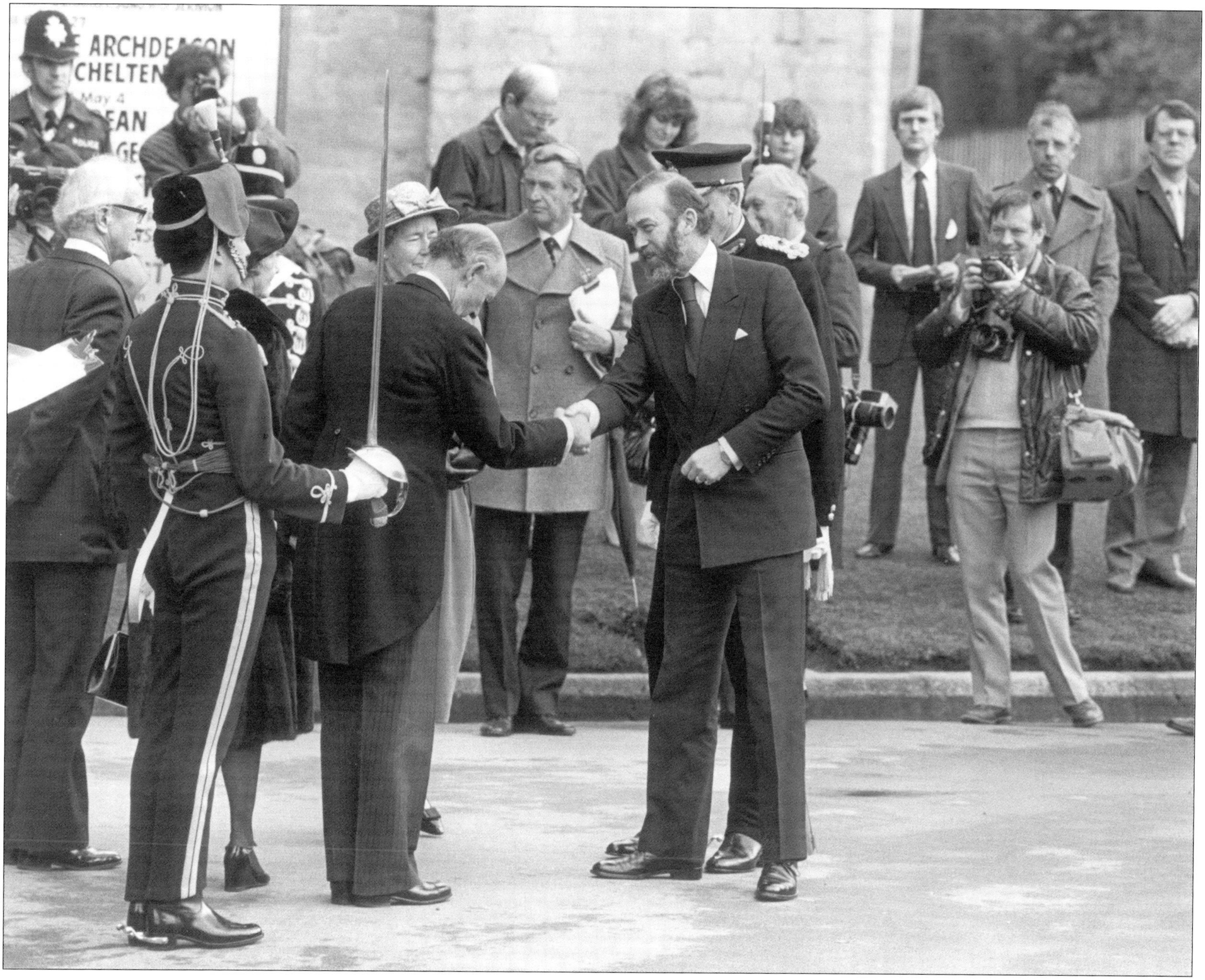

The Prince and the Press
Prince Michael of Kent takes his leave after the Cathedral service in memory of the 10th Duke of Beaufort. In the background, an informal gaggle of press are seen recording the occasion. After the service, the Queen and Duke of Edinburgh went on to meet staff and pupils at Widden school in Gloucester.

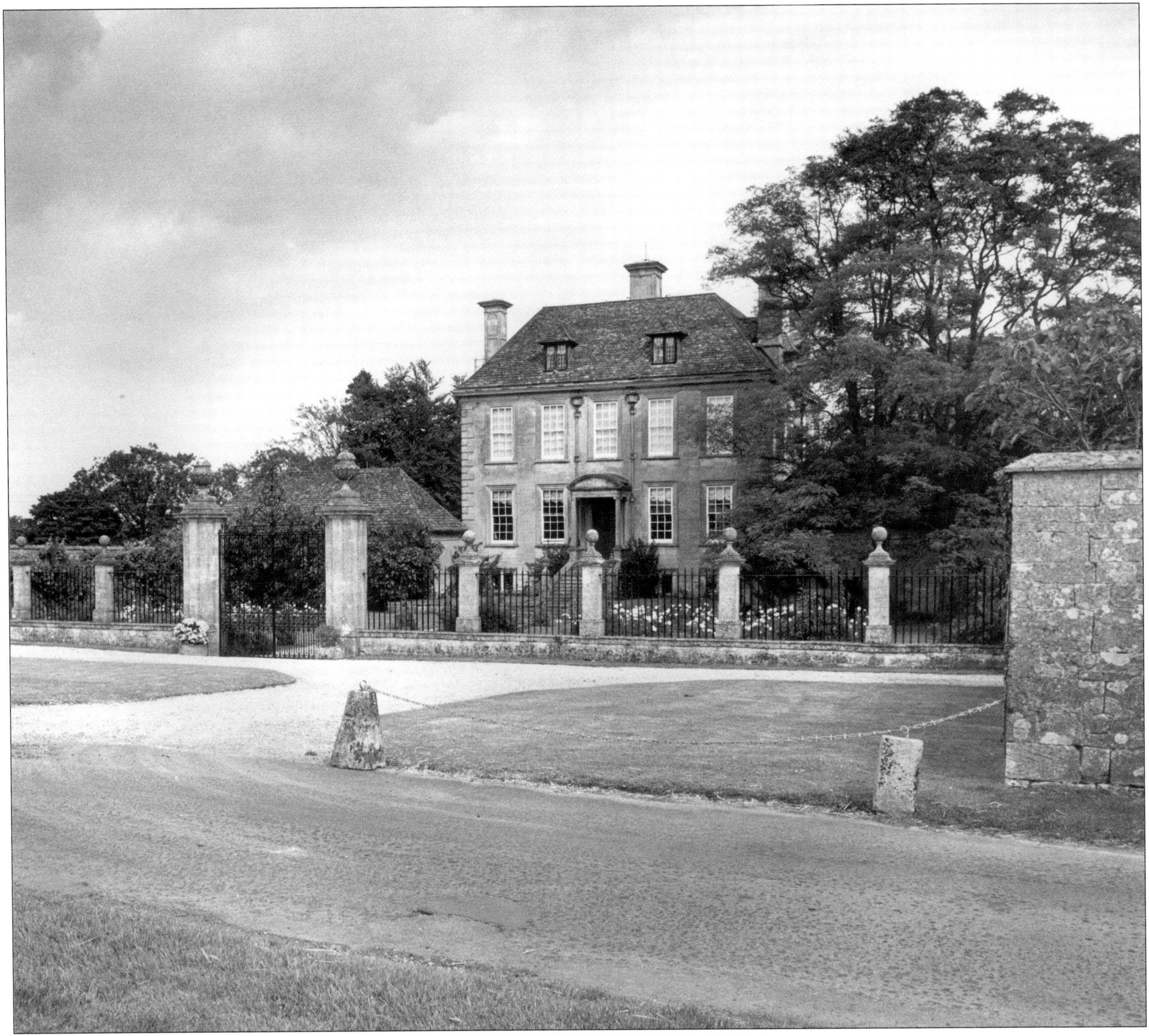

Opposite: *Ghostly Home*
Nether Lypiatt near Stroud, Gloucestershire, 1981 – the year it became home to the Prince and Princess Michael of Kent. This charming house is reputed to have a darker side to its history, and legend says that on certain nights of the year, a ghostly coach and horses can be seen galloping past the imposing front gates. In the garden of this beautiful house are the graves of past faithful pets; cats, dogs and even a horse! Some years ago, the Princess let it be known that she had lost one of her favourite cats and spent hours searching for it. *The Sun* newspaper then joined the hunt, and sent a reporter decked in full 'White Hunter' garb wielding a giant butterfly net. I was also in tow to capture the exclusive, elusive pussy. Sad to say, even the power of the almighty *Sun* was unable to find the missing cat!

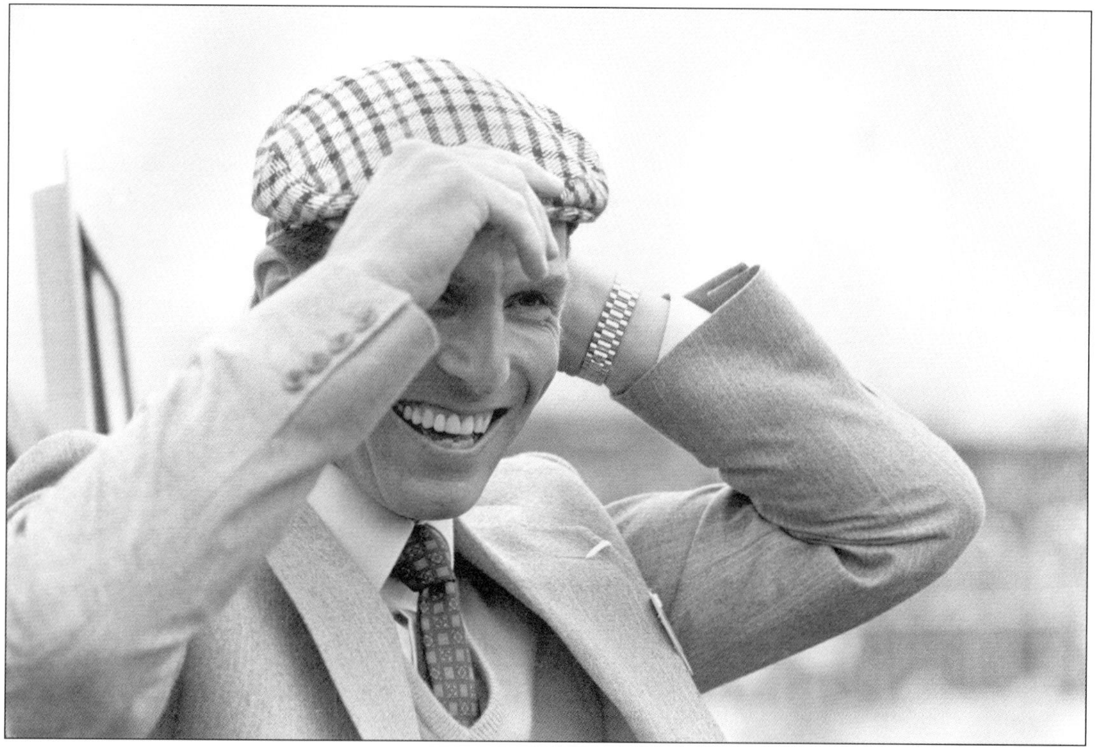

Top: Roving Ambassador
A jovial Captain Mark Phillips arrives at Cheltenham Racecourse for a special Land Rover promotion in May 1983.

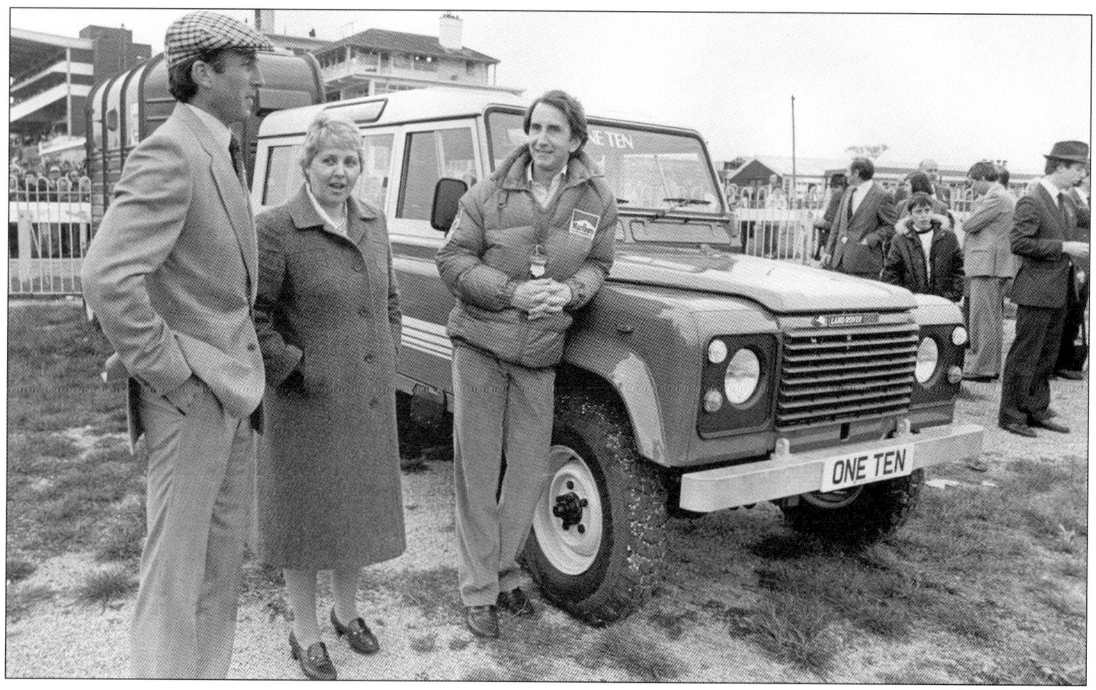

Horsepower Brokers
Horse trainer Jenny Pitman in conversation with Mark Phillips and John Watson, during the same Land Rover promotion organized by Captain Phillips at Cheltenham Racecourse in 1983.

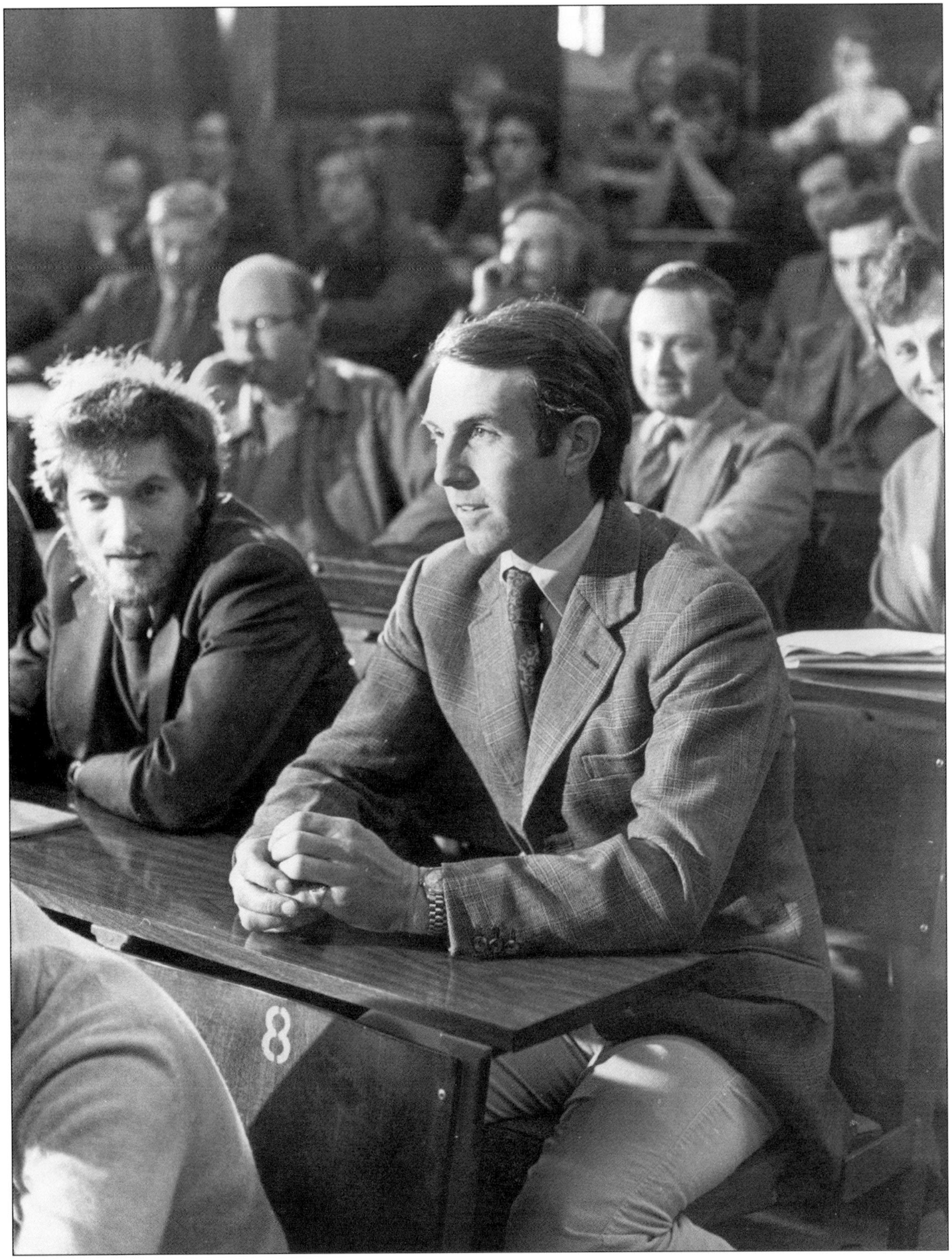

The New Boy
Captain Mark Phillips on his first day of lessons in 1977, when he joined the Royal Agricultural College, Cirencester, for an intensive farming course.

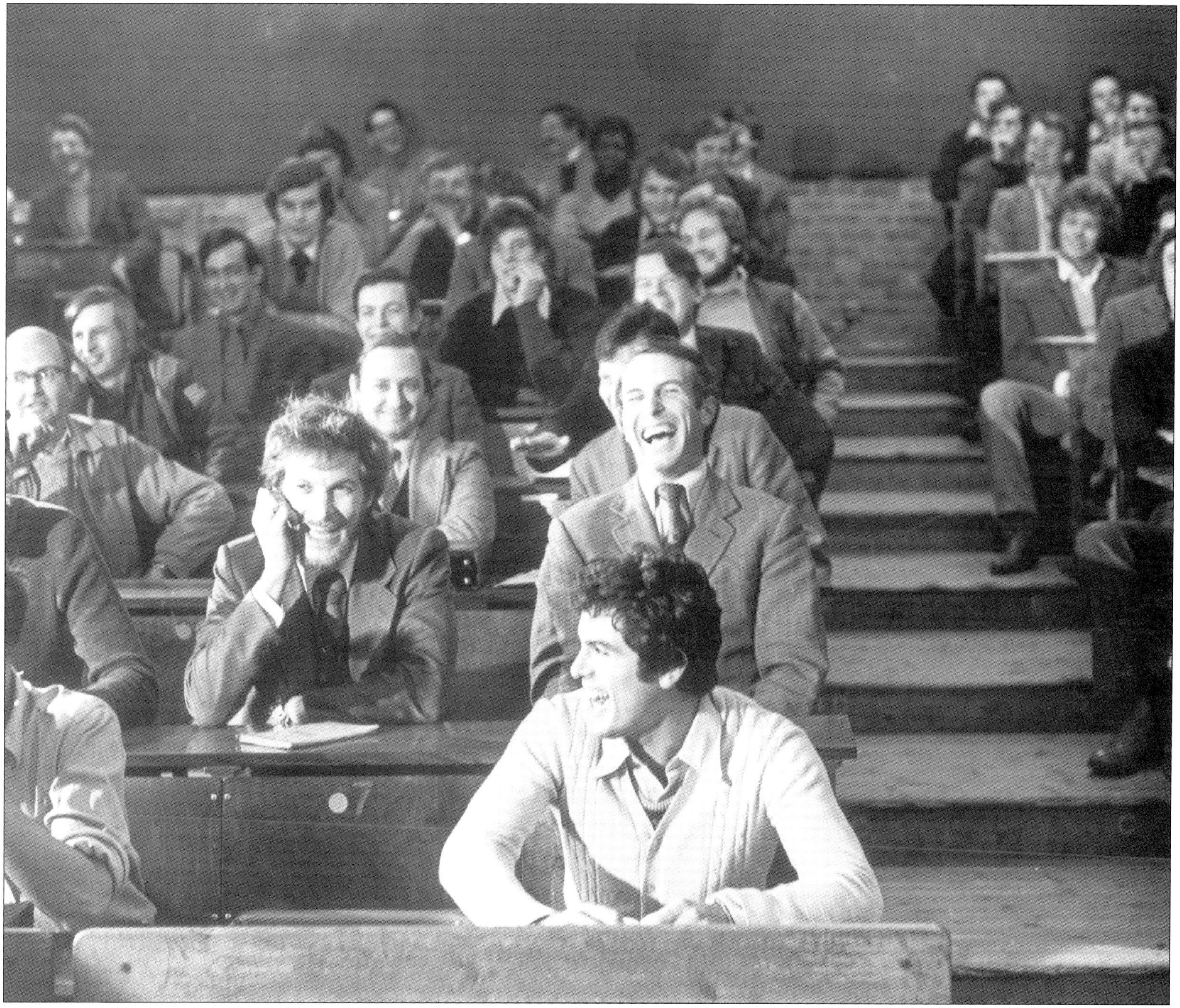

Agricultural Fun
Mark Phillips enjoys a joke with his fellow students.

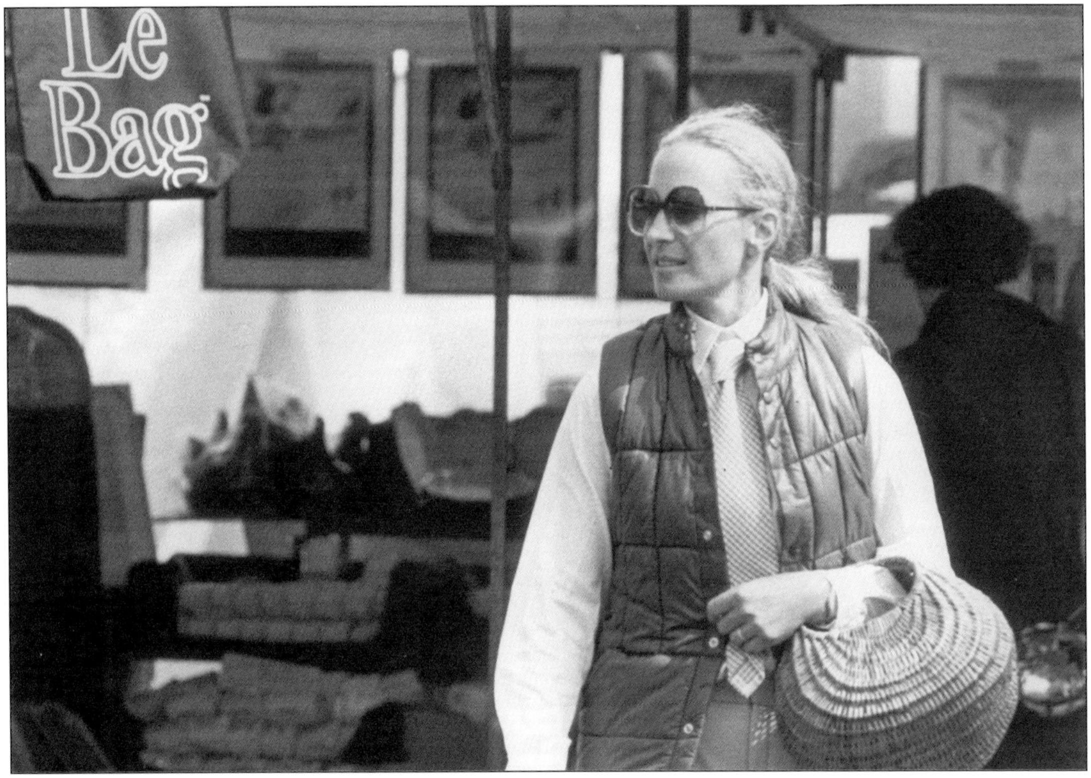

Early Morning Shopper
A stroll around the showground stalls for Princess Michael of Kent during the horse trials at Cirencester Park in the 1980s.

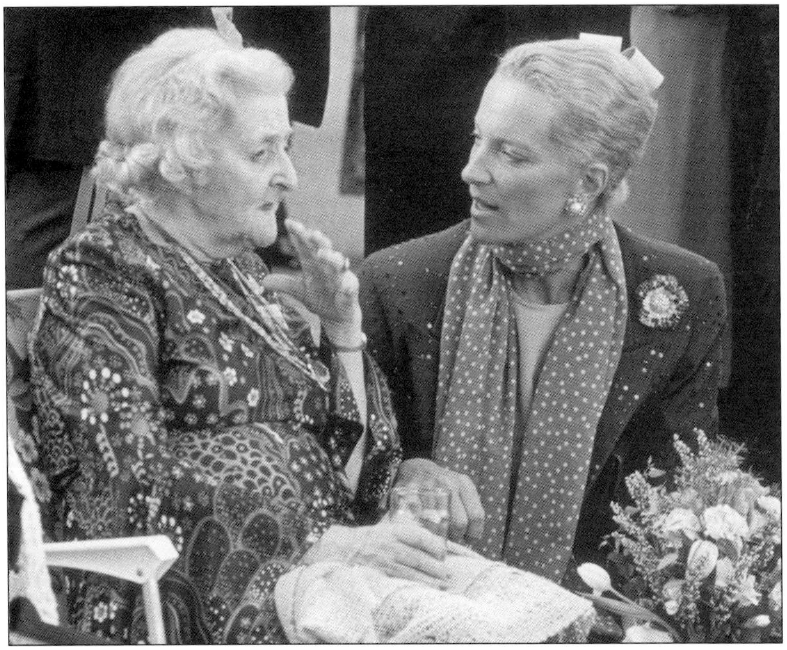

Holding Court
An attentive Princess Michael in discussion with Cheltenham fundraiser Audrey Truscott, famed for her charity functions in the country involving members of the Royal Family. This picture was taken at Elmore Court near Gloucester, the home of Sir John Guise. The reception was held to raise funds for the Regiments of Gloucestershire Museum which is situated in Gloucester Docks.

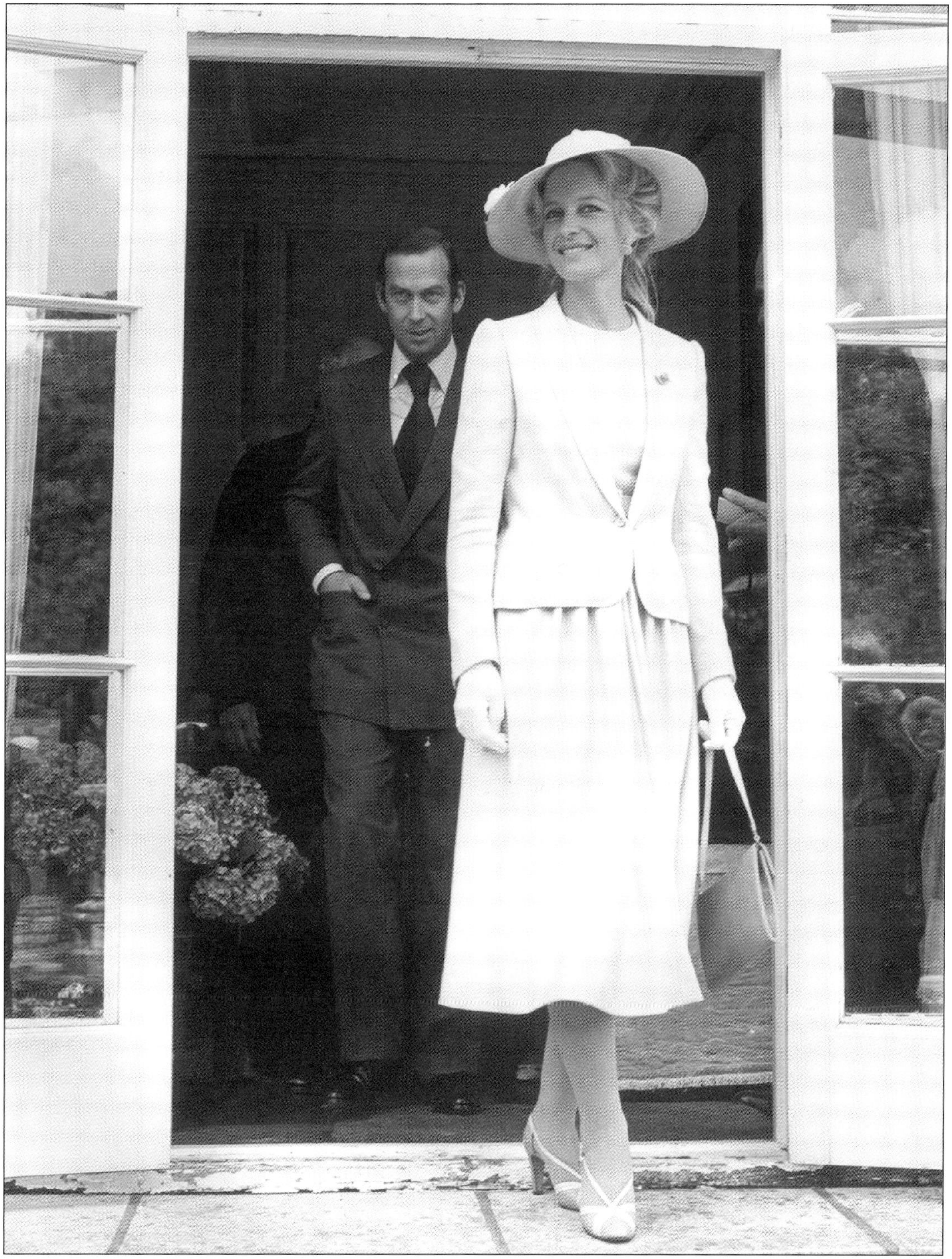

Royal Garden Party
Prince and Princess Michael of Kent arrive for a fundraising garden party at the Ewen home of Colonel and Mrs Martin Gibbs near Cirencester in 1992.

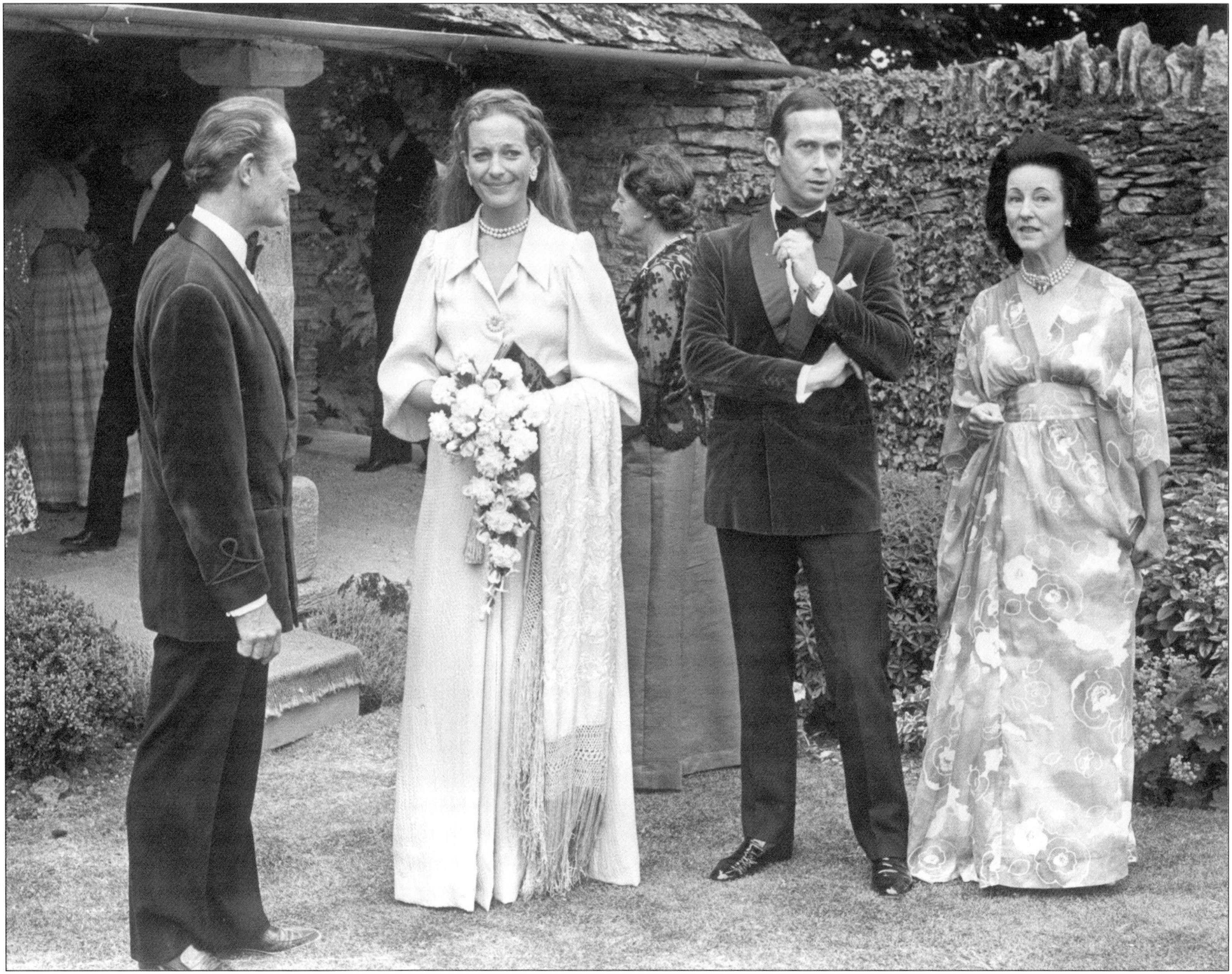

A House of Music
Sir Guy and Lady Holland welcome Prince and Princess Michael of Kent on one of their first social engagements after moving to the county. They were attending a musical evening at Sheepsbridge Barn, near Coln St Aldwyn, the home of Sir Guy and Lady Holland in whose house the living space was restricted to just three or four rooms, the major part of the house being designed to provide a small concert hall where many fundraising, musical soirées took place in the 1970s and '80s.

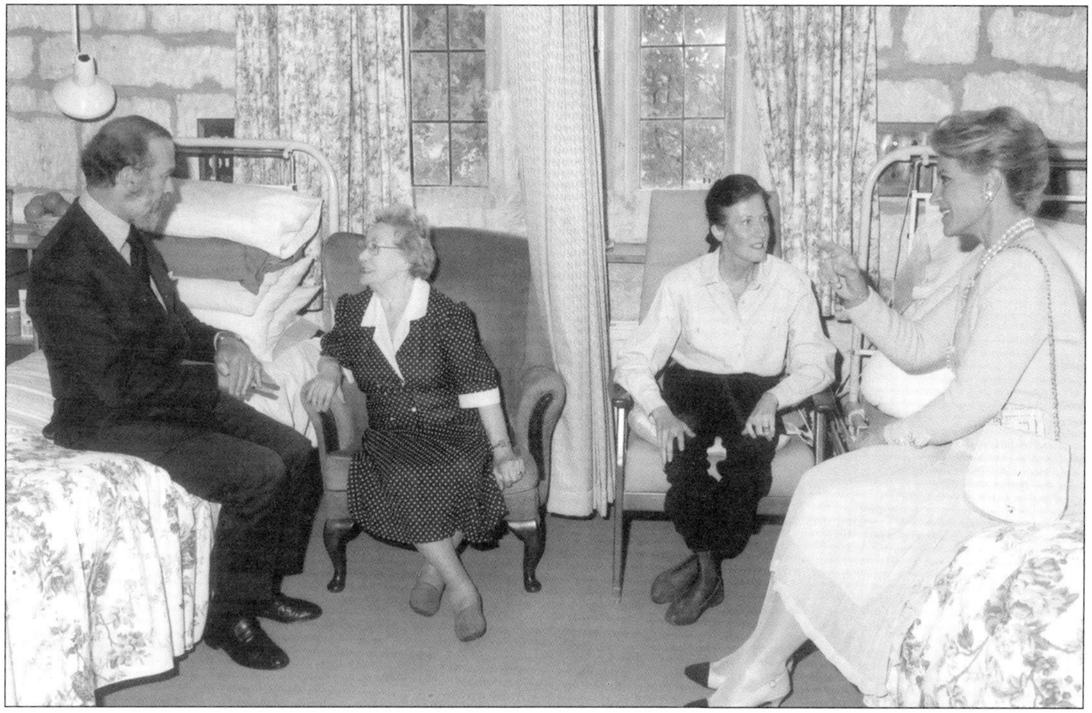

Bedside Manner
Prince and Princess Michael of Kent chat with patients at the Sue Ryder Hospice at Leckhampton Court in Cheltenham in June 1993, prior to attending an art exhibition held in the hospice chapel.

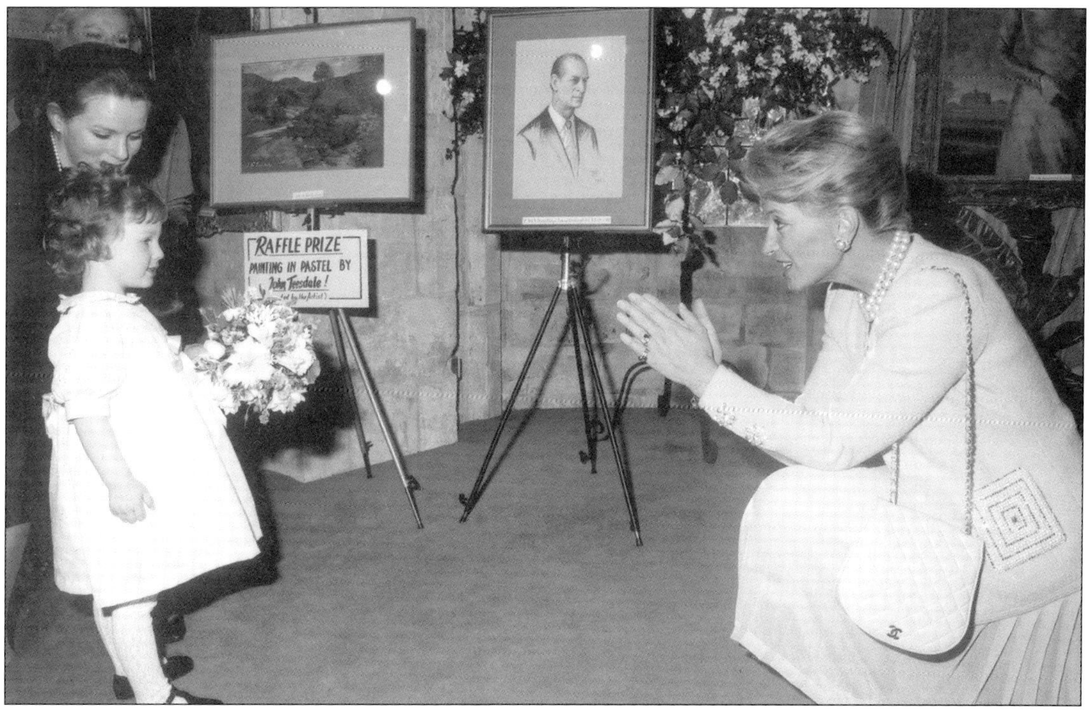

Stage Fright
After meeting patients Prince and Princess Michael of Kent attended an exhibition showing the work of well-known Gloucestershire artist John Teesdale at the chapel of Leckhampton Court. Here a rather shy Anna Goldingham, granddaughter of the artist, is being unsuccessfully tempted by the Princess to hand over the bouquet.

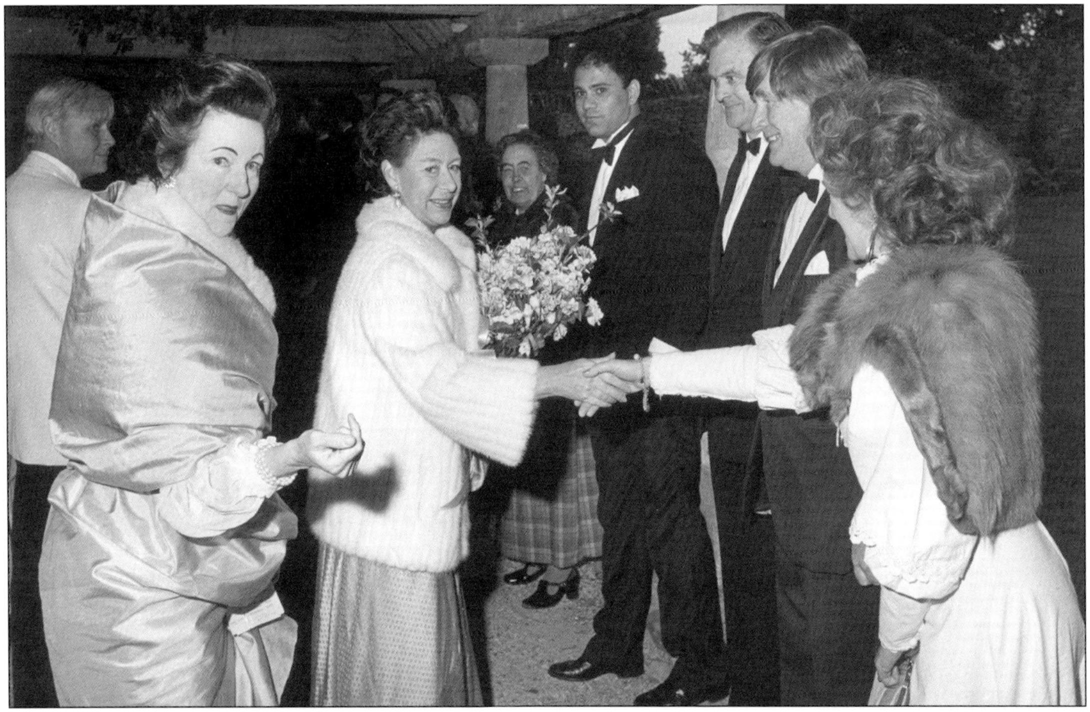

Principal Guest Meets Principal Girl
Lady Holland and Princess Margaret paused as I recorded their meeting with Cheltenham actress Hazel Rayward who often played at the Everyman Theatre during the Pantomime season. Also in the photograph is the actress' husband Michael, Cheltenham Tourist Officer and Brian Wynn, Cheltenham's Town Clerk. This occasion, during the 1980s, was another of Lady Holland's charity musical events, played out in the delightful concert hall in their Cotswold home near Coln St Aldwyn.

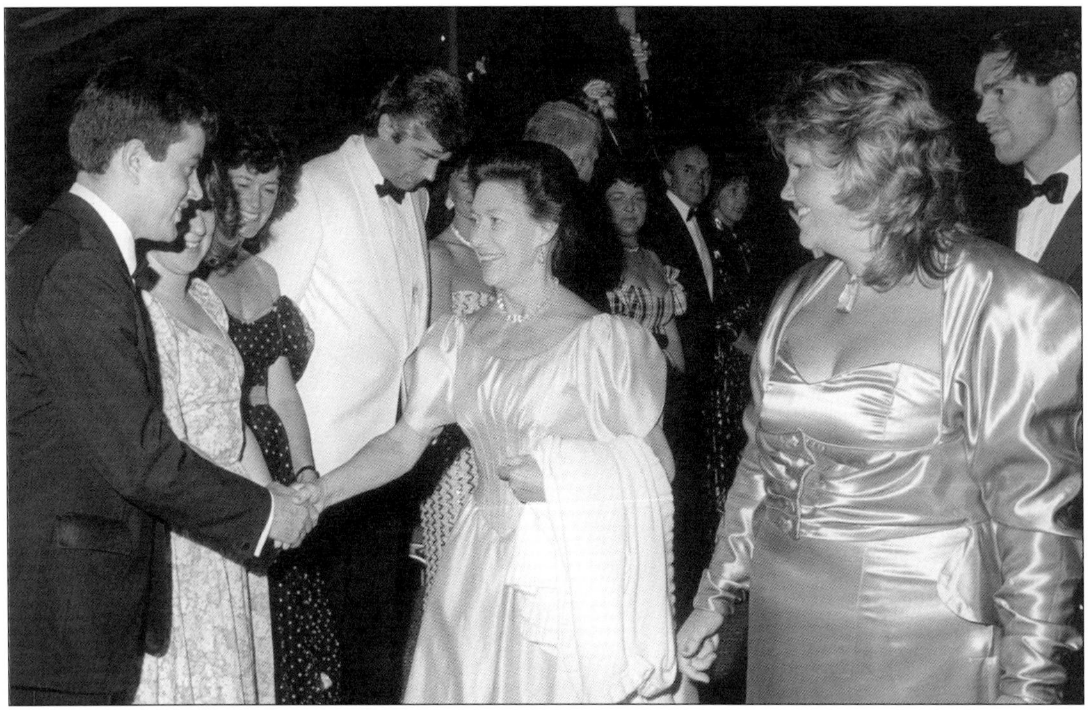

Ball Gowns
Princess Margaret being introduced to NSPCC guests and supporters by party organizer Pam Cadbury at the Grand Ball at Overbury Court in July 1988 which was held in aid of the children's charity.

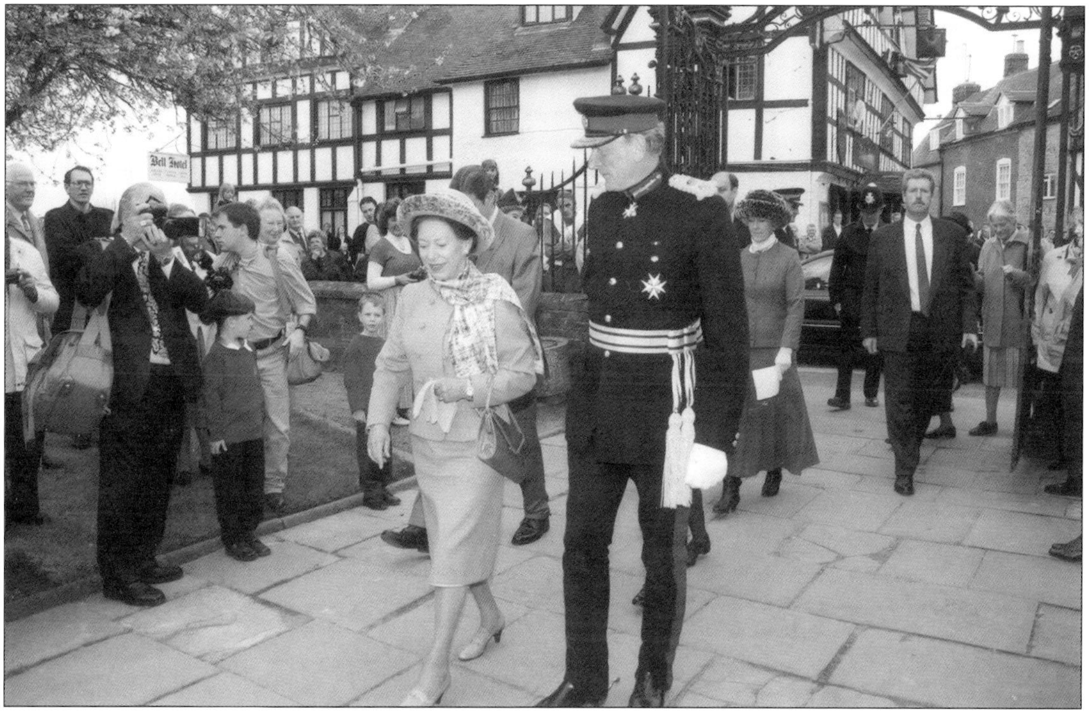

Appealing Princess
In 1997 Princess Margaret was guest of honour at a special Tewkesbury Abbey service of dedication to mark the raising of over £1.6 million to rebuild the seventeenth-century church organ and provide a new visitors centre in the grounds of the abbey. The Princess is seen here arriving for the service accompanied by Henry Elwes, Lord Lieutenant of Gloucestershire.

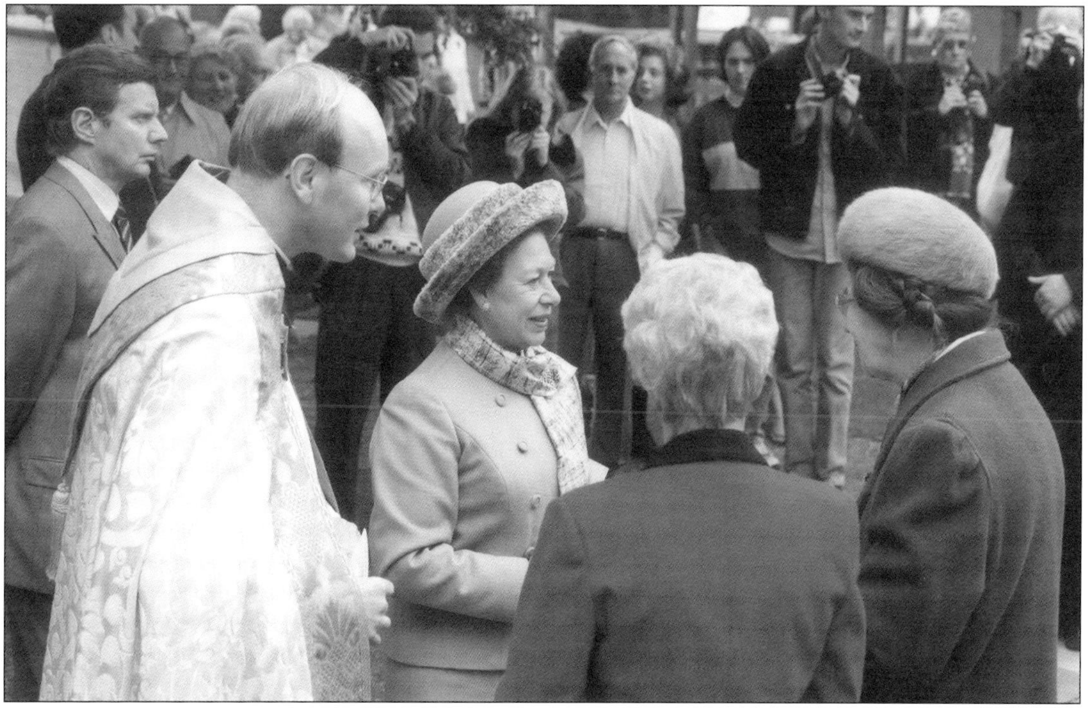

Abbey Walk
The Vicar of Tewkesbury, The Reverend Michael Tavinor, introduces Princess Margaret to parishioners in the grounds of the abbey in 1997, after the service of dedication.

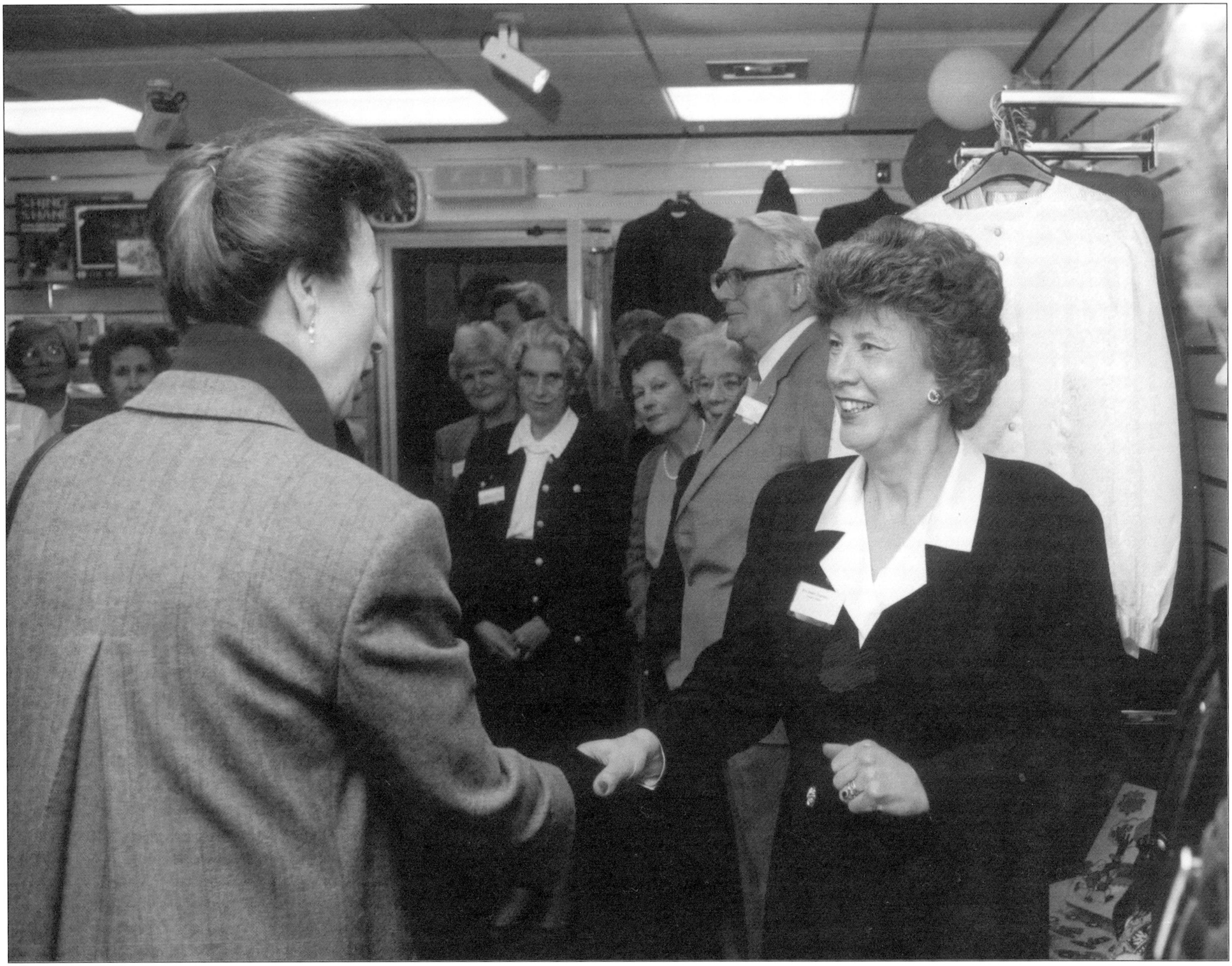

Years of Service
In March 1995, Princess Anne made one of her frequent visits to Cheltenham – this time to meet up with volunteer staff at the Save the Children charity shop in Regent Street, where, in her capacity as the fund's President, she presented three long-service awards to staff. Here, the Princess meets Anne Dimmer who had served thirty years on behalf of the charity.

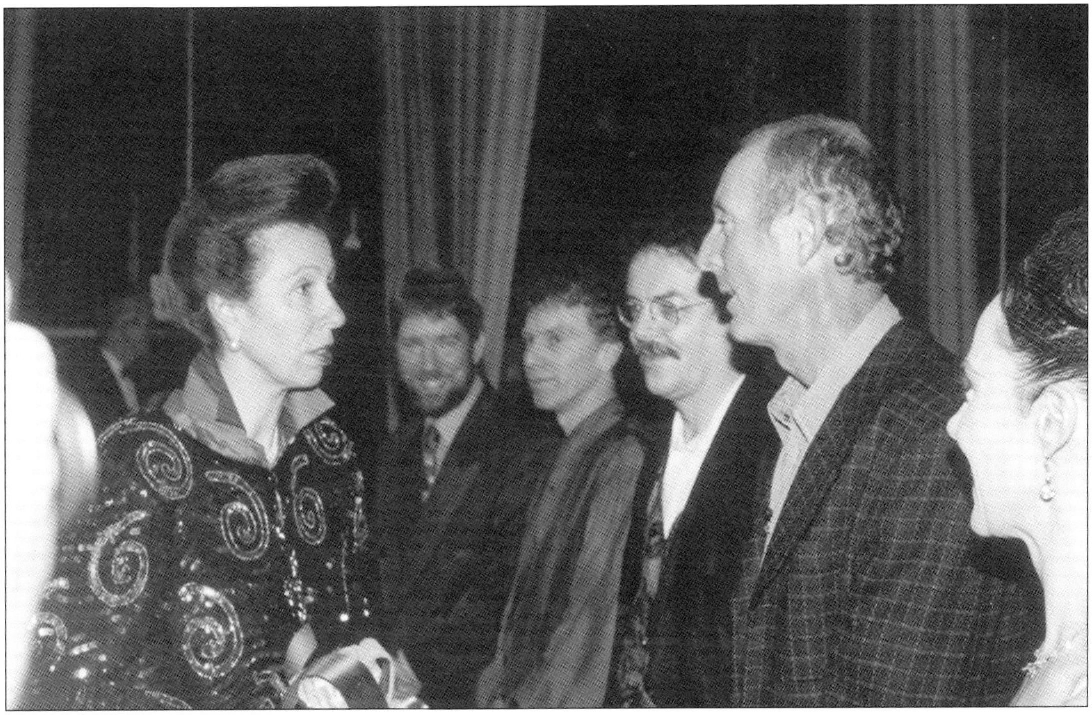

The Princess and the Comic
Princess Anne goes backstage – this time at the Roses Theatre, Tewkesbury with her new husband Captain Tim Laurence, for a Gala Concert in 1997 to mark the twenty-first anniversary of the theatre's opening. The cast combined professional and amateur acts, headed by the comedian Jasper Carrott, pictured here in conversation with the Princess.

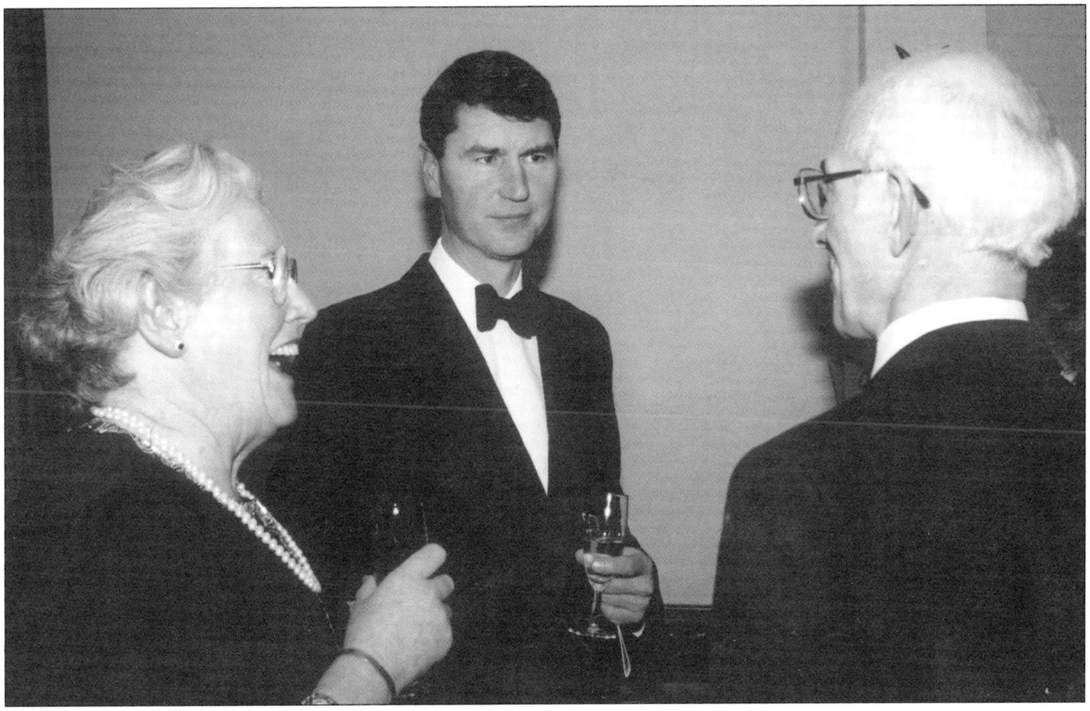

Birthday Celebrations
Anne Cadbury, OBE, JP and Patron of the Roses Theatre Trust is seen here with Princess Anne's husband, Captain Tim Laurence, at the reception held at The Roses Theatre during the Gala Concert in 1997.

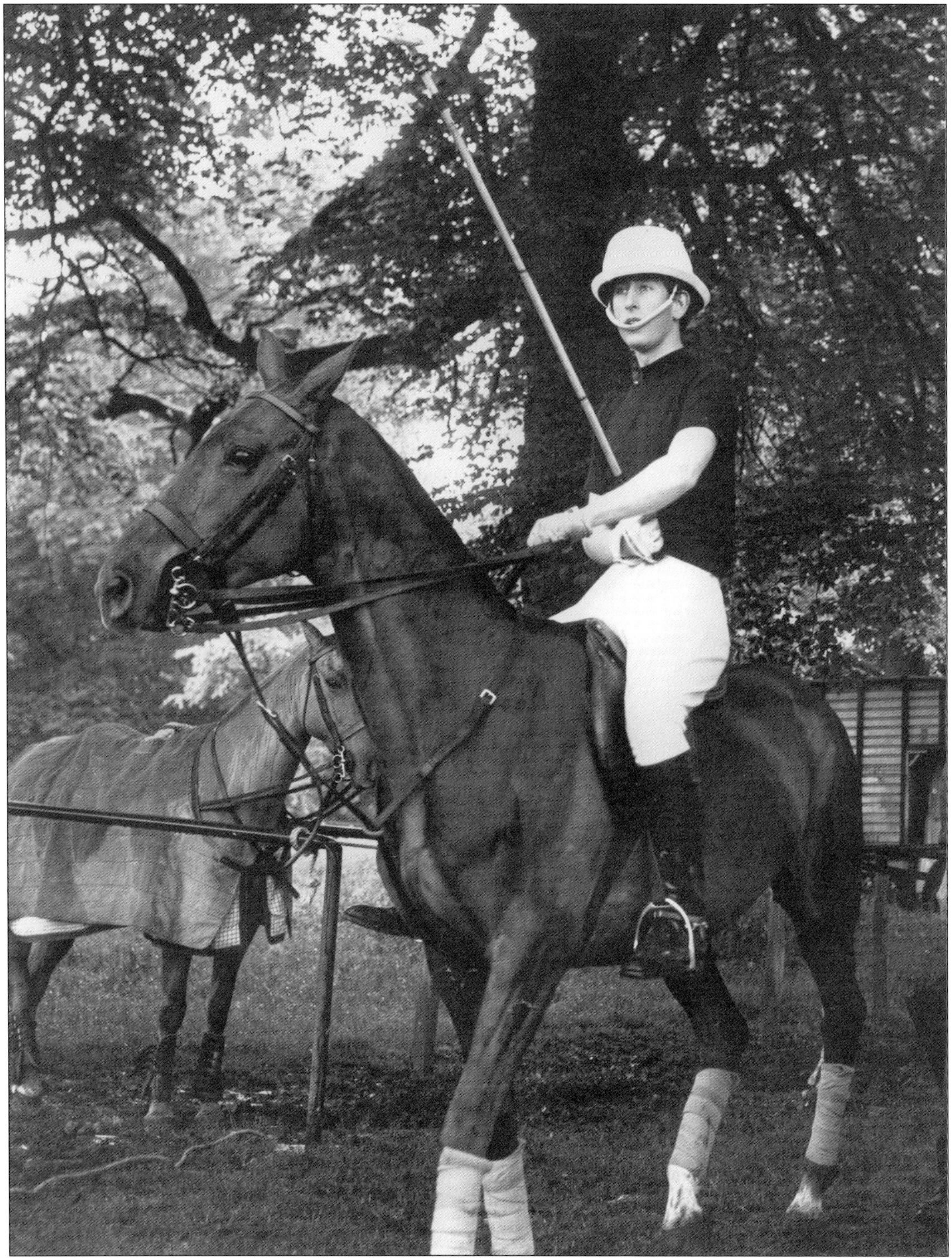

Princely Shelter
Prince Charles shelters from the rain prior to a polo match held at Cirencester Park in 1969. The match had to be abandoned due to continuous rain, much to the disappointment of the large crowd and no doubt the Prince himself. This image was taken by my wife Gillian, who as a photographer worked with me on many assignments before our son, Daniel, was born. Photo: Gillian Charity

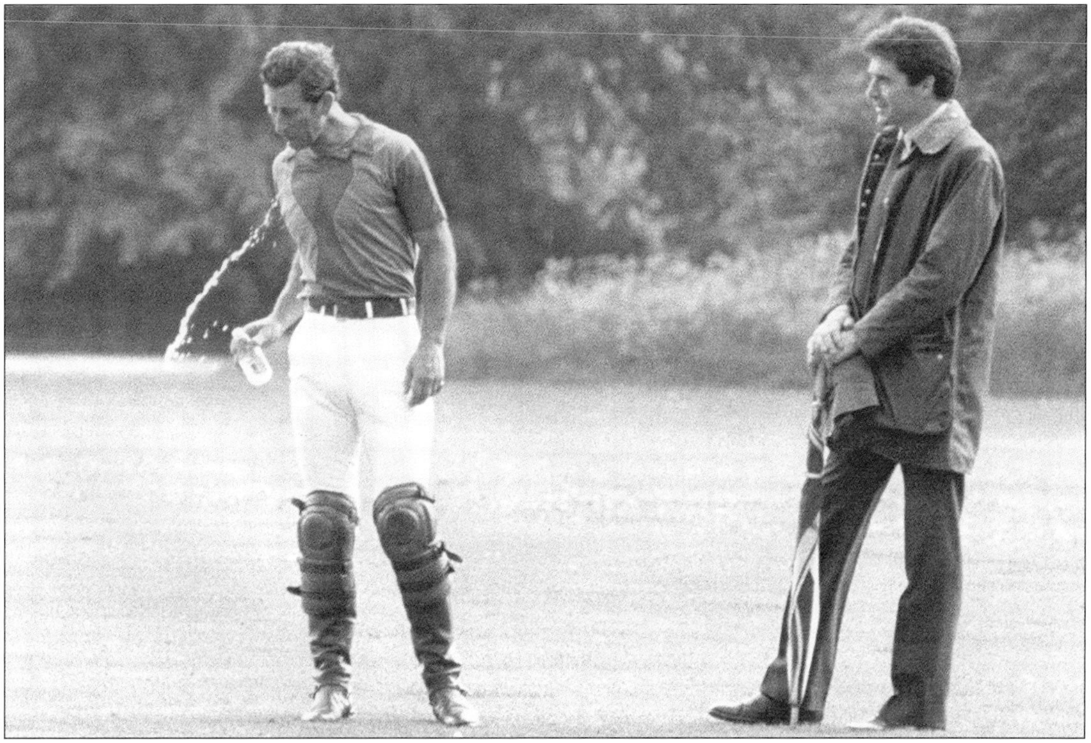

Cool Prince
Prince Charles' detective looks on as the Prince attempts to cool down during a polo match interval at Cirencester Park in the 1990s.

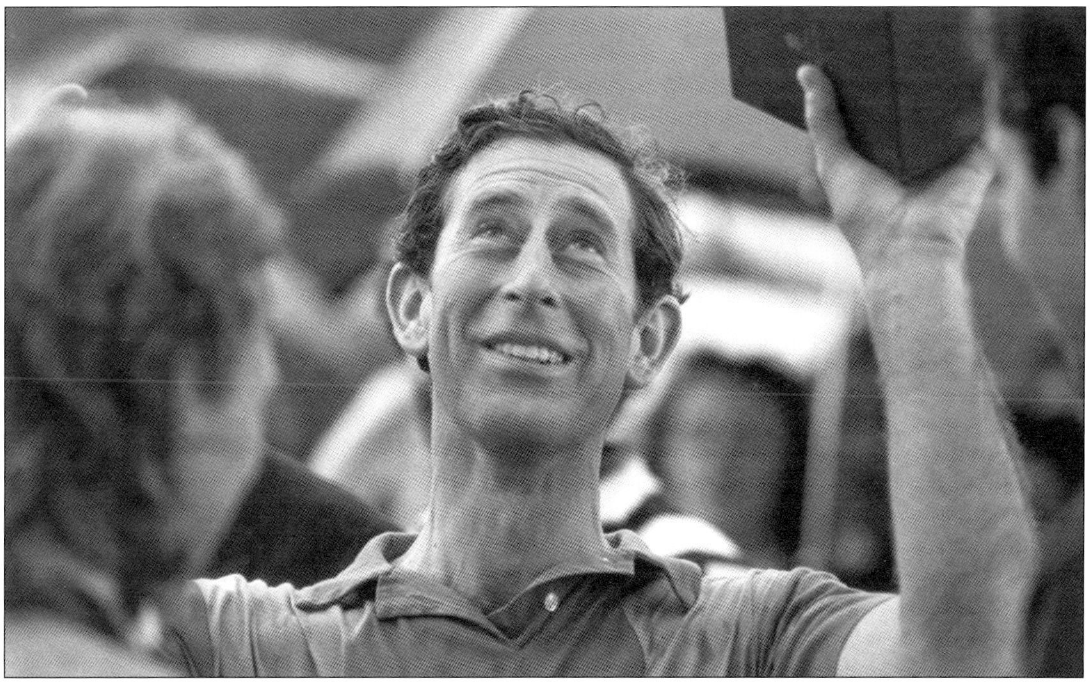

Highly Prized
A delighted Prince Charles holds his trophy aloft during polo match presentations following a charity game at Cirencester Park in the 1990s in aid of the Sue Ryder Hospice.

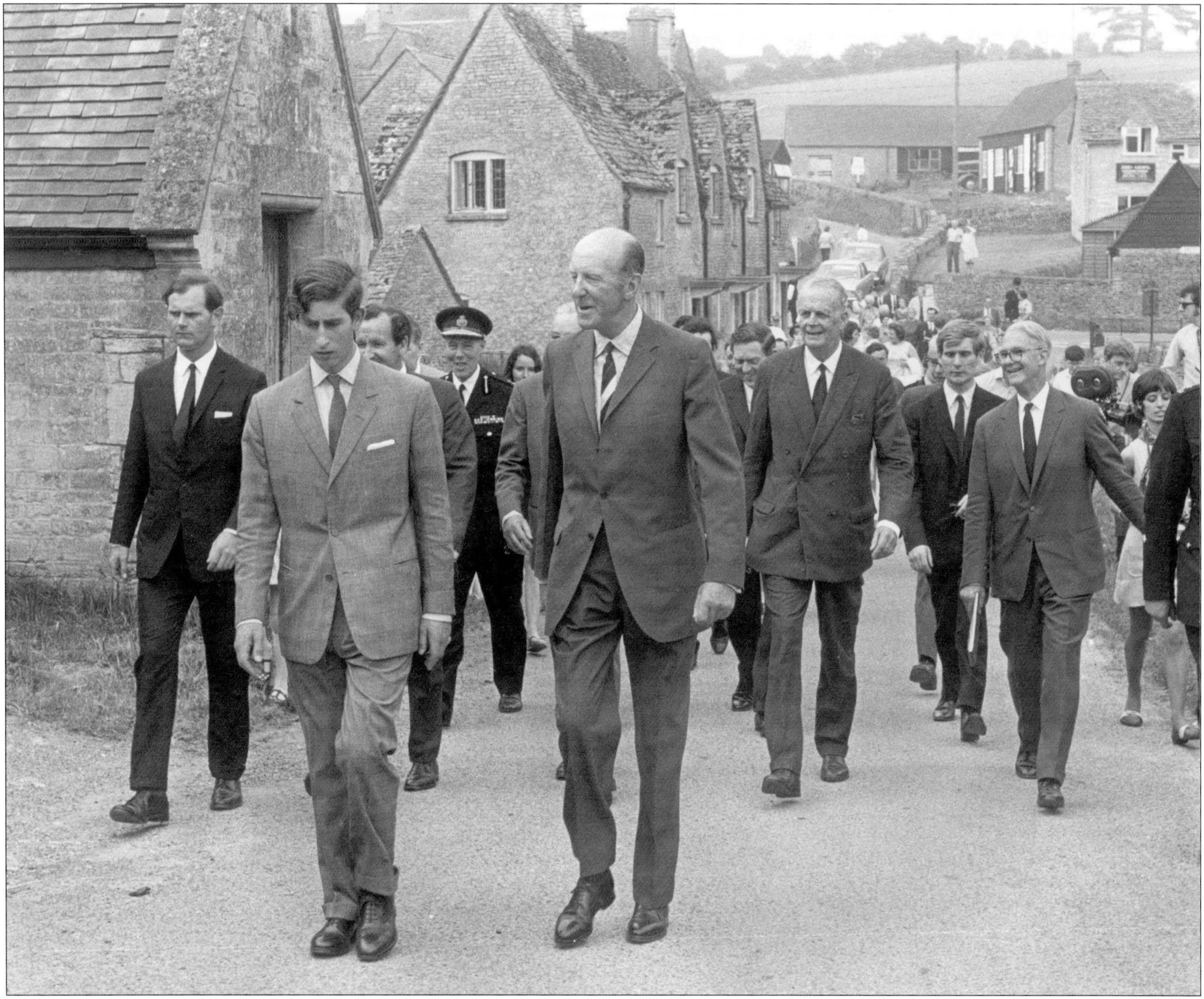

Walk This Way, Sir
The young Prince strolls through the normally serene village of Daglingworth near Cirencester with the Duke of Beaufort during a tour of Duchy of Cornwall property in the Cotswolds in 1969.

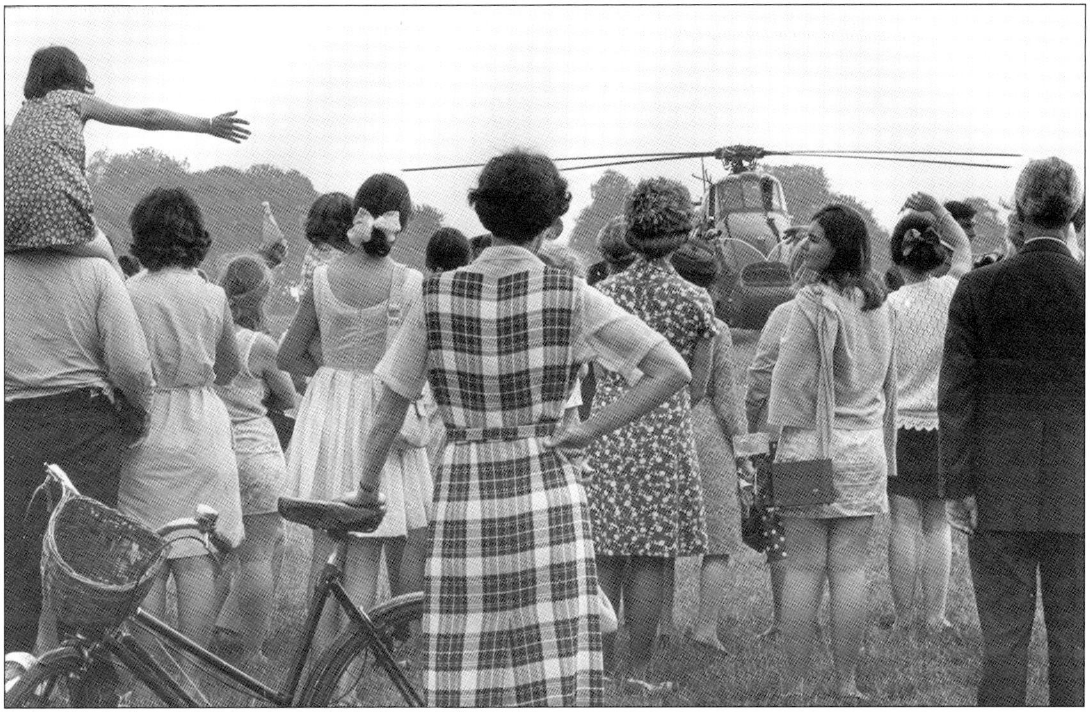

Waiting
Villagers wait expectantly as Prince Charles arrives in his helicopter at Daglingworth in 1969 for a tour of the Duchy estates.

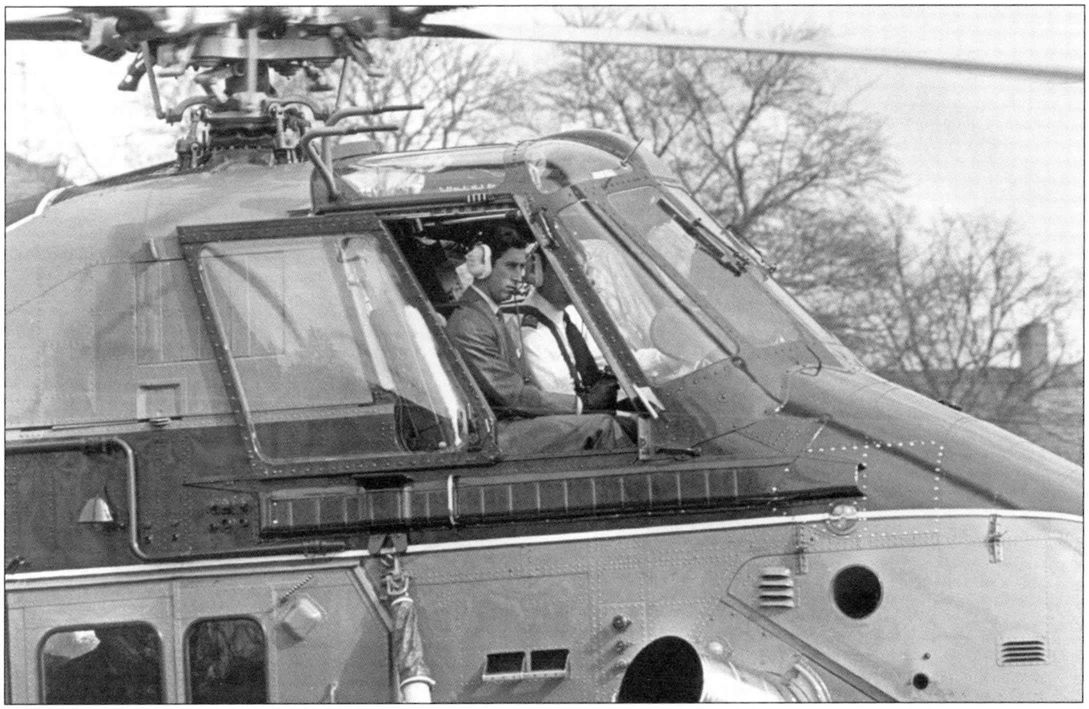

High Flyer
Prince Charles in the pilot's seat of his helicopter, after landing in a field at Daglingworth in 1969.

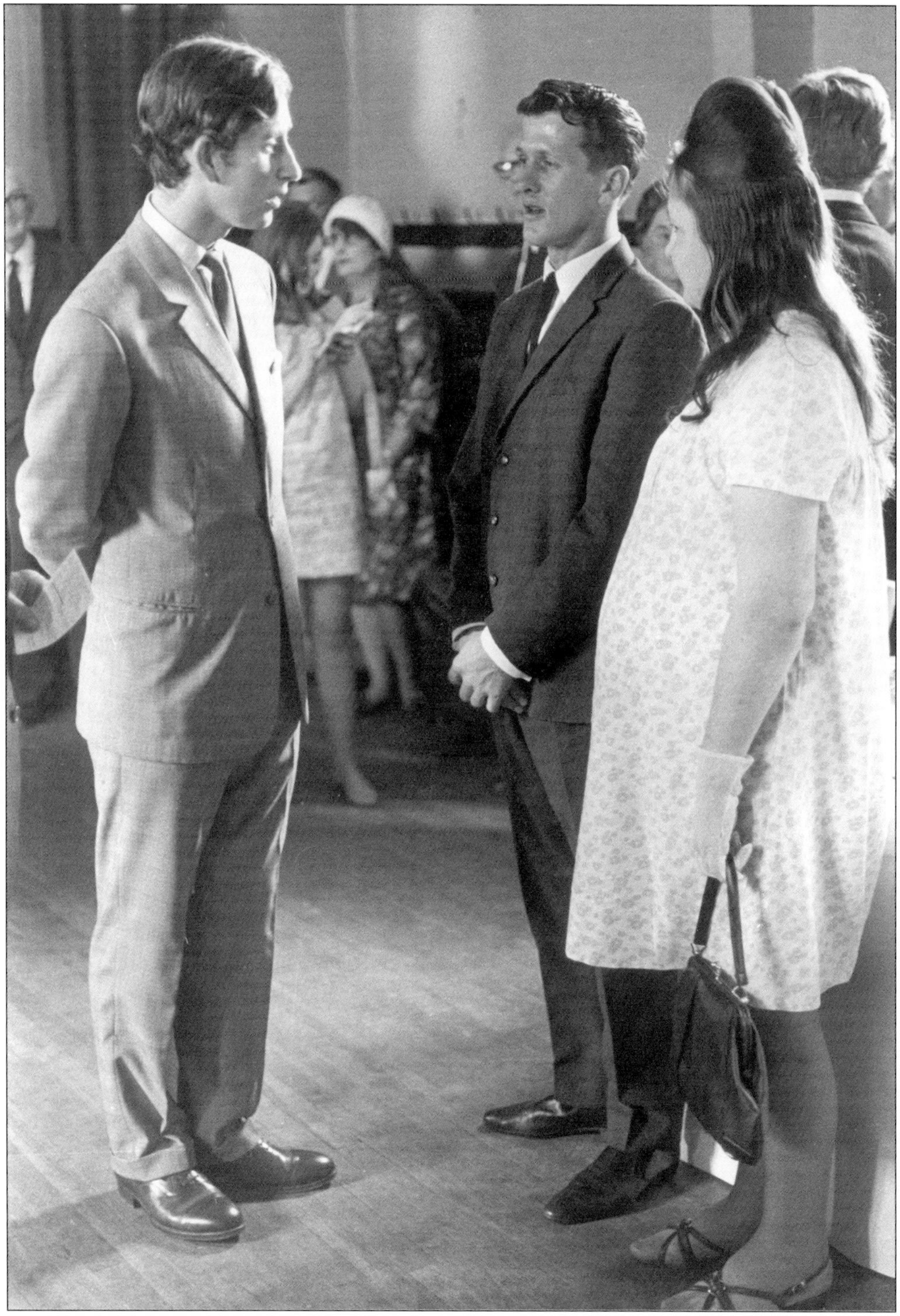

Pregnant Pause
Over informal tea and cakes in Daglingworth village hall, a young Prince Charles mingled with villagers during his 1969 visit. Here is seen chatting here with a village couple who seemed set to increase the local population!

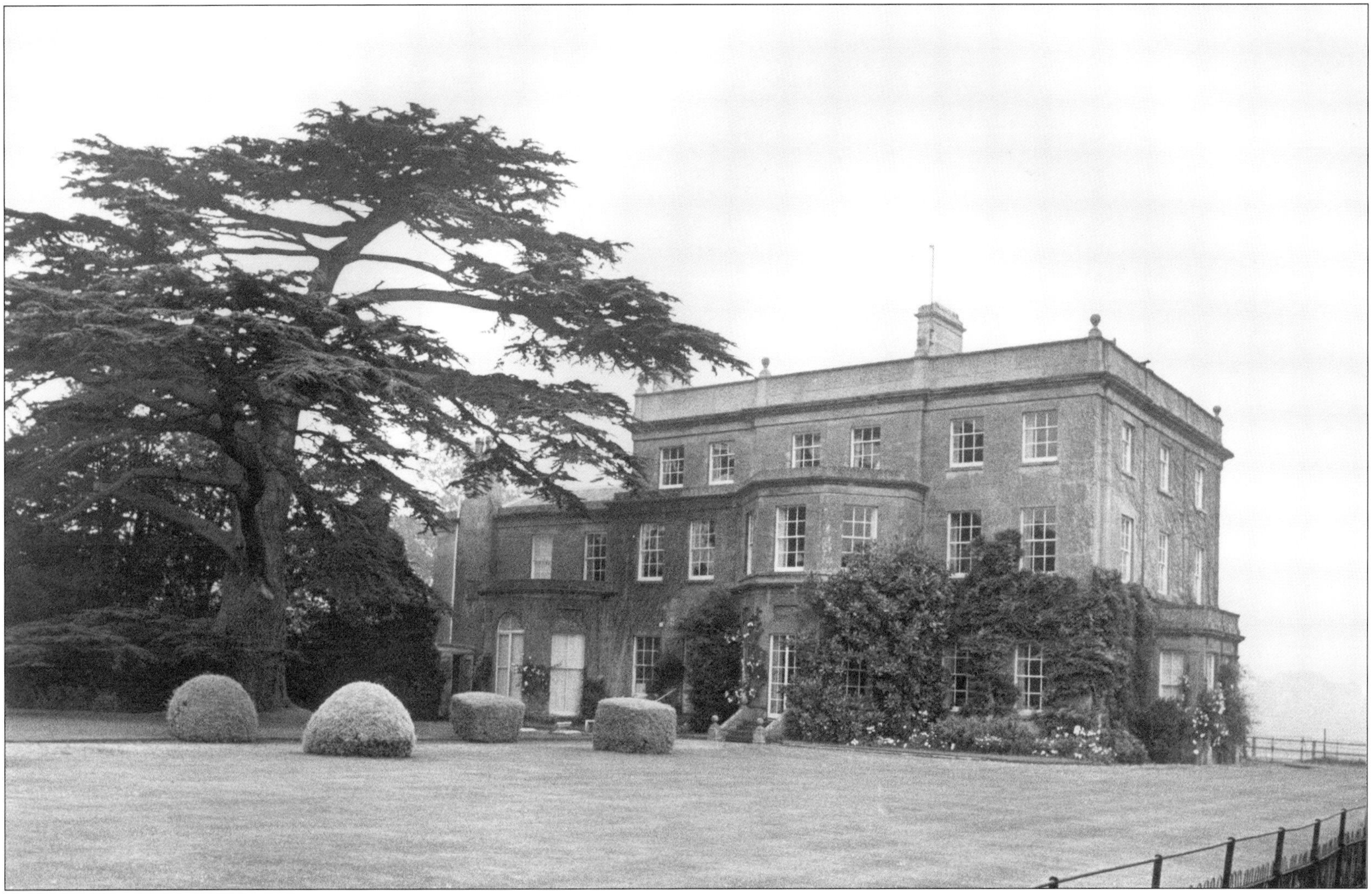

Put 'em Up!
The quiet market town of Tetbury became the centre of the world's media attention when, in 1971, the Duchy of Cornwall bought Highgrove House, situated in the tiny hamlet of Dougton on the outskirts of Tetbury, reputedly for around £1 million. The property already had illustrious connections; the Macmillan family trust purchased the estate for £89,000 in 1965 and it was occupied for a time by Maurice Macmillan, son of Prime Minister Sir Harold Macmillan. It had also been the home of the son of President Roosevelt for over two years. The purchase completed the third side of Gloucestershire's 'royal triangle', comprising Gatcombe Park, Nether Lypiatt Manor and now Highgrove.

With our pictures in the bag, we were politely requested to leave the grounds but some of us refused until other snappers, lurking deep in the undergrowth, also left. As we made our protests, a royal correspondent, James Whittaker, called me a '[expletive] sneak' and raised his fists in a classic pugilist pose. I retorted that I would not lower myself to brawl on the lawn of the heir to the throne and this seemed to take the wind out of his sails. Fortunately, for me at least, he calmed down, for it did appear that he might have been quite useful in a boxing ring.

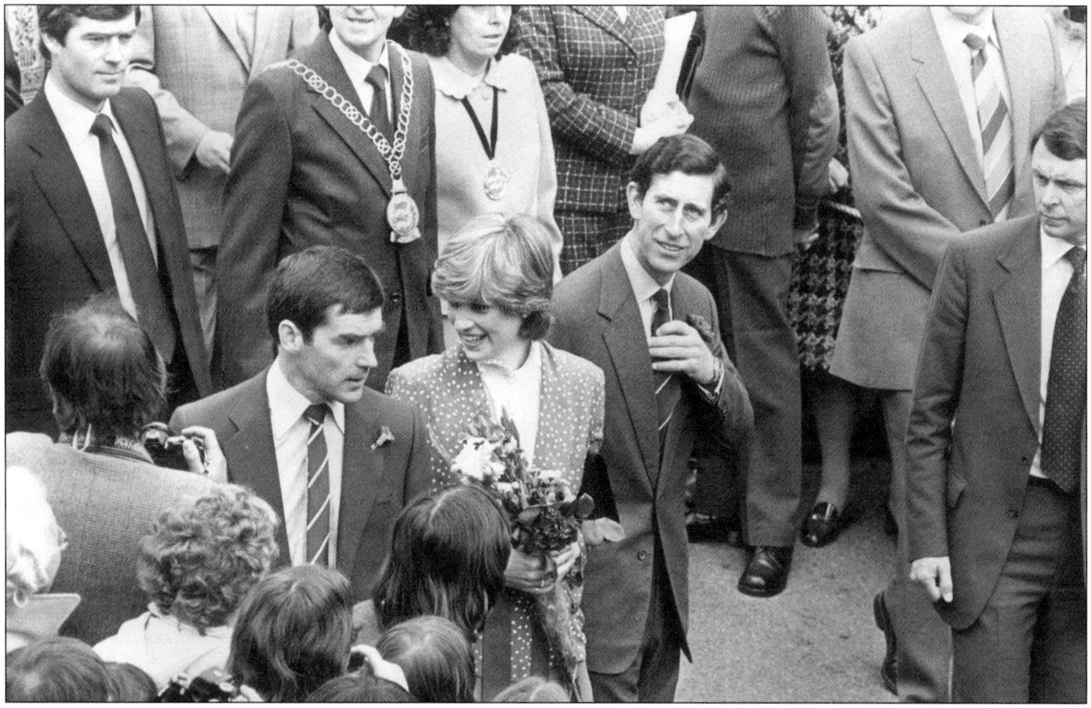

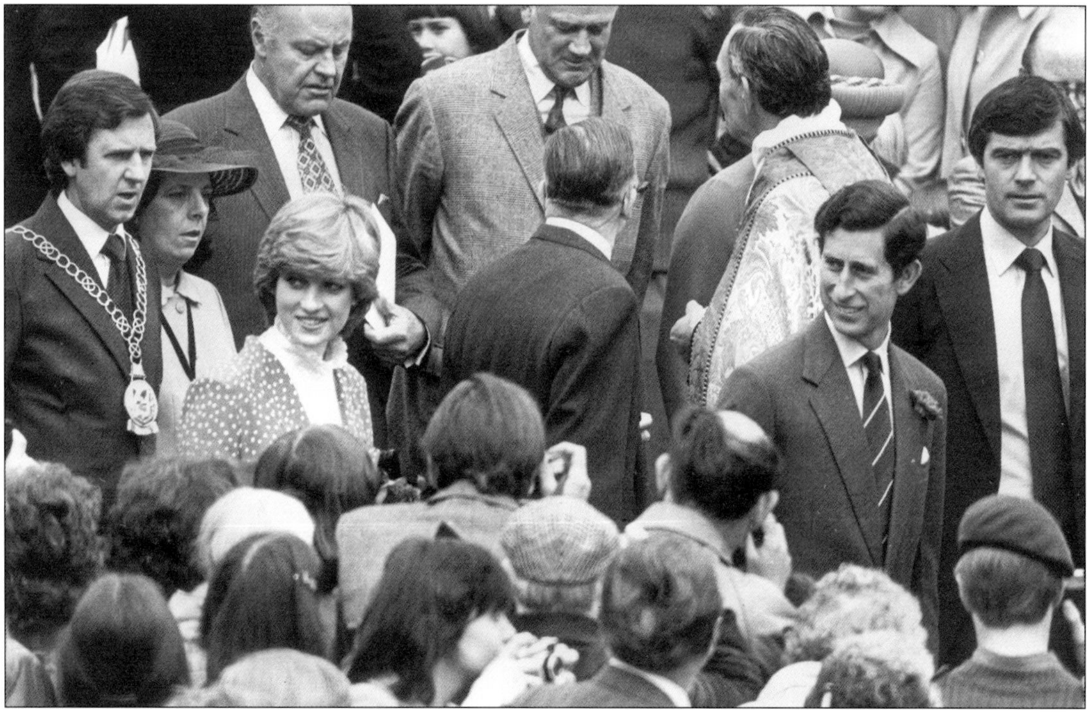

Charming Tetbury
Prior to their marriage in 1981, the Prince of Wales and Lady Diana Spencer brought Tetbury to a standstill with an informal walkabout much in the style of European royals. The streets were thronged with locals and sightseers desperate to get a glimpse of the world's most famous couple. They were accompanied on the walk by the Mayor and Mayoress of the town, Councillor and Mrs Brian Kimber.

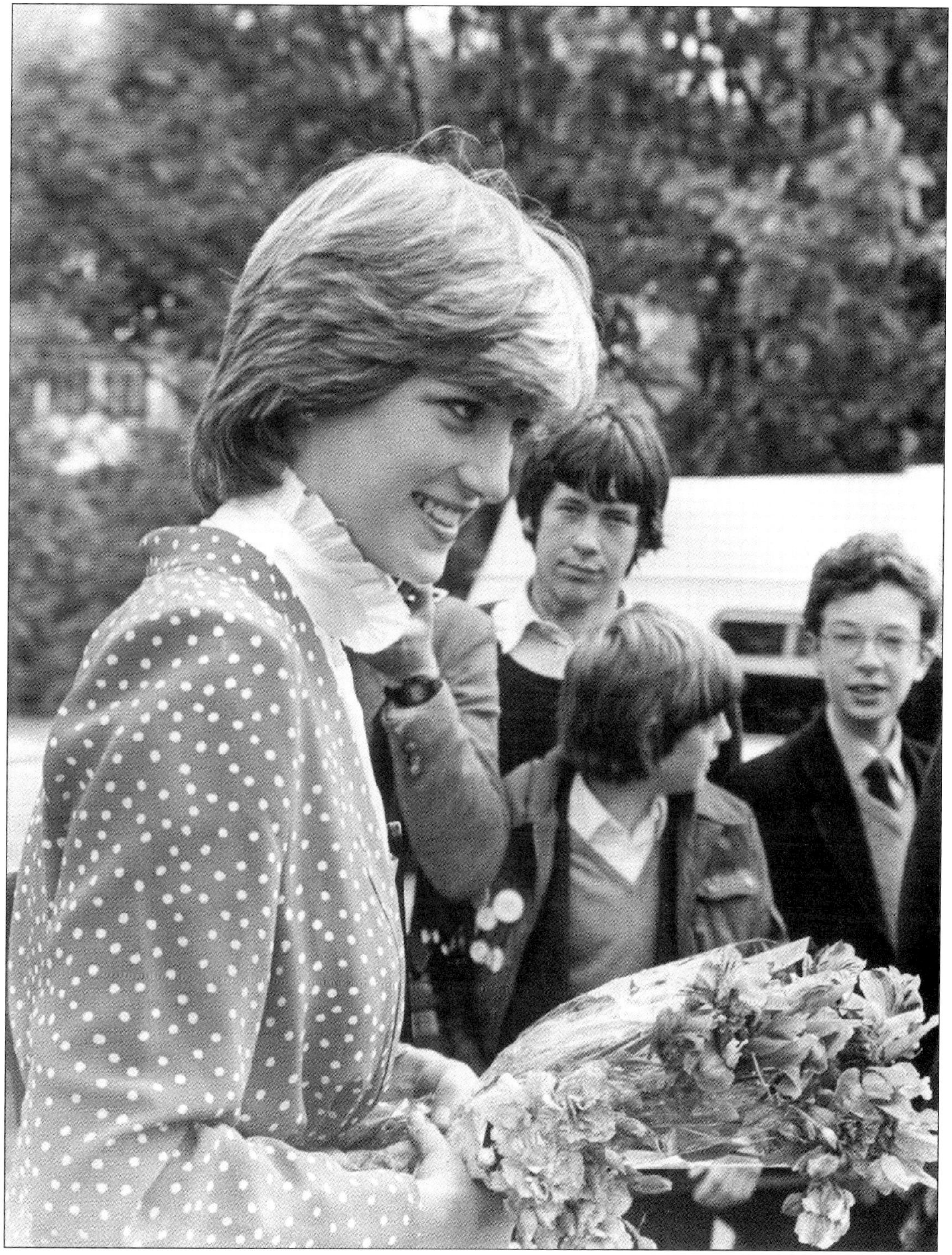

Flowering Princess
The beautiful young Lady Diana strolls through the streets of Tetbury with the panache of a seasoned royal.

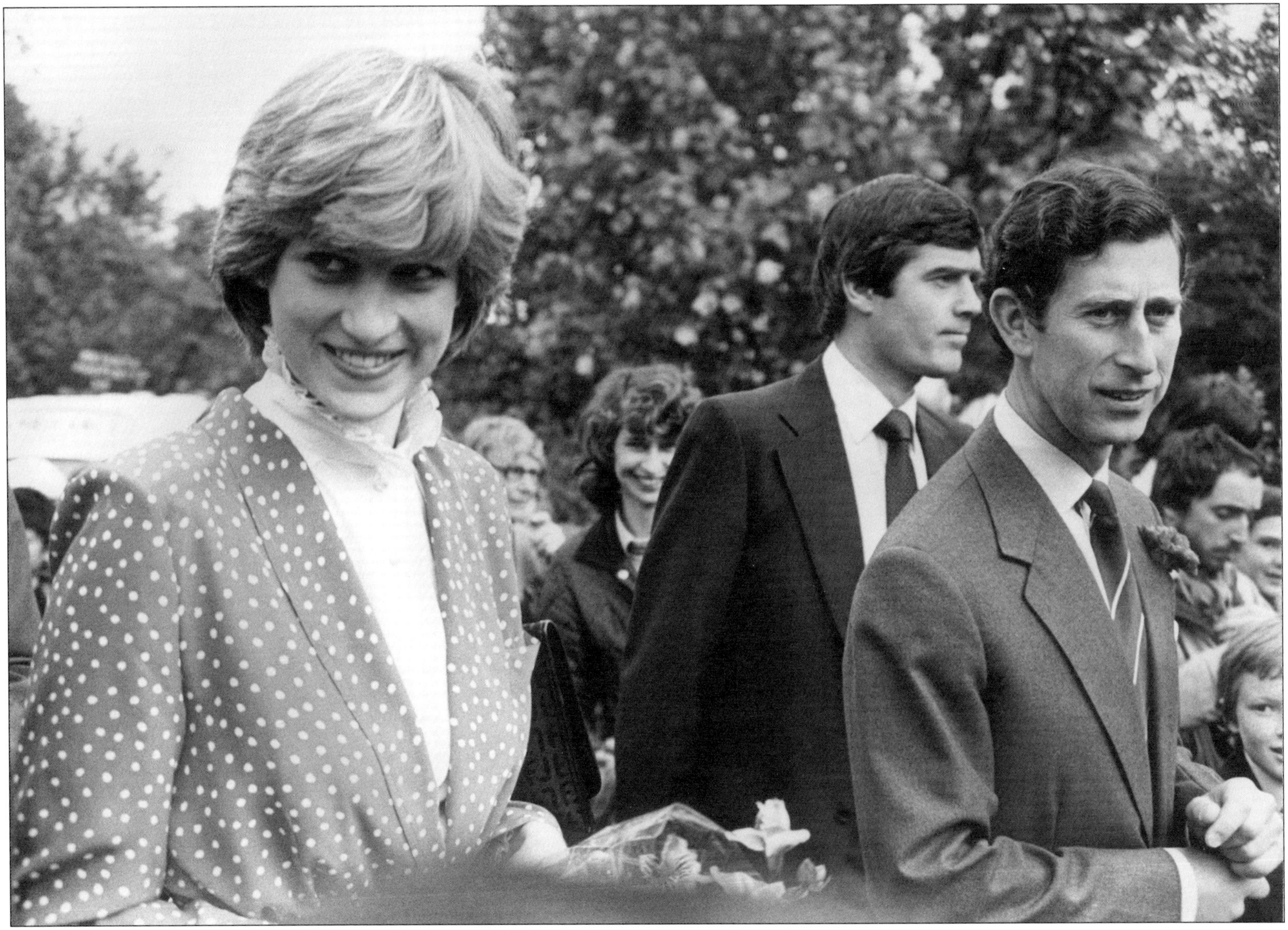

The Prince's Princess
A slightly coy Diana with a confident Prince Charles on their stroll through Tetbury in 1981.

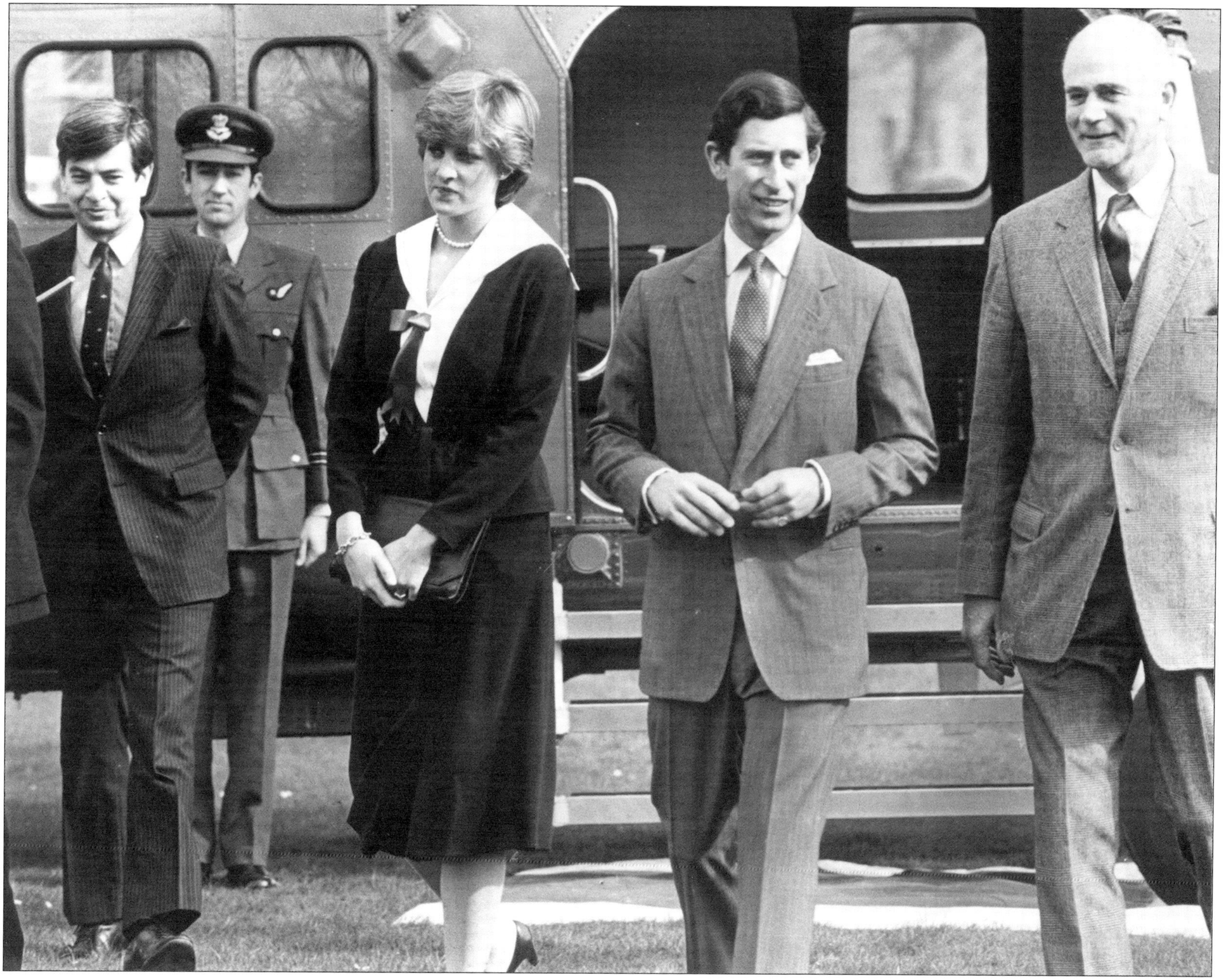

Flying Visit
The Prince of Wales and Diana Spencer arrive by helicopter to visit Dean Close School in 1981. Alongside the Prince is Colonel Martin Gibbs, Lord Lieutenant of Gloucestershire.

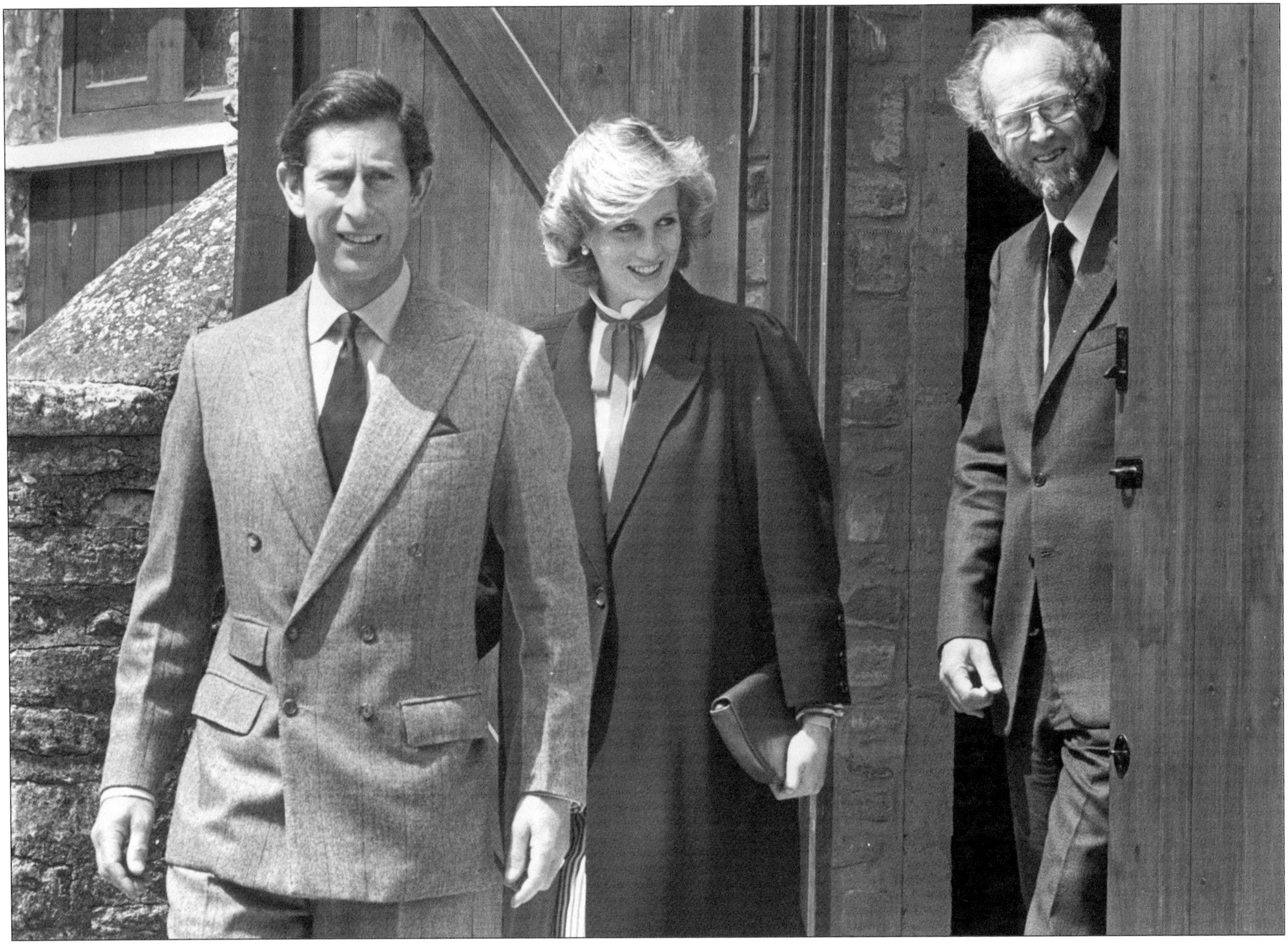

Royal Landlord
The completion of a project dear to the heart of the Prince Charles came to fruition in 1984, when in the company of the Princess of Wales he opened the Street Farm workshops at Highgrove. After eighteen months of building work, the former derelict farm buildings on the Prince's estate were turned into a cluster of workshops that would provide economical, rented facilities from small business users. The Prince told guests at the opening ceremony that 'If you had seen Street Farm two years ago, you would have written them off as a rather charming, quaint collection of collapsing farm buildings'. The scheme was a welcome opportunity for first-time businesses to get a foot on the ladder, and its first tenants were two young ladies who specialized in restoring damaged items of porcelain and pottery. The Prince and Princess of Wales are pictured touring the newly-opened workshops.

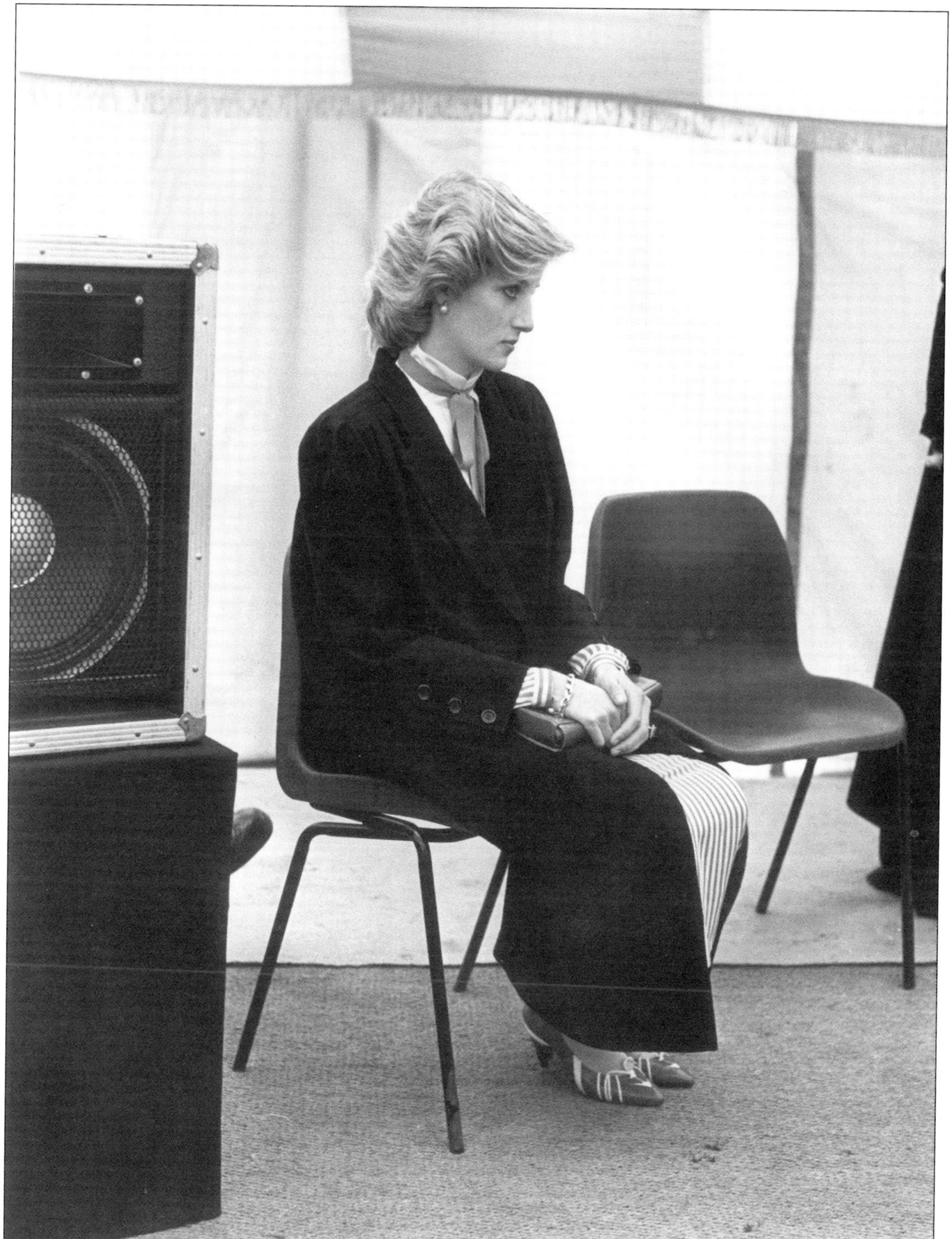

Patient Princess
Princess Diana listens to speeches at the opening of the Street Farm workshops at Highgrove in 1984.

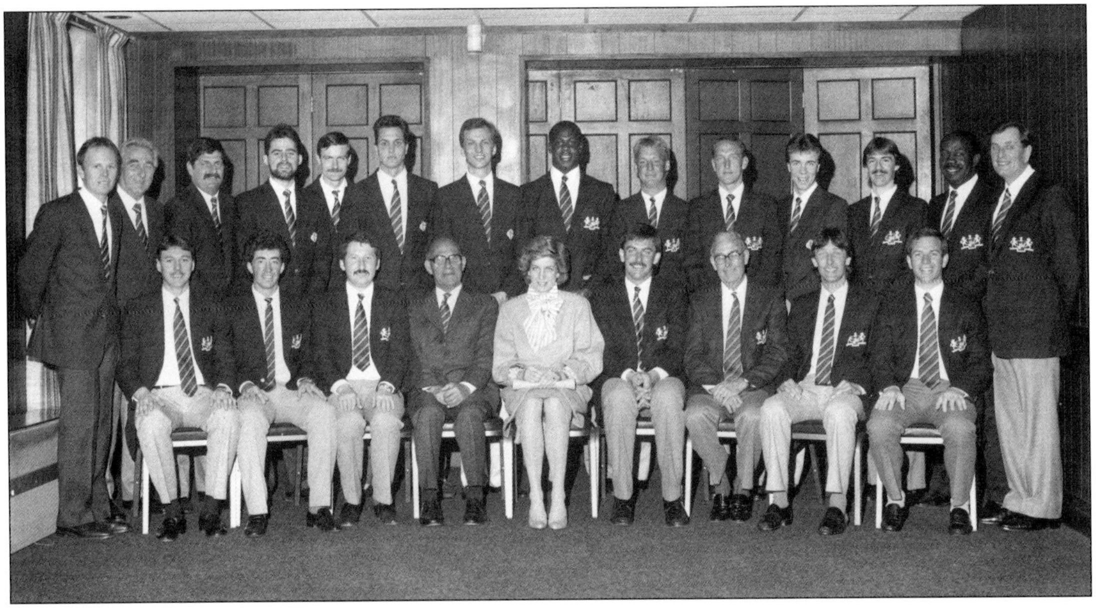

The Princess' Eleven
Because of my associations with the Gloucestershire County Cricket Club and I was kindly asked in the spring of 1986 to be the official photographer for the visit of the Princess of Wales, who in her role as Patron of the club was visiting the Bristol ground to meet players and officials at a special luncheon. When the day came I waited along with my Fleet Street colleagues for the Princess to arrive, all of us hoping to capture that elusive, exclusive snap that would wing its way around the world's news desks. You can imagine their surprise when, a short time later, I was called from the pack by a royal detective and escorted to the boardroom for the team photograph – but with an extra person in the group – the Princess of Wales! The team entered the room and took their places, while I waited nervously for the royal guest. A few minutes later she entered the boardroom, and on passing me, whispered 'I hope you're going to make us laugh'. How I wish I'd had the nerve to tell a joke!

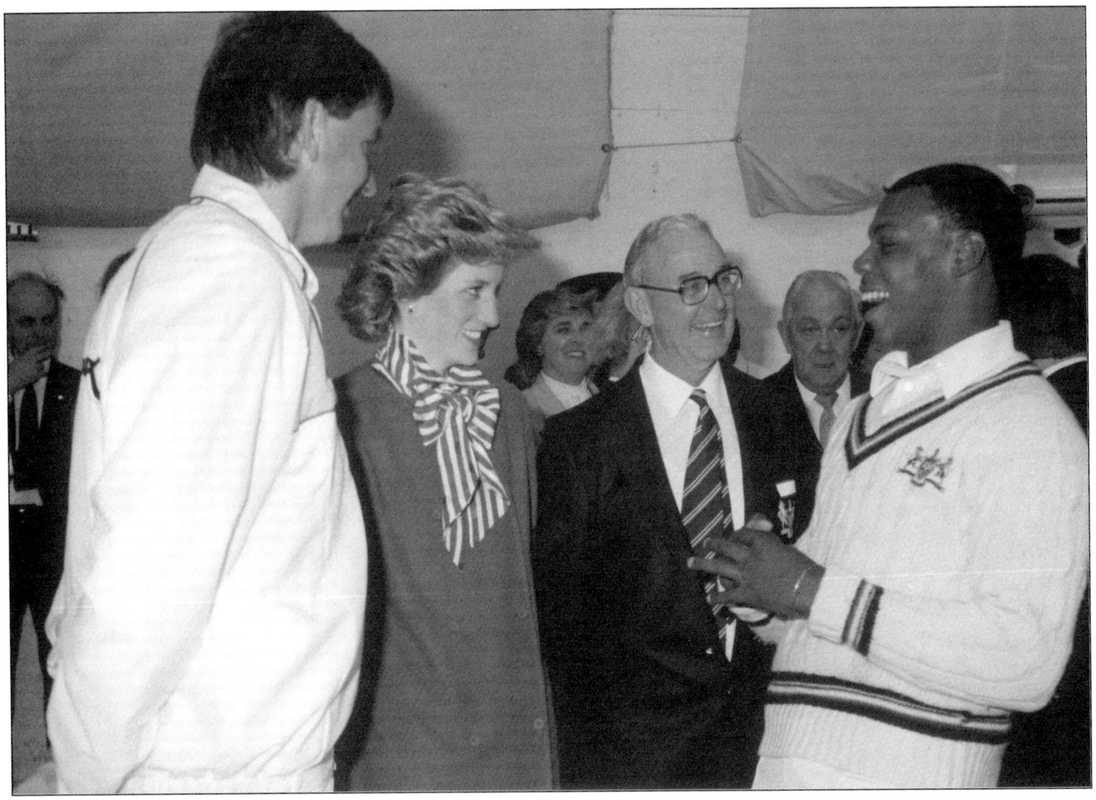

Bowling Them Over
The Princess's visit to the club was a memorable one. She was totally at ease with everybody, and obviously enjoyed the occasion. She presented David Lawrence, the team's fast bowler, with a Young Cricketer of the Year award on behalf of the Cricket Writer's Association, and joked with players as she toured the gym and training areas. Here she is seen with club captain David Graveney, chairman Don Perry and David Lawrence, known to his colleagues and fans as 'Syd'.

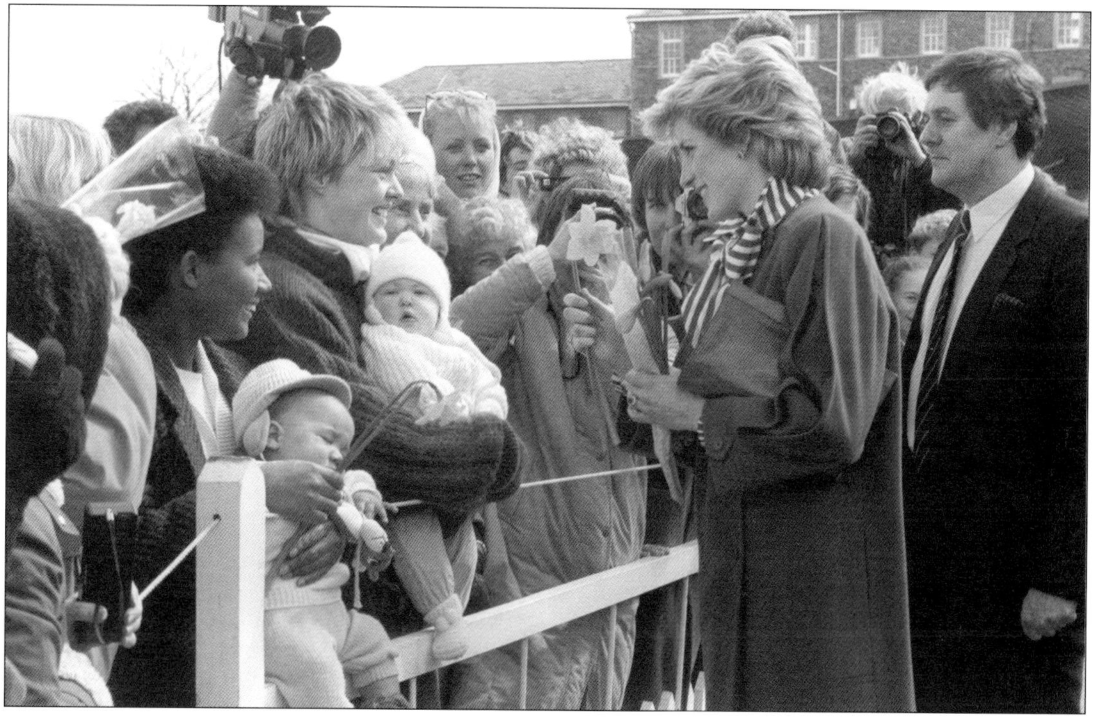

A Welcome in the Vale
After the official ceremonies were over, Princess Diana stopped before leaving the ground to meet up with club supporters and players' families lined around the pitch. One of the onlookers presented the Princess of Wales with a single daffodil.

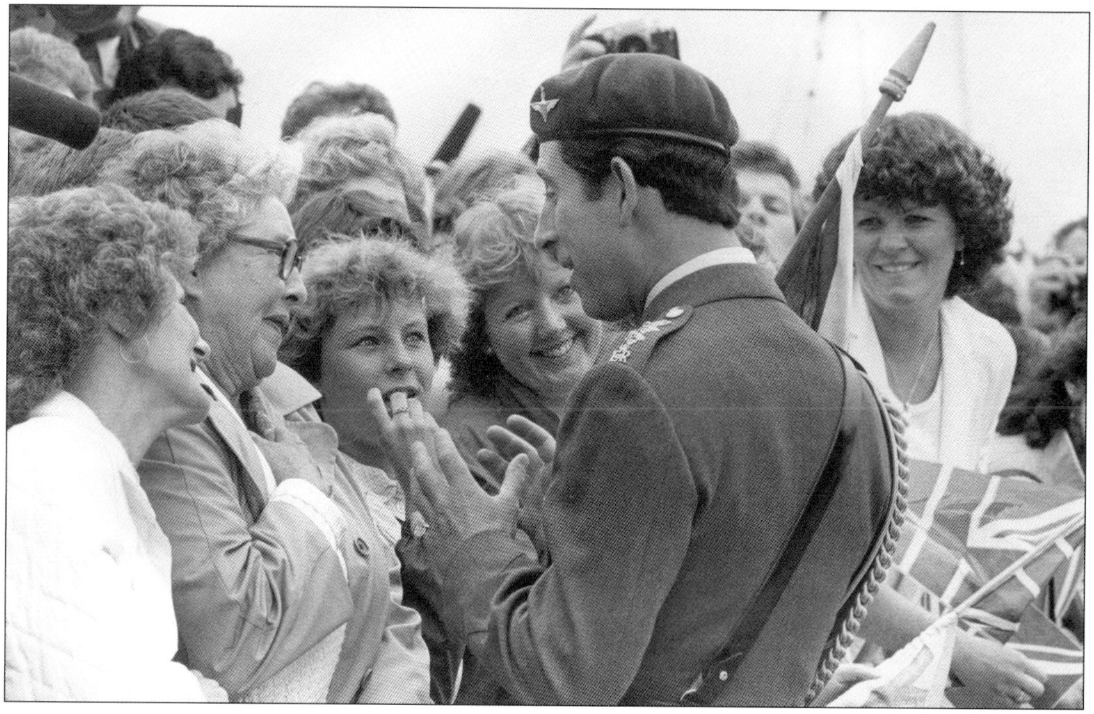

Homecoming
The Prince of Wales engaged in animated conversation with forces families as they wait at RAF Brize Norton for their loved ones to come home from the Falkland War, in 1982.

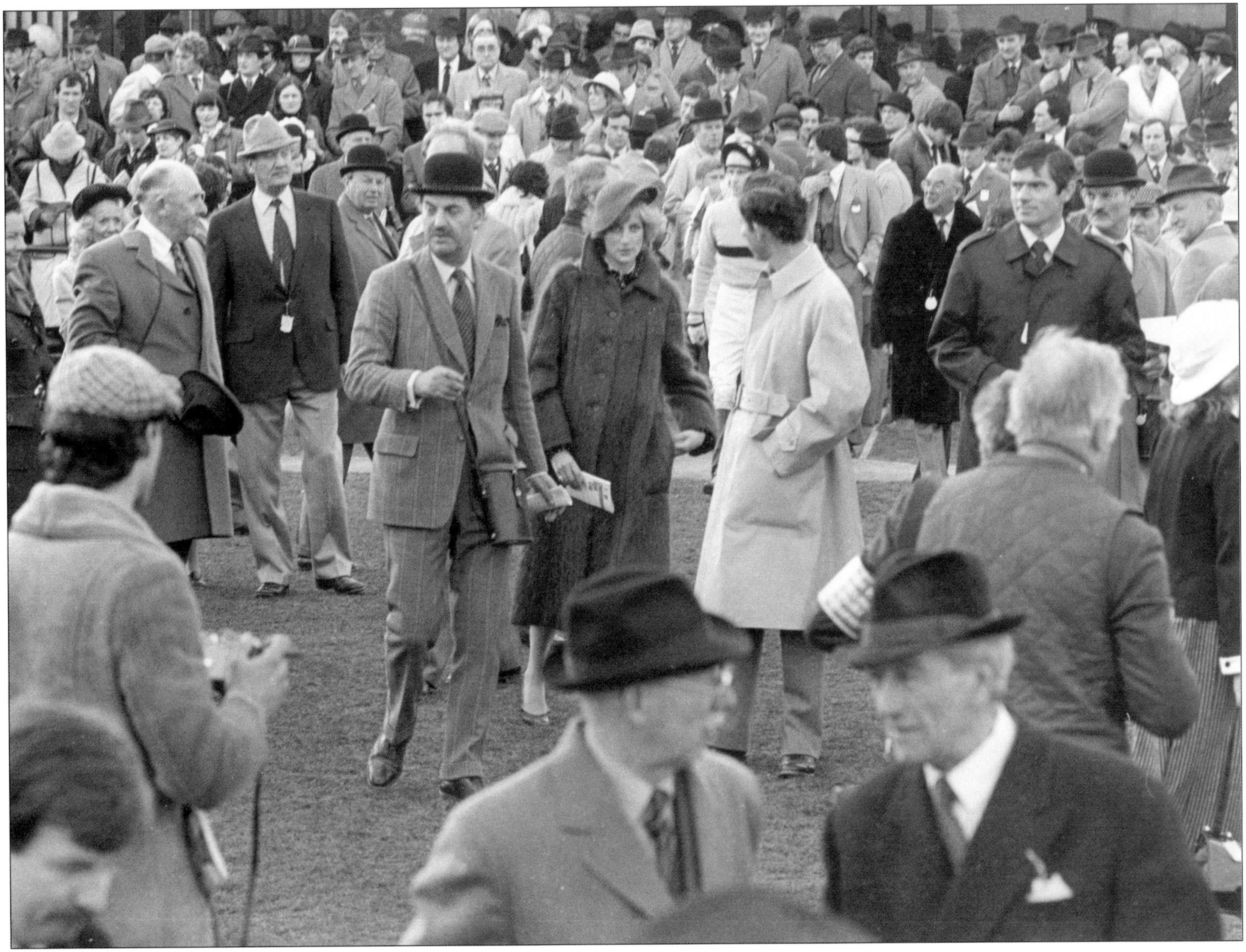

All at Sea
Horse racing was probably not a particularly fond pastime of the Princess of Wales – she is seen here with Sir Piers Bengough and Prince Charles, seeming rather lost amid a sea of race-goers in the parade ring during a Cheltenham Gold Cup meeting in the 1980s.

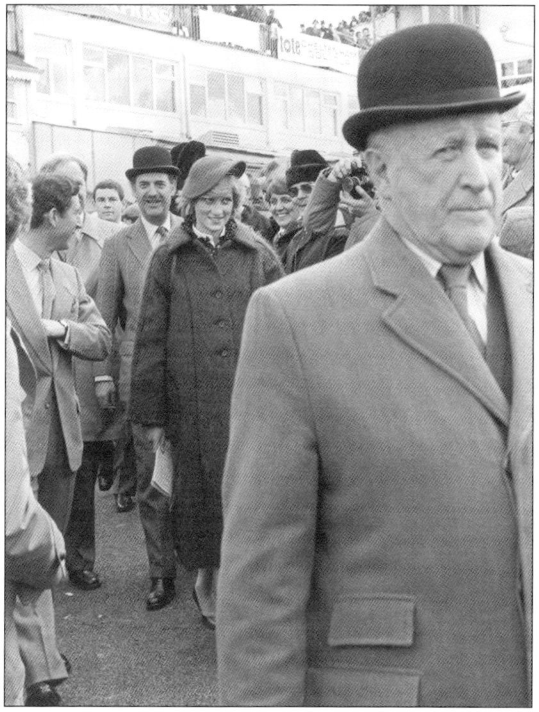

Faces in the Crowd
The Prince and Princess of Wales make their way through a crowd of race-goers at a 1980s Cheltenham Gold Cup meeting. They are led by Sir Desmond Plummer, Chairman of the Levy Board, and following the Princess is Sir Piers Bengough, a director of the Cheltenham Racecourse Company.

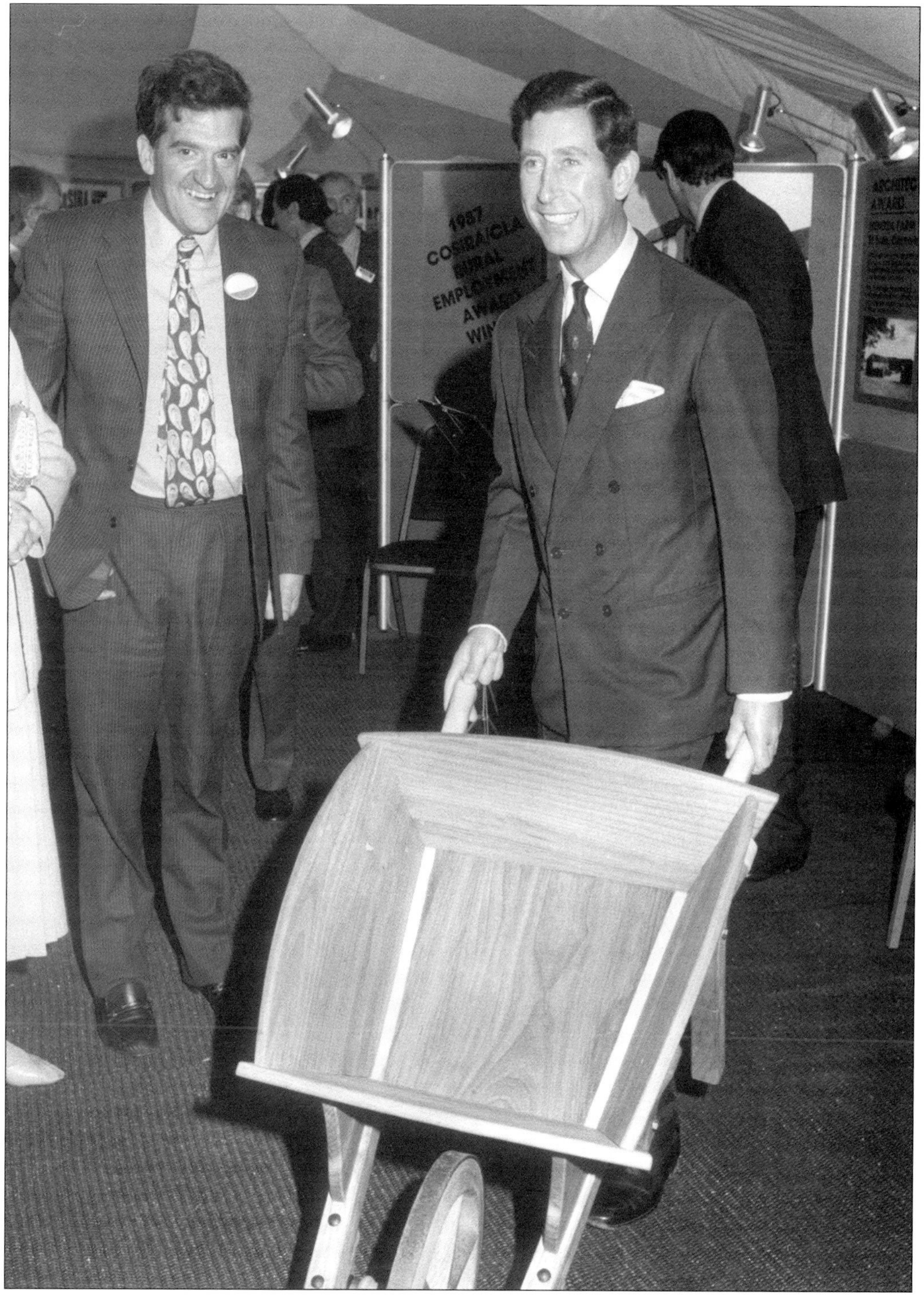

Barrow Boy
An apparently delighted Prince of Wales is presented with a gift of a bespoke wheelbarrow for his beloved garden at Highgrove, during a Rural Industries Exhibition held at his home in 1987.

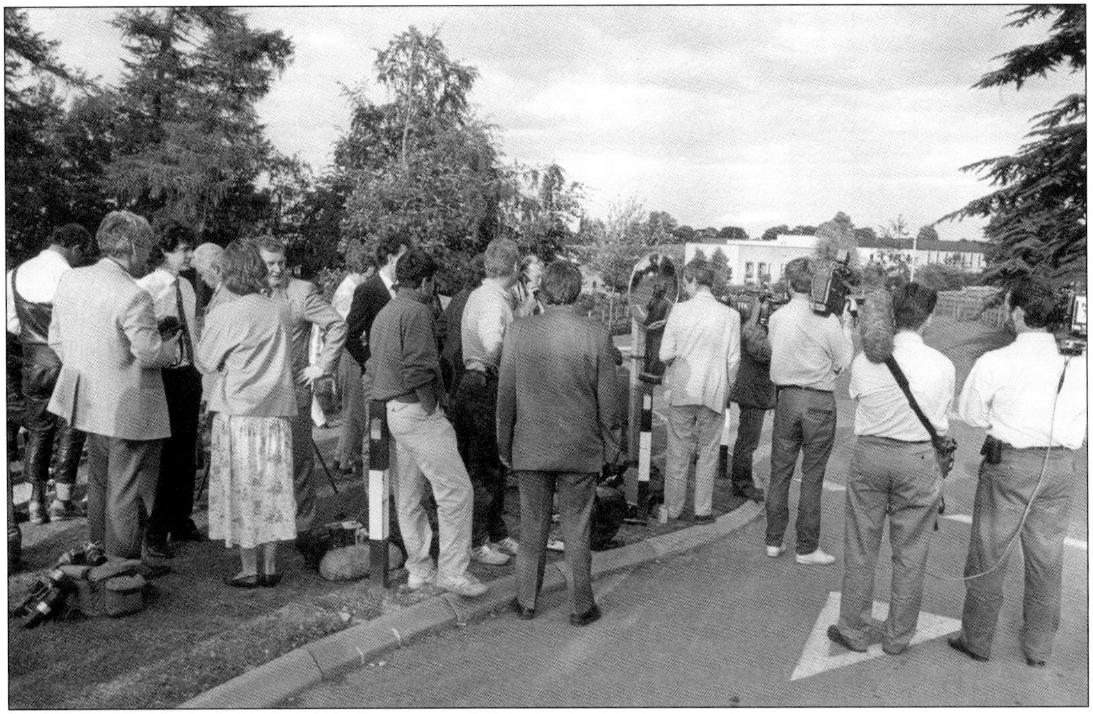

Press Posse
The media descended on Cirencester Hospital in great numbers when Prince Charles was injured in a polo match at Cirencester Park in 1990. Impatiently they waited, for any morsel of news that would keep their editors happy.

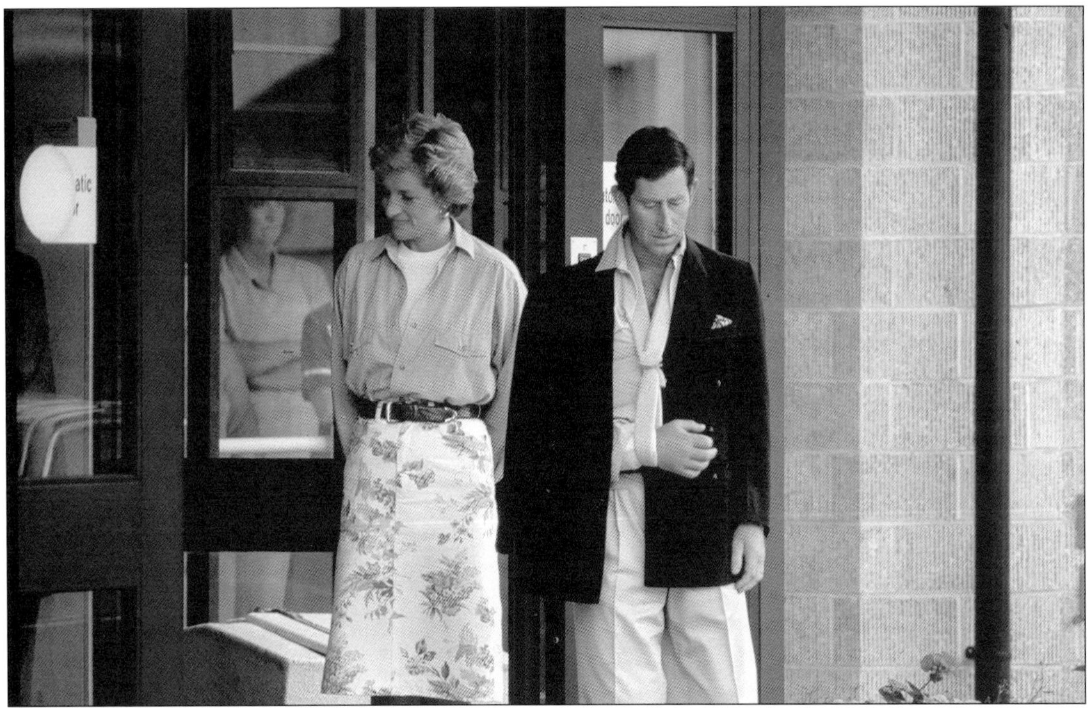

On the Mend
Prince Charles accompanied by the Princess of Wales, leaves Cirencester Hospital with his arm in a sling after a two-night stay following his polo accident in 1990.

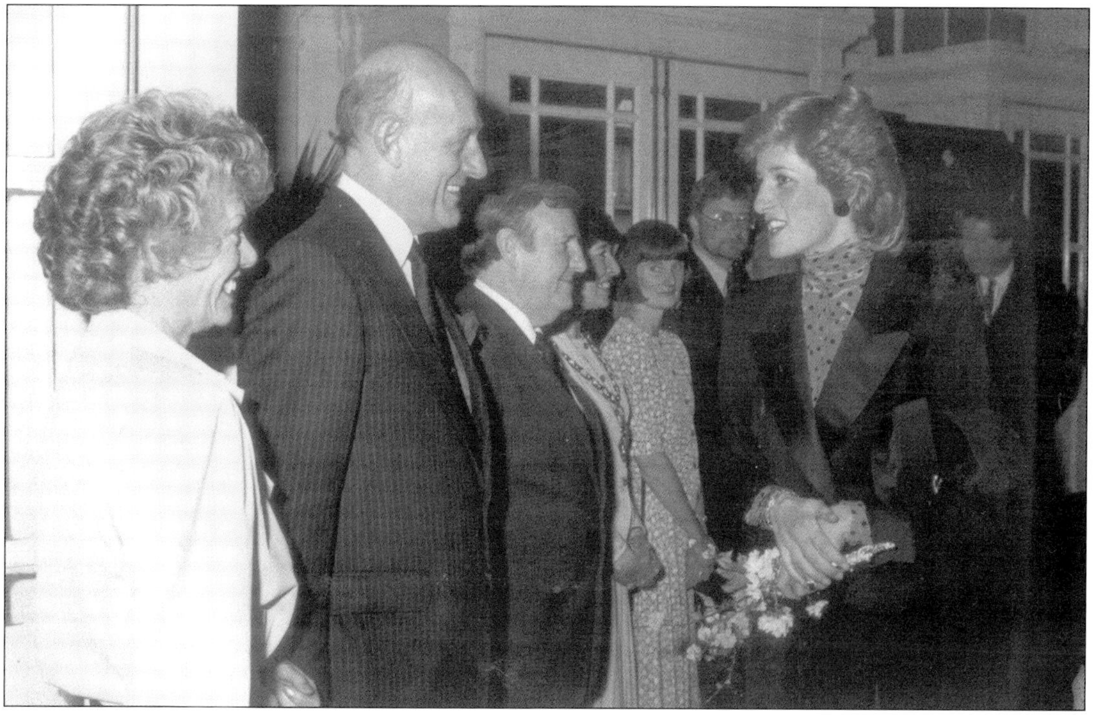

The Princess and the Policeman
The Chief Constable of Gloucestershire Constabulary, Albert Pacey and his wife Ann, meeting the Princess of Wales at Cheltenham Town Hall in 1989, when the Force celebrated their 150th anniversary year.

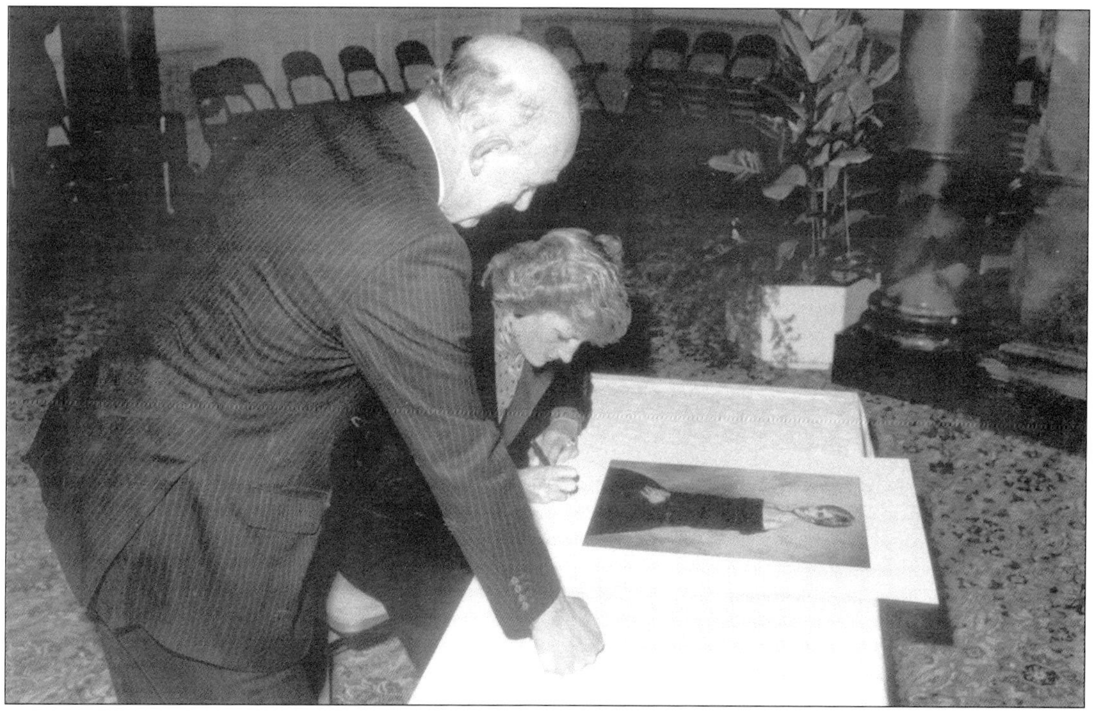

Wall Hanging
The Princess signs a portrait of herself for Chief Constable Albert Pacey at the exhibition. The picture was destined to take pride of place at Cheltenham's Landsdown Road Police Headquarters.

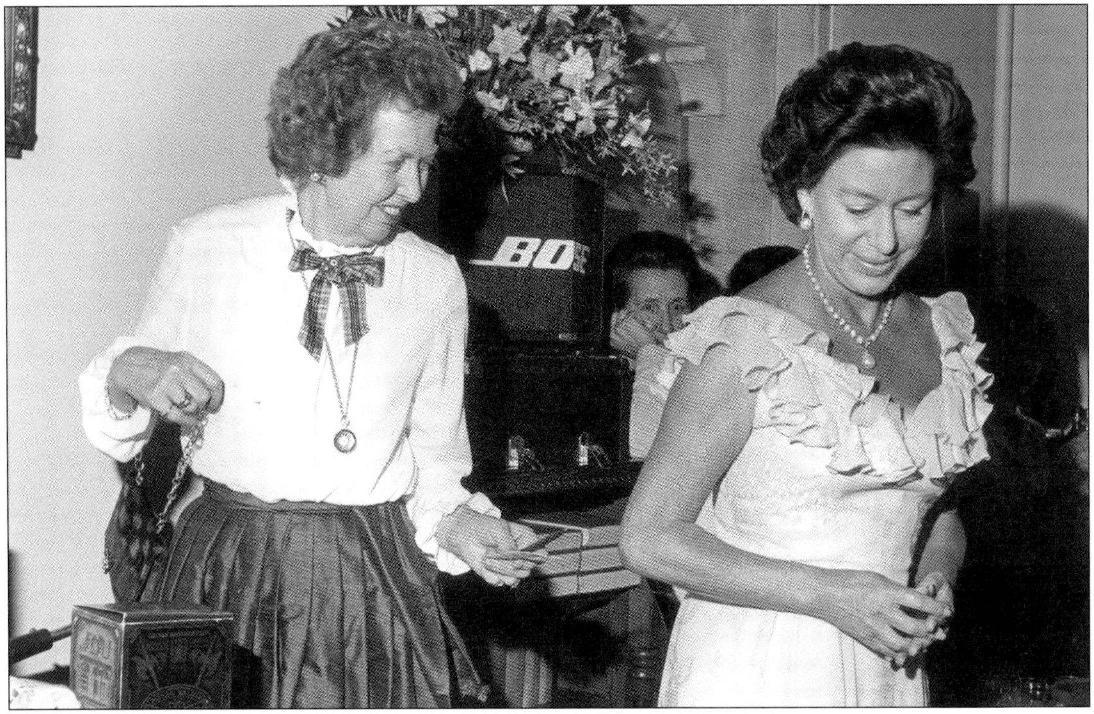

Prize Princess
Princess Margaret with her close friend Lady Holland-Martin, photographed during the grand prize draw ceremony at a fashion show held in aid of the NSPCC at the Cheltenham Ladies College in 1982.

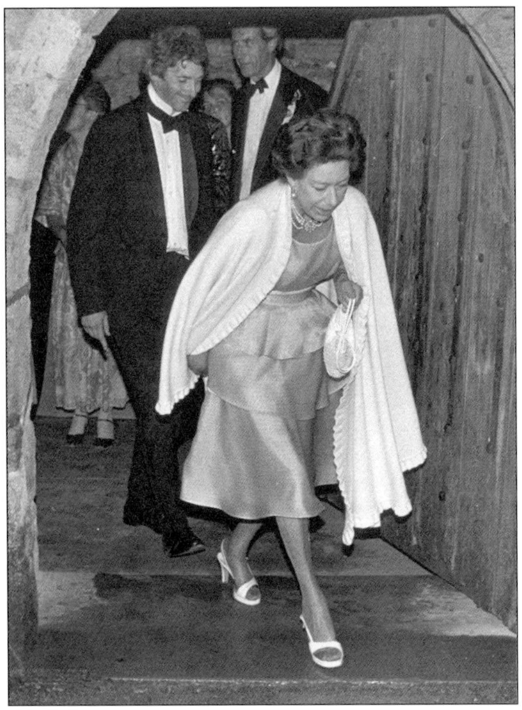

All That Jazz
Princess Margaret with Lord Neidpath at his family seat Stanway House near Winchcombe, making their way from the estate's tithe barn in a downpour, after an evening of jazz provided by Humphrey Lyttelton and his band, organized by the Winchcombe District Committee for the NSPCC in 1992.

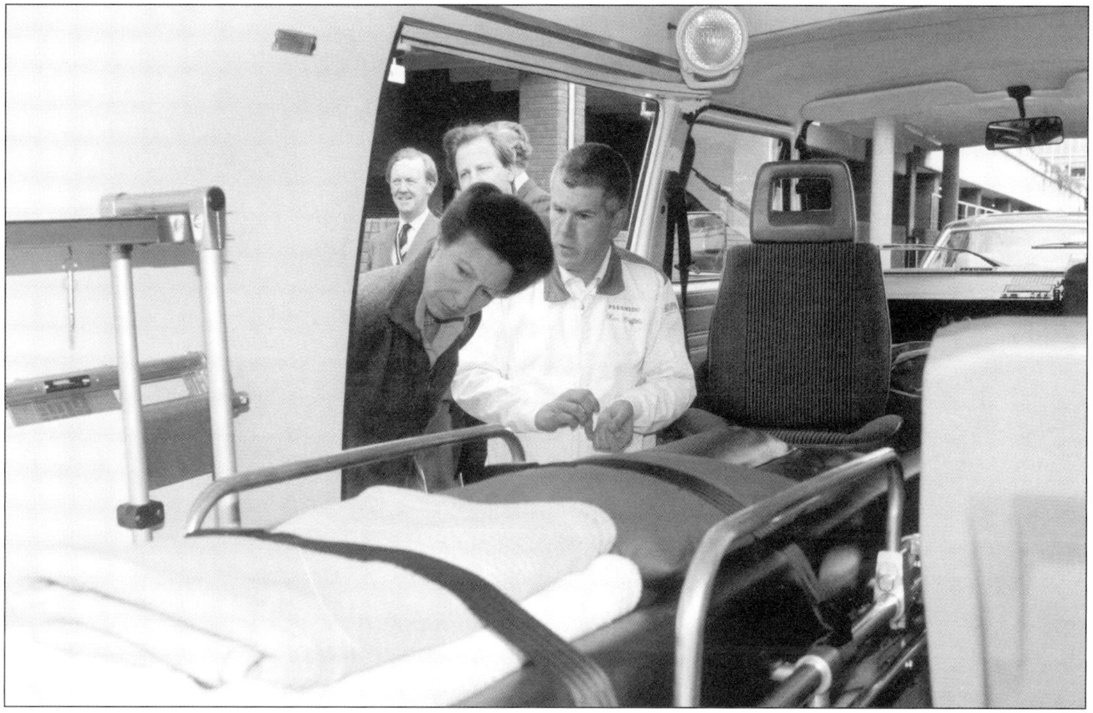

Is it Comfortable, Ken?
Princess Anne, a regular visitor to Cheltenham racecourse, attended a special medical conference held there by BUPA in 1991, where they unveiled a purpose-built ambulance for injured jockeys. The Princess, herself a keen horsewoman, naturally showed great interest in the vehicle and its equipment as she was shown around by BUPA paramedic Ken Griffiths.

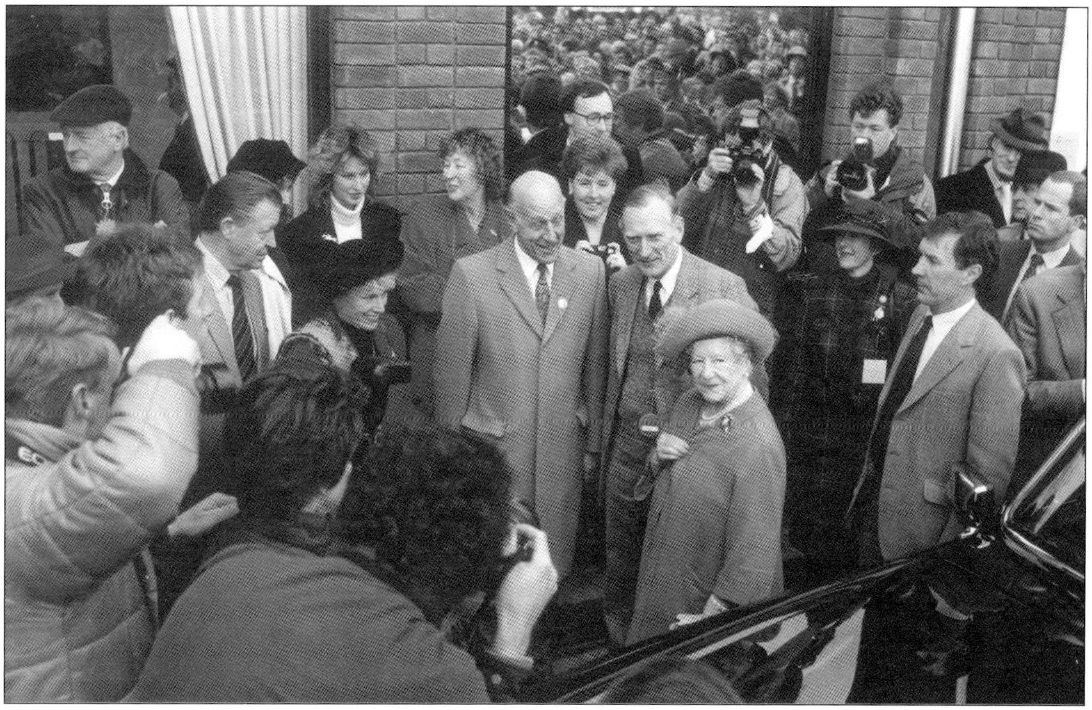

Racecourse Favourite
The Queen Mother arrives at Cheltenham racecourse for the 1993 Gold Cup meeting. Photographers started snapping away as she alighted from her car to be introduced by the Lord Lieutenant of Gloucestershire, Henry Elwes, to Gloucestershire's Chief Constable Albert Pacey and his wife, Ann.

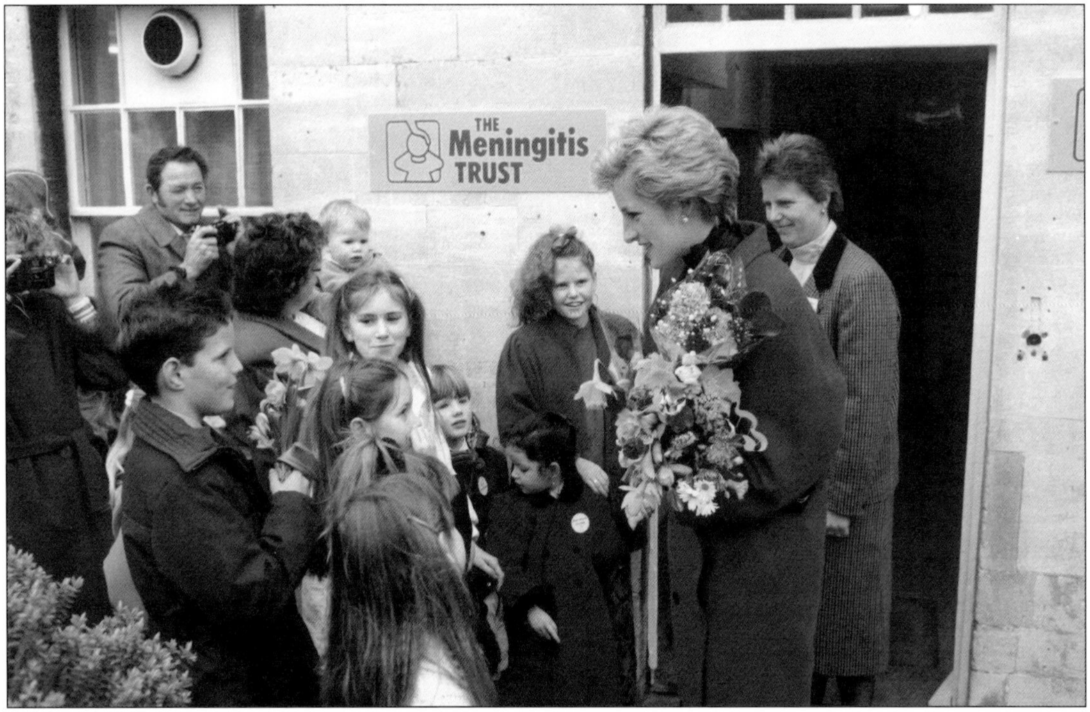

Trust in Stroud
The Princess of Wales brightened up an overcast day when she visited the Meningitis Trust in Stroud in 1990. The trust has achieved major in-roads in the battle to overcome the deadly disease, and the royal visit took place shortly after the Princess became President of the charity. After touring the Trust's headquarters, the Princess ignored the inclement weather to meet with children who had waited patiently in the rain to present her with flowers.

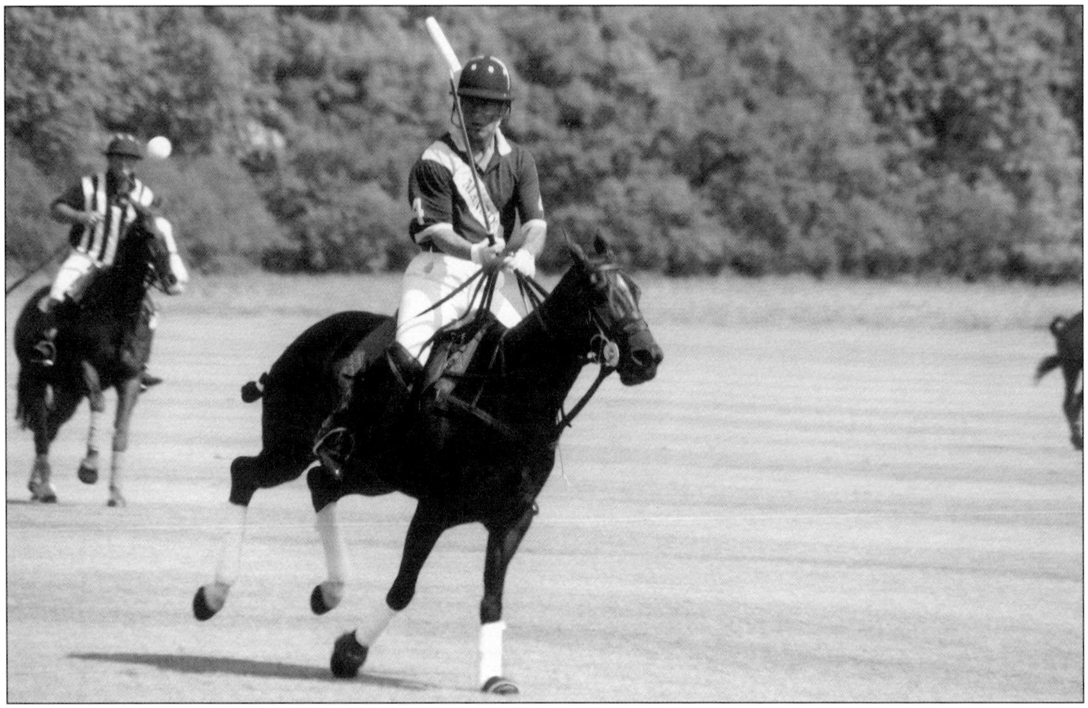

Spot the Ball
Prince Charles is seen here in action during a charity game held at the Cirencester Park polo ground. Each year, the Prince sets aside one match during the polo season when all the proceeds are donated to a deserving organization. The Cheltenham Sue Ryder Hospice was the recipient on this occasion.

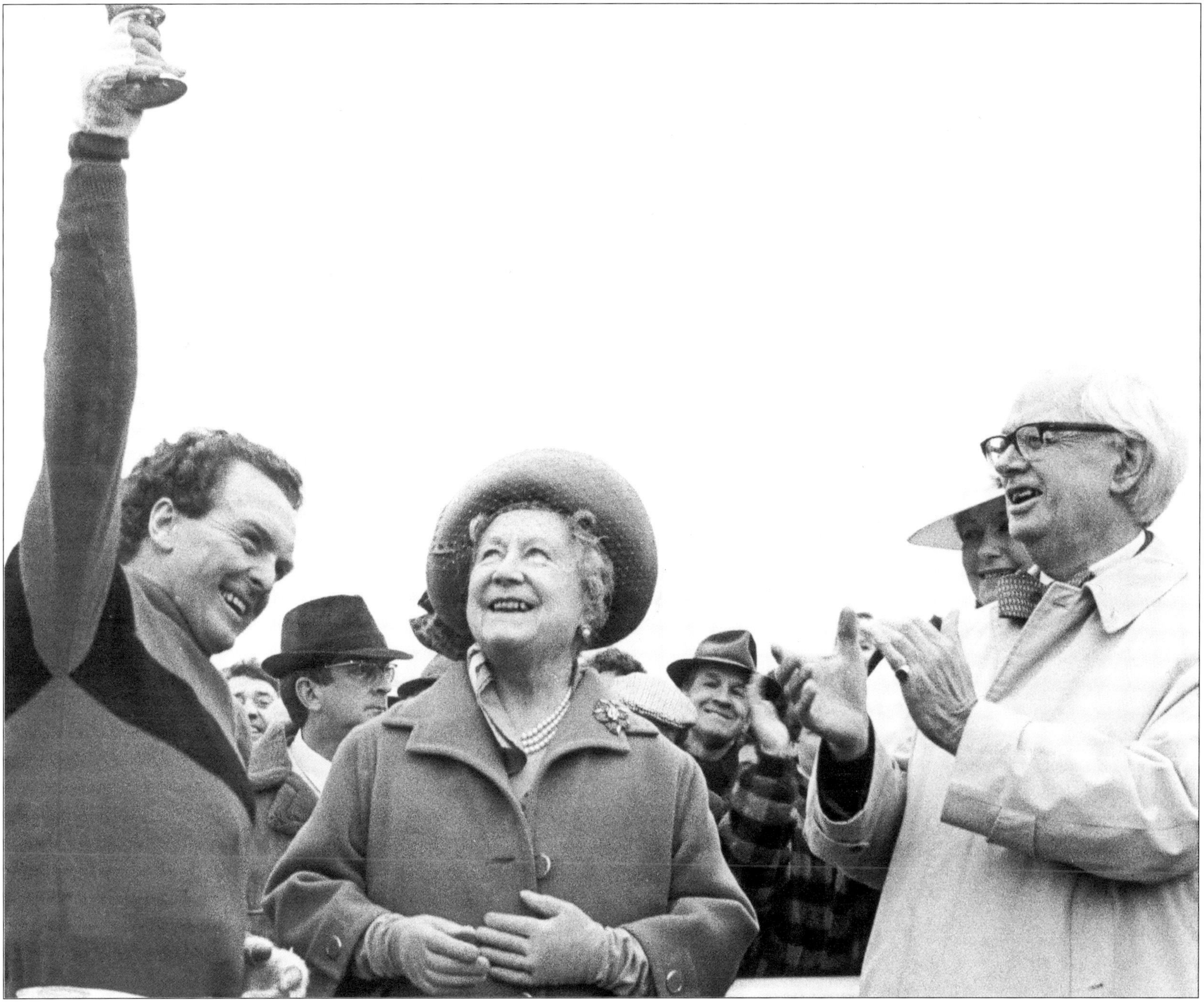

The Cup That Cheers
Top jockey Jonjo O'Neil holds the Gold Cup aloft, to the delight of the Queen Mother after she presented him with the coveted prize for triumphing on Dawn Run at Cheltenham in 1986.

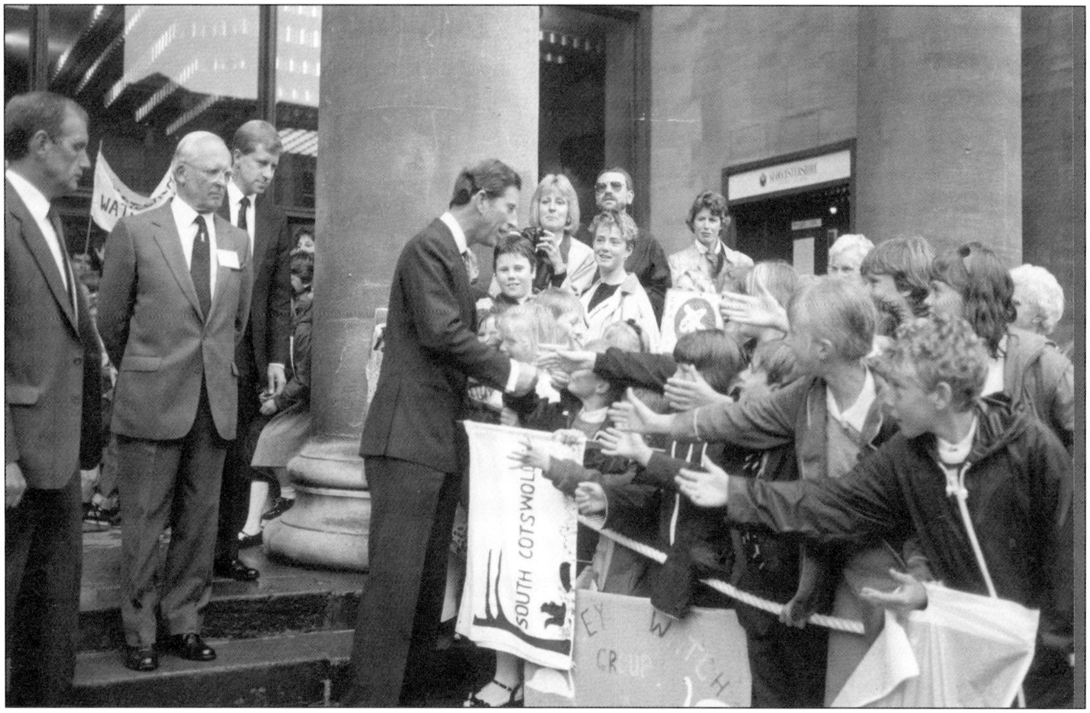

Take my Hand
Youngsters were eager to shake the hand of their future King when the Prince of Wales visited an exhibition by the Nature Conservation Trust at the Shirehall in Gloucester.

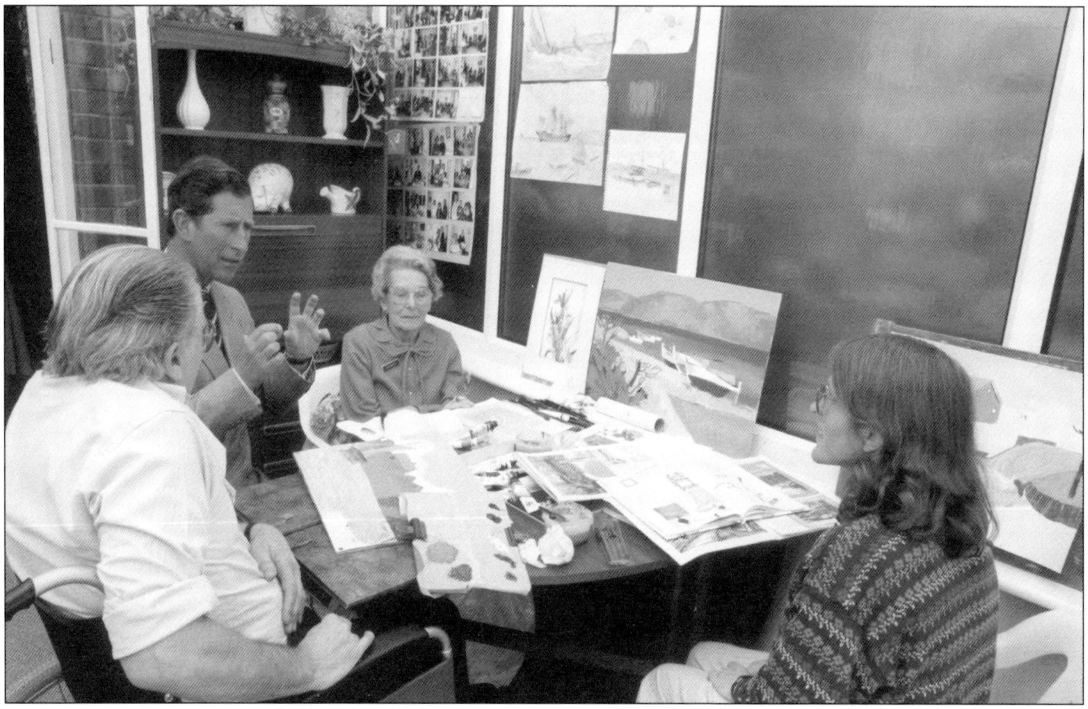

Art for Art's Sake
After opening the new Wheatstone Centre in Gloucester in 1992, Prince Charles – an artist himself – joined in with fellow painters at the day centre's art class.

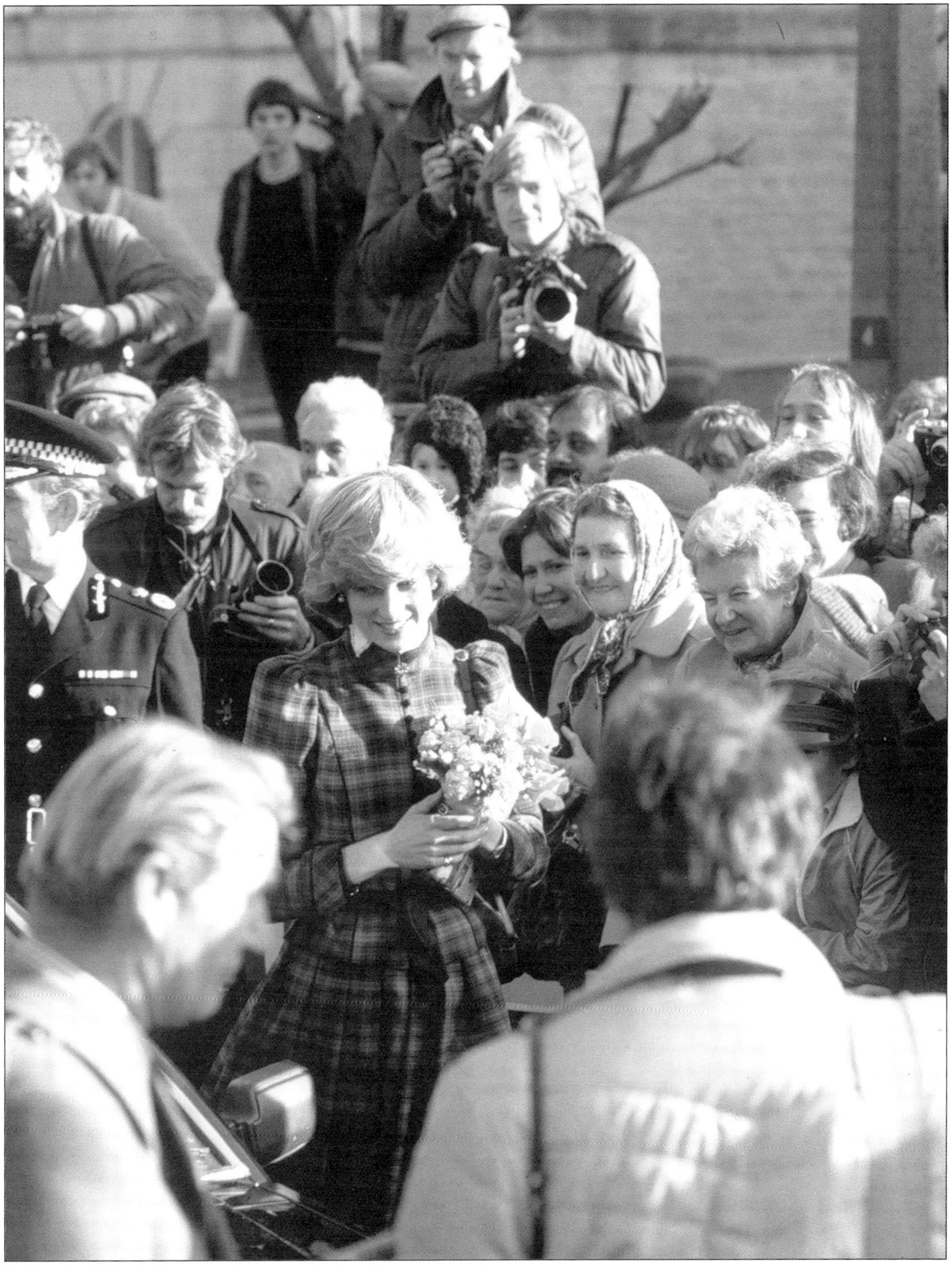

Plaid Princess
Princess Diana was the centre of attention when she called into the Lewis Lane Playgroup at Cirencester in 1982. The world's best known ex-kindergarten teacher quickly became immersed in the playtime children's activities, reading stories, playing games and swapping notes with helpers. The popular Princess delayed her departure to meet with folk in this crowded back street.

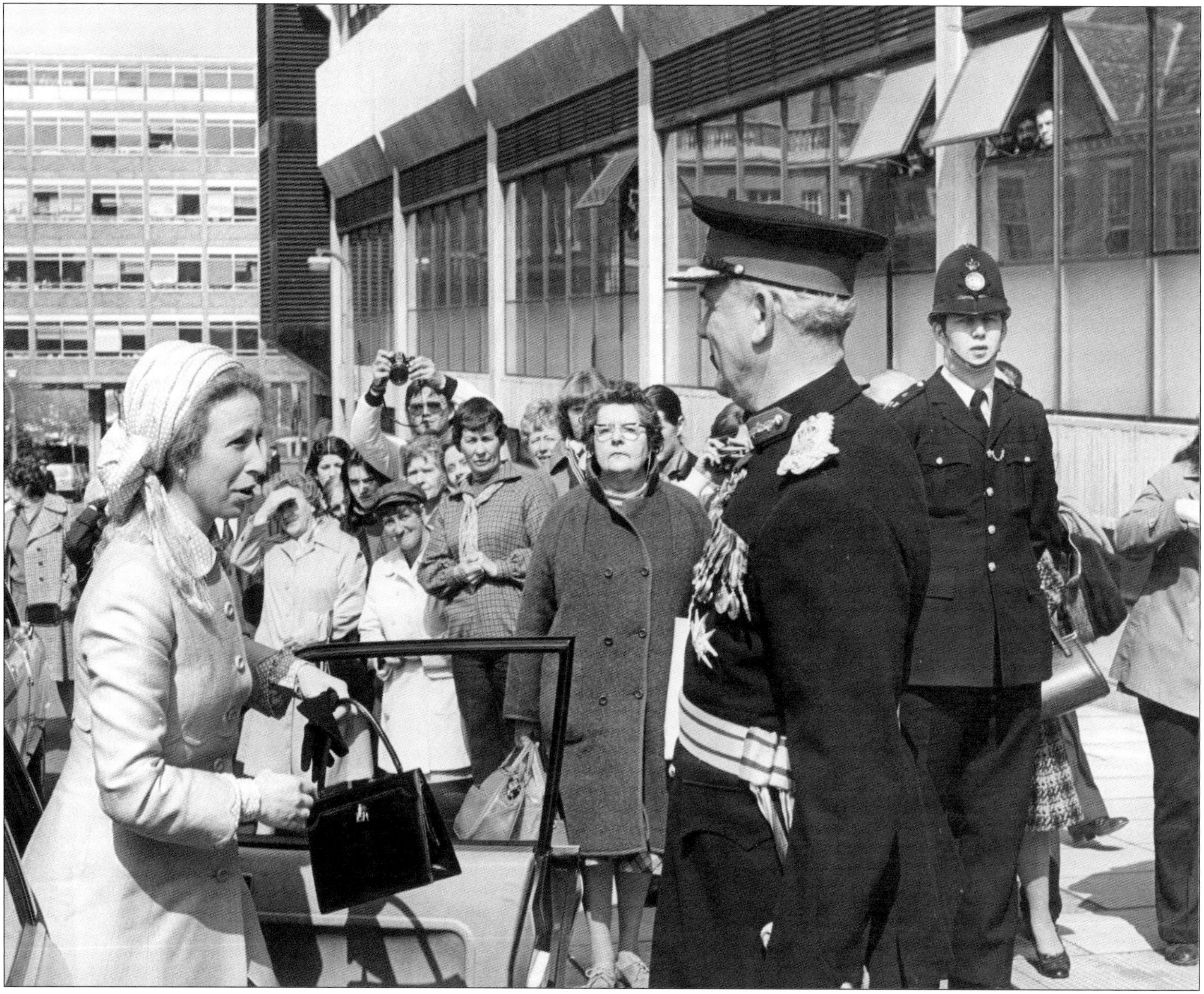

Royal Watchers
Crowds gathered in Gloucester to see Princess Anne on her visit to the city in 1974. Here she is being by Lord Lieutenant Colonel Martin Gibbs as she alights from her car near Westgate Street.

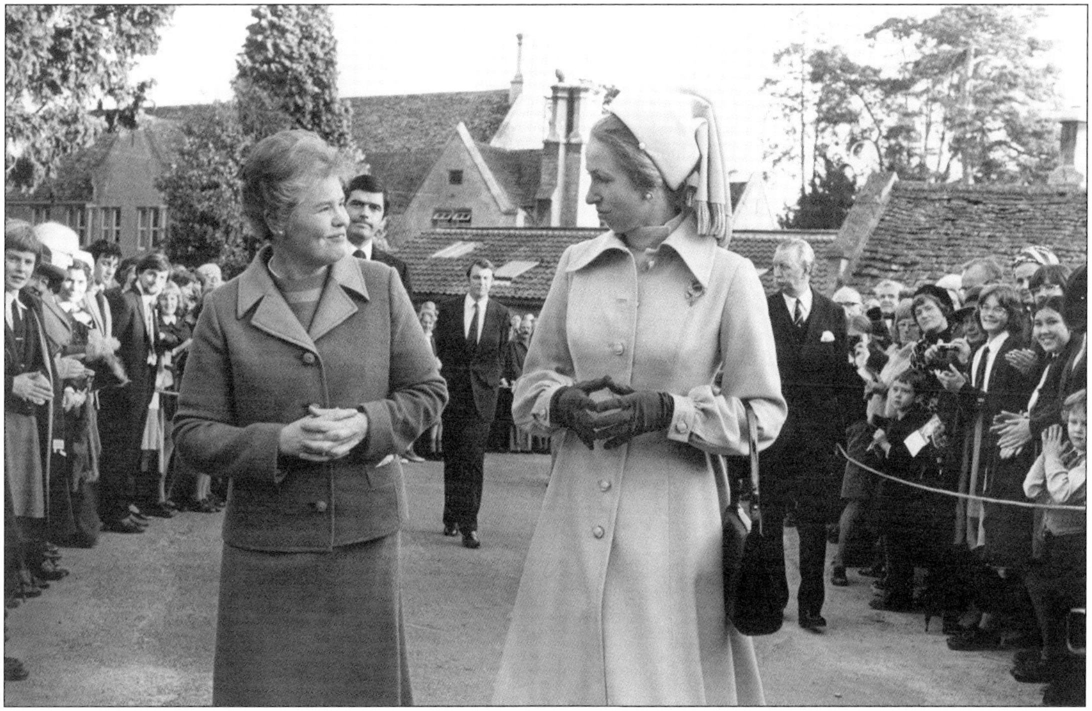

Back to School
The completion of new school facilities prompted a visit to Westonbirt School near Tetbury in October 1975. Here the Princess strolls through the school grounds with Headmistress Miss Margaret Newton, before officially opening the new buildings.

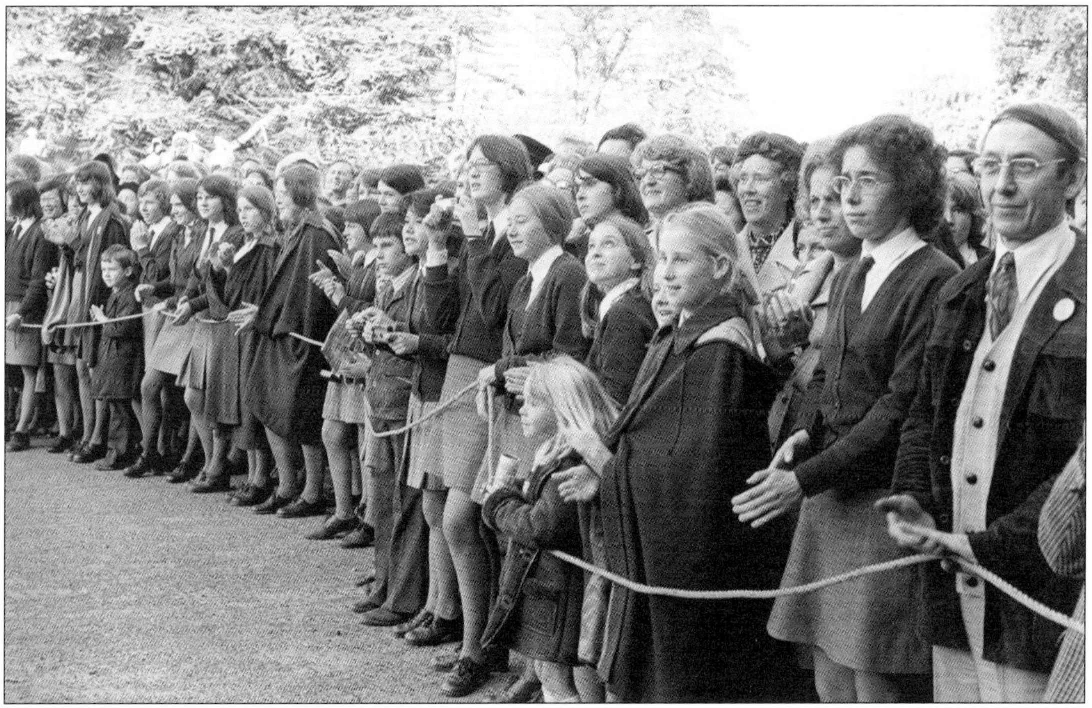

Class of '75
Westonbirt School pupils wait to meet Princess Anne on her visit to open new classrooms built at a cost of £84,000 in October 1975.

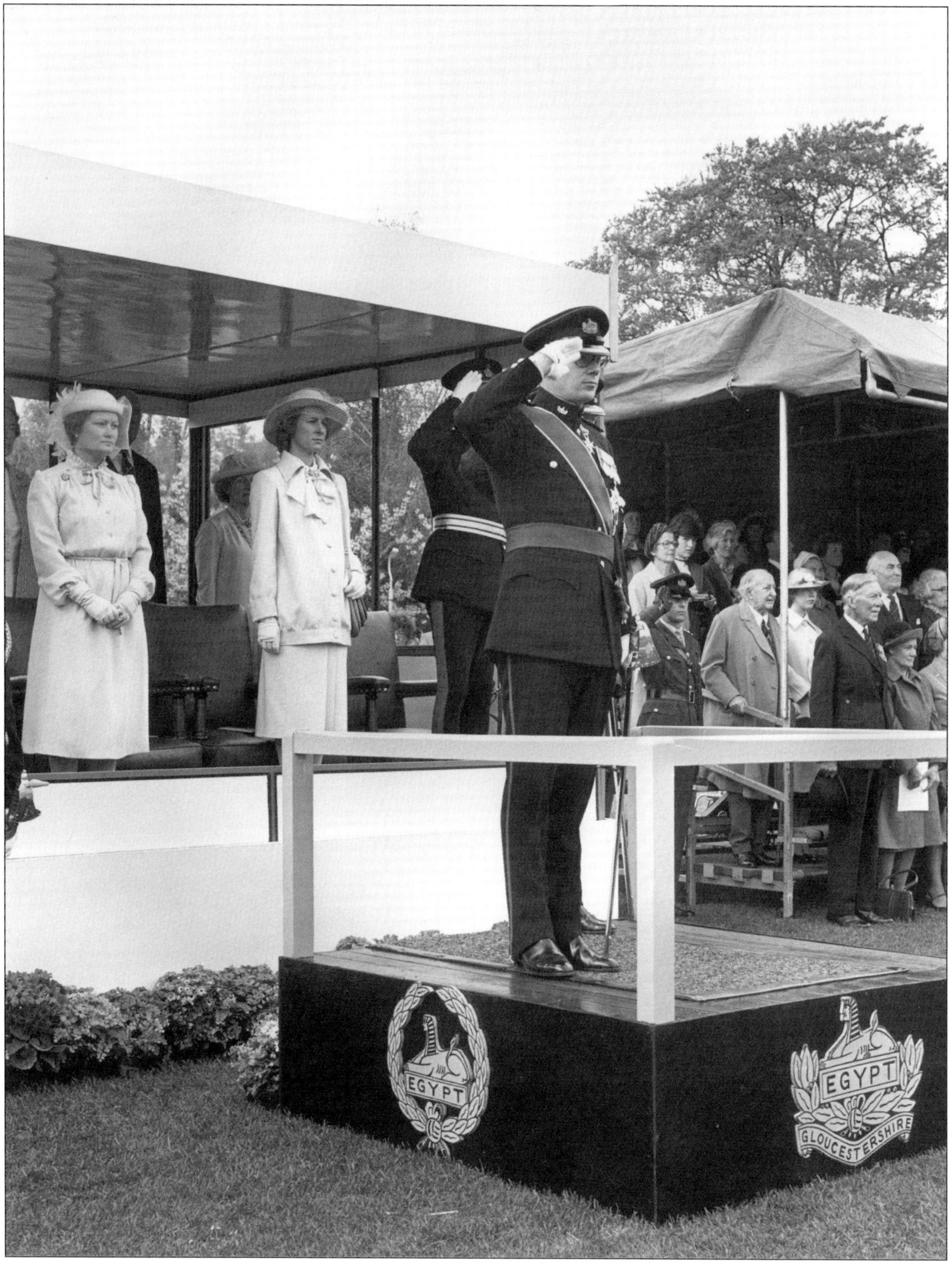

Glorious Glosters
The Duke and Duchess of Gloucester take the royal salute during the march past in Gloucester Park, when the 1st Battalion of the Gloucestershire Regiment held their Freedom of the City Parade in 1982. On the right, wearing a dark suit is Colonel Carne, VC, DSO, famed for his part played with the 'Glosters' in the Korean campaign.

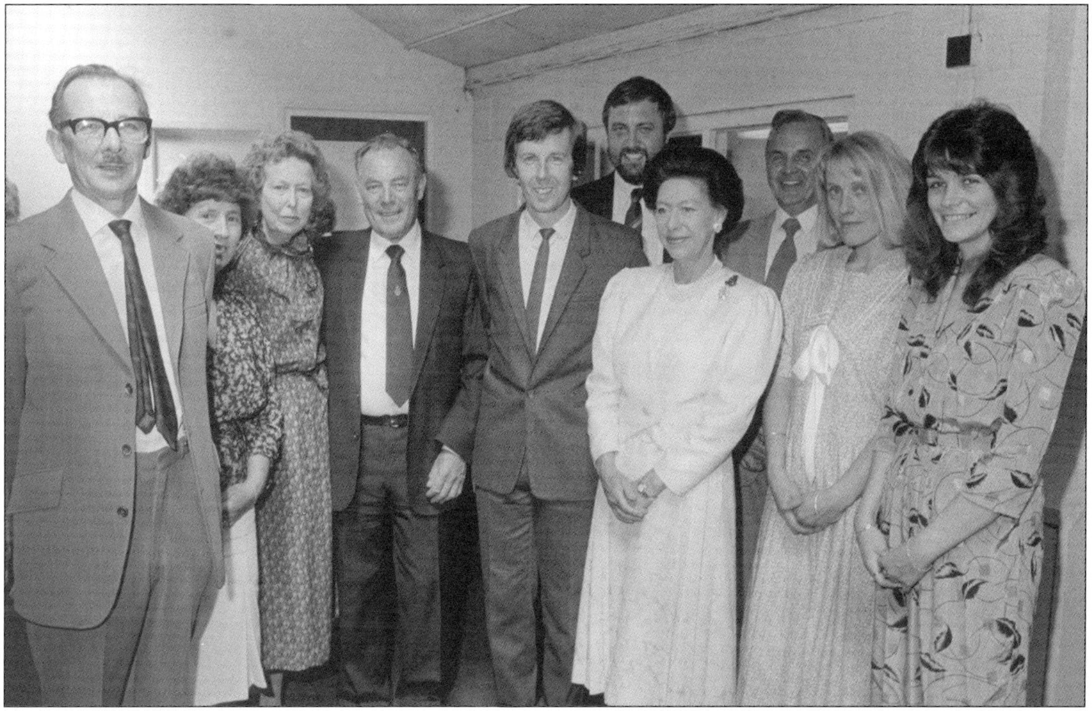

Suffer the Little Children
Staff of the Gloucestershire branch of the NSPCC, members of the Child Protection team, photographed with Princess Margaret when she opened the society's Holland-Martin Centre in Llanthony Road, Gloucester in 1985. Lady Holland-Martin, a great supporter of the NSPCC, is third from the left in the picture.

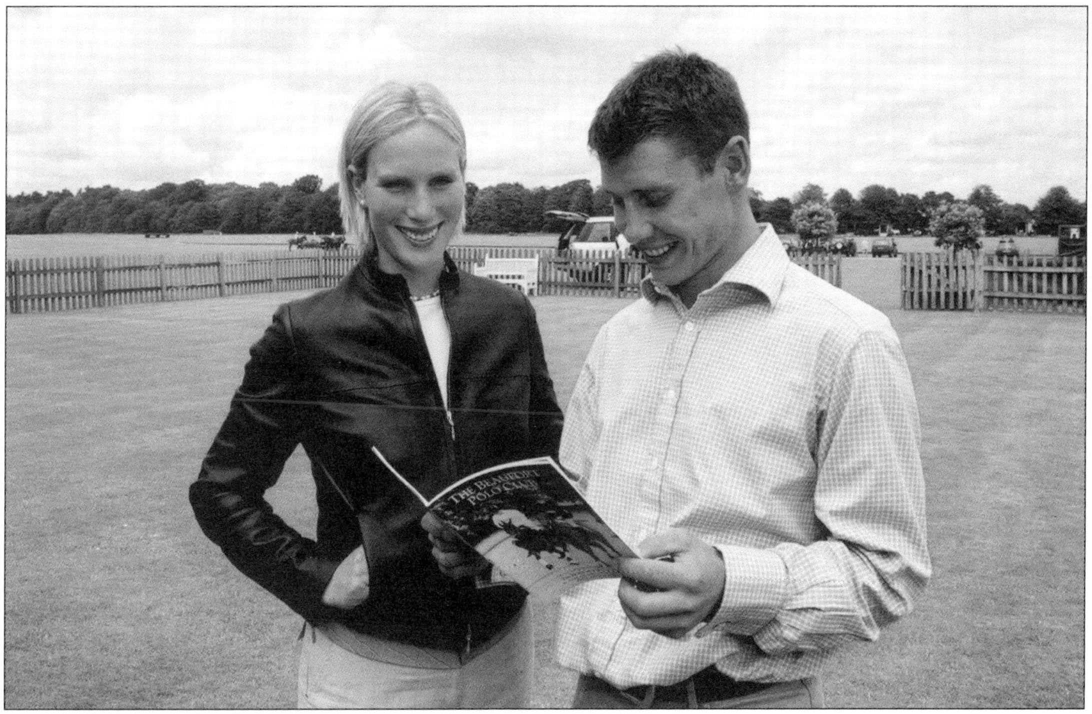

Love Match
Princess Anne's daughter Zara Phillips, pictured with her boyfriend, well-known jockey Richard Johnson, at the Beaufort Polo Club in July 2002. The event was a charity match in aid of the Animal Health Trust, a leading veterinary organization dedicated to developing new techniques to treat diseases in cats, dogs and horses.

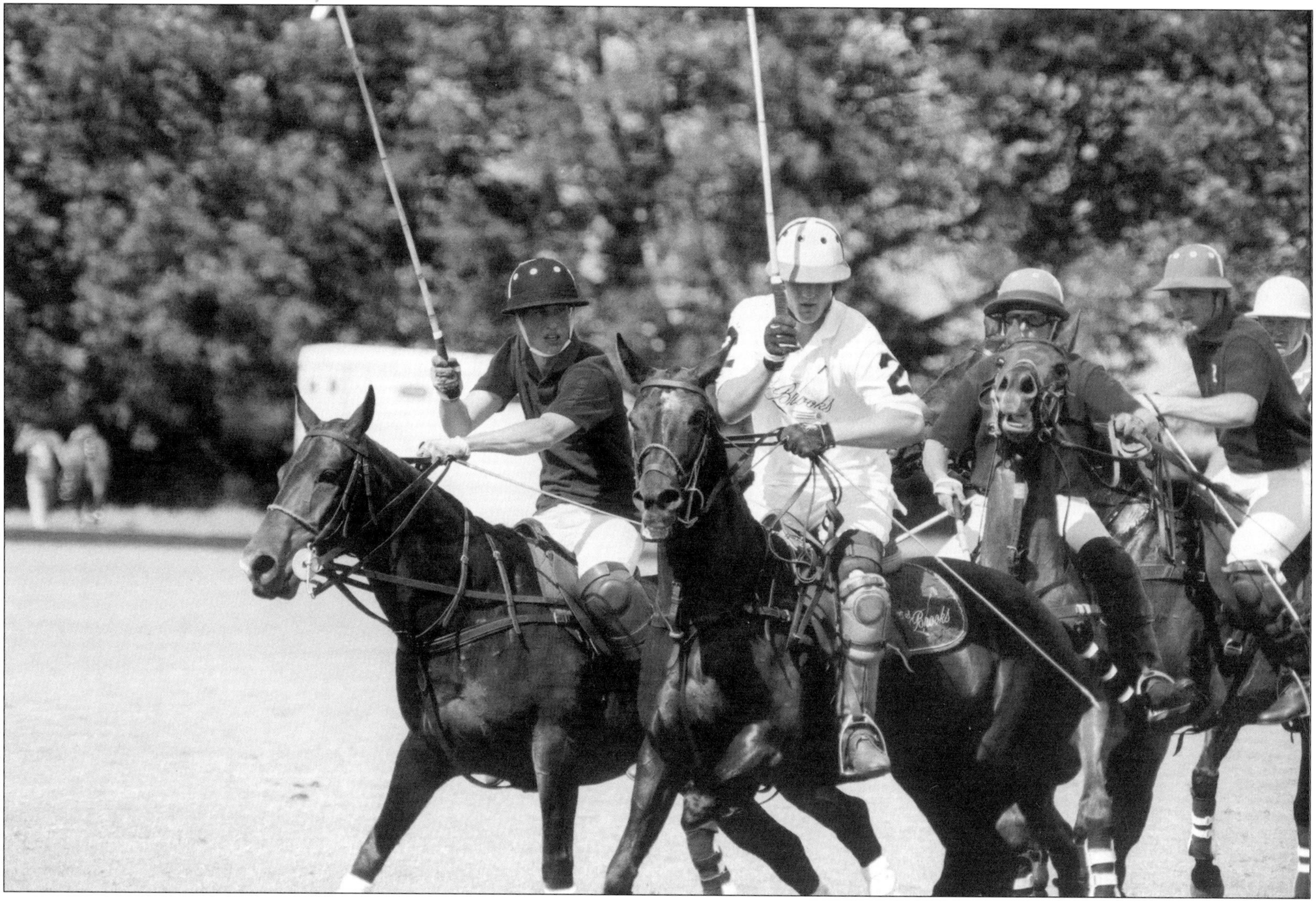

In His Father's Hoof Steps
Prince Charles and his son Prince William teamed up in July 2002 to play in a charity polo match in aid of the Countryside Foundation for Education. The match was held at the Beaufort Polo Club at Westonbirt, and was sponsored by Calcot Manor. The image shows the young Prince on the left, getting into the action.

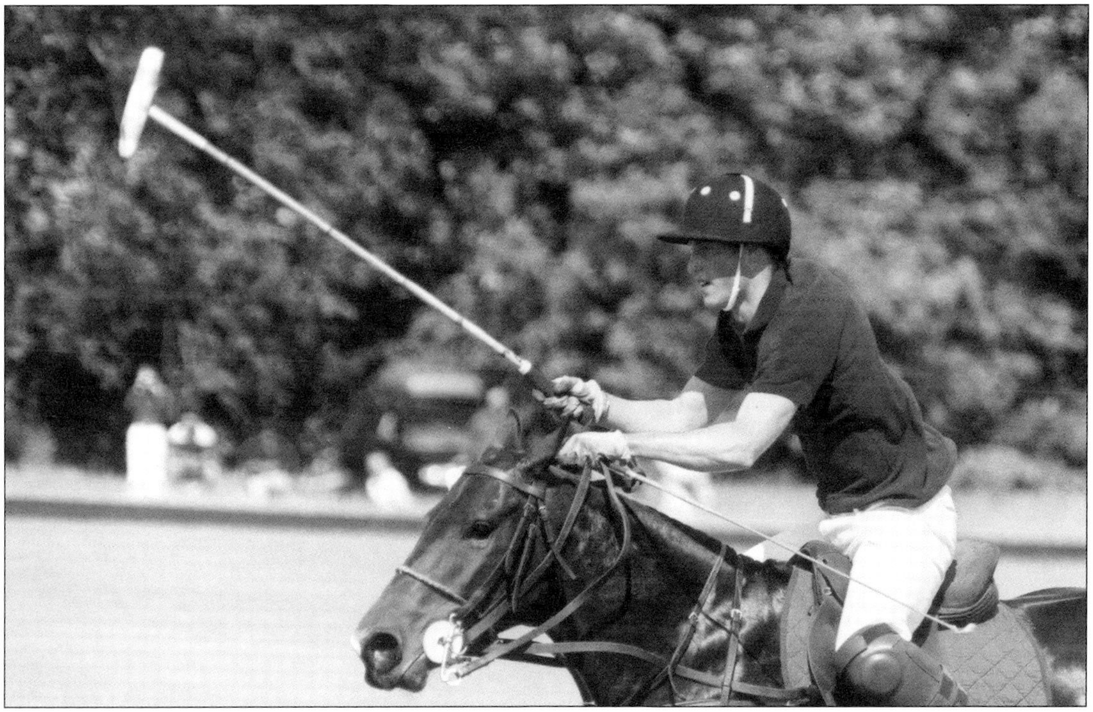

Princely Horsemanship
Prince William storms across the polo ground during a chukka.

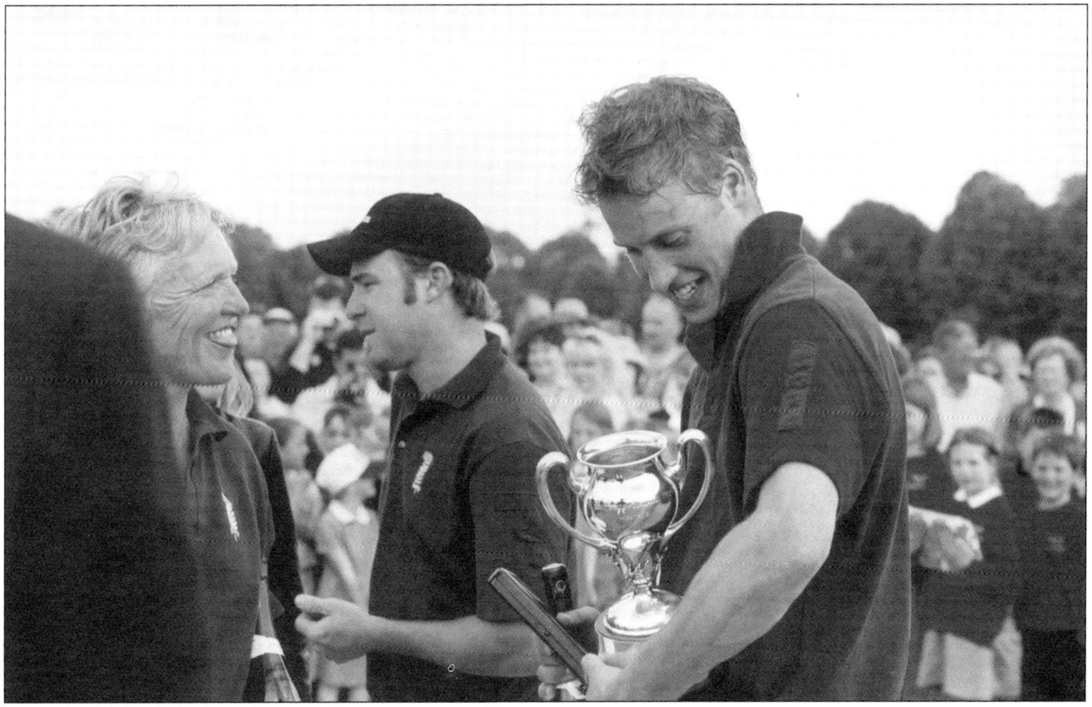

Winning Smile
An elated Prince William admiring his side's winning trophy with team mate Claire Tomlinson.

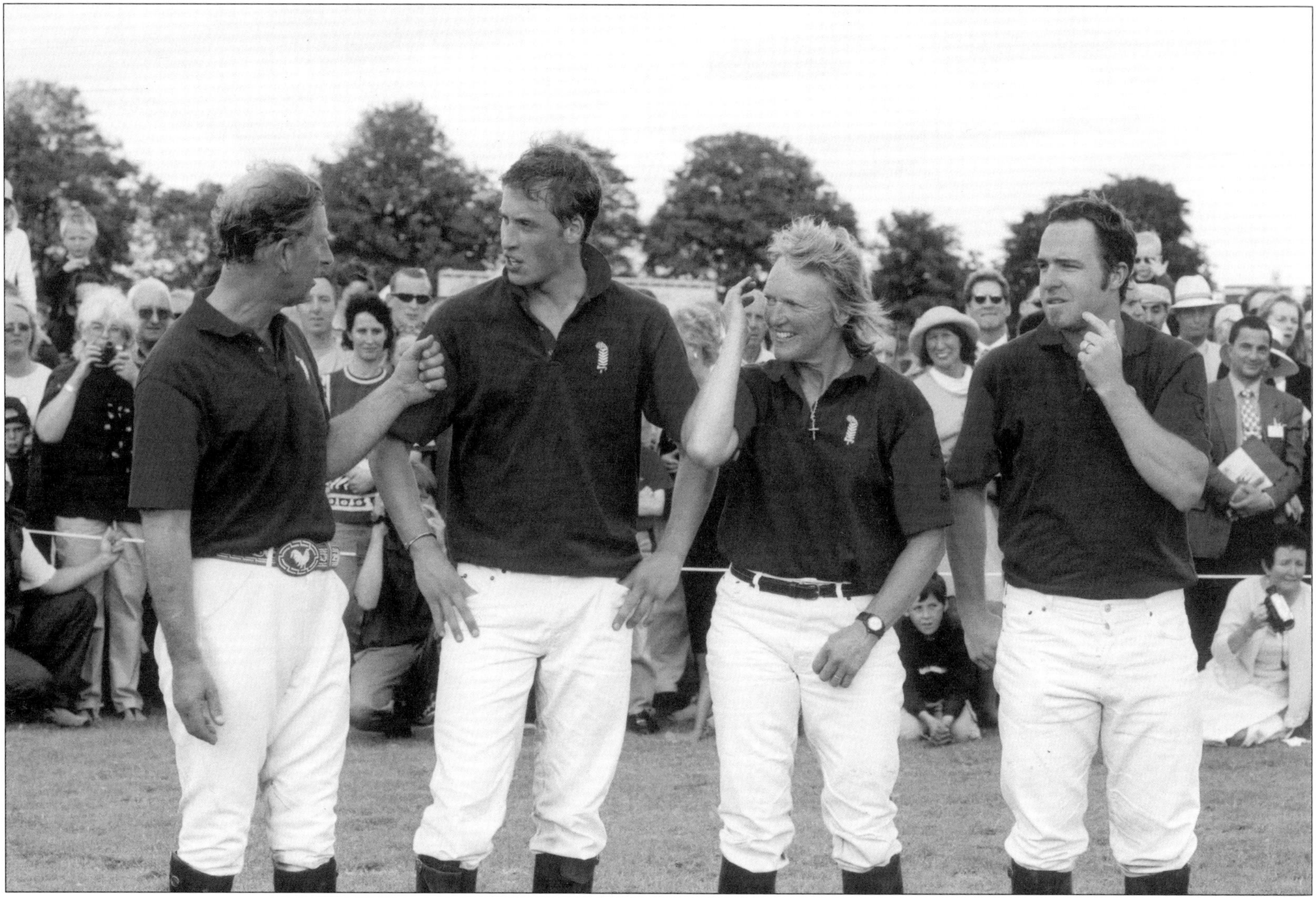

Smile Please
After the match – Prince Charles and Prince William line up with team-mates for the official team photograph.